Charles M. Schulz

PEANUTS

Happiness is a Warm Blanket, Charlie Brown!

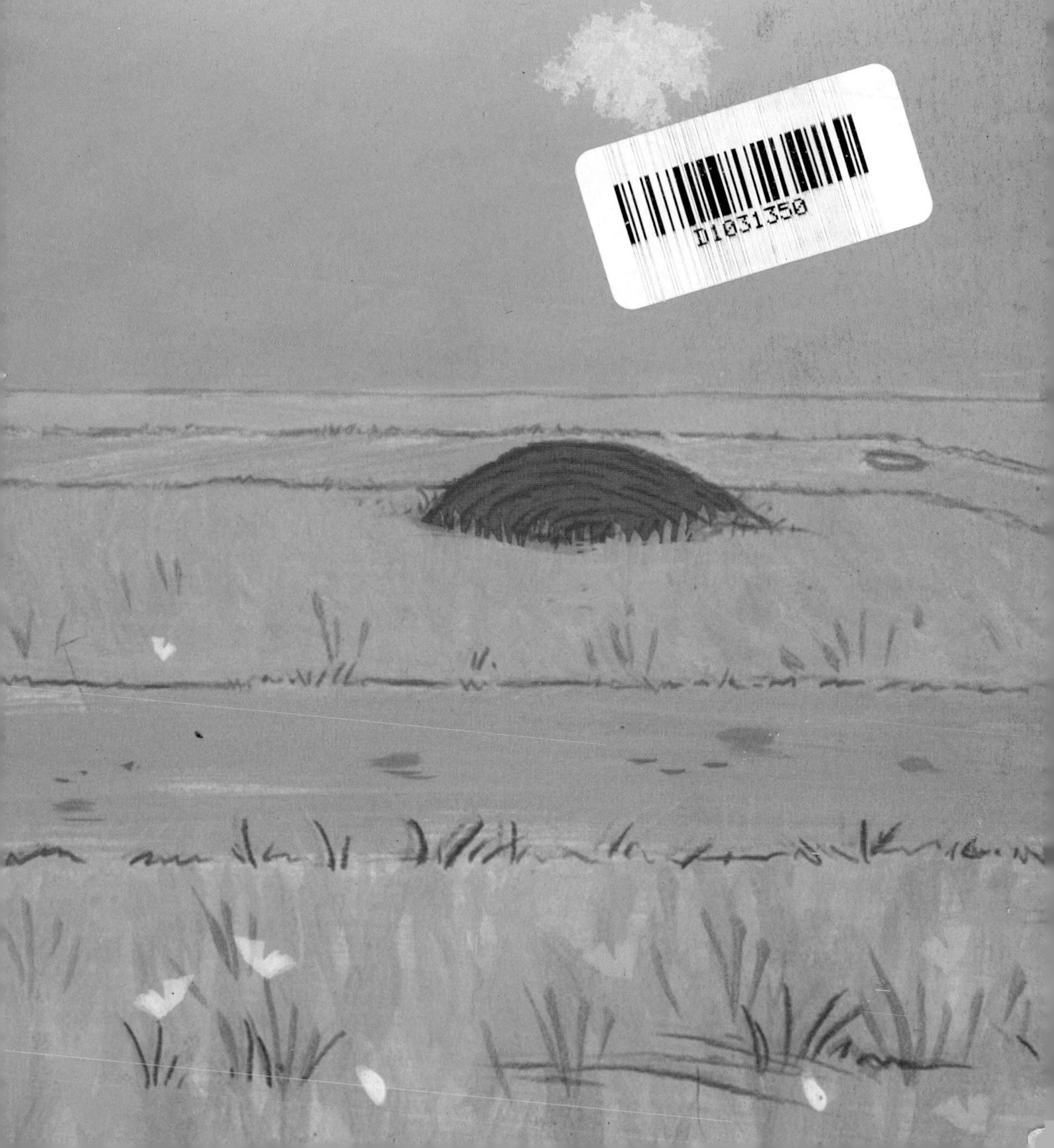

Ross Richie - Chief Executive Officer
Matt Gagnon - Editor-in-Chief
Adam Fortier - VP-New Business
Wes Harris - VP-Publishing
Lance Kreiter - VP-Licensing & Merchandising
Chip Mosher - Marketing & Sales Director

Bryce Carlson - Managing Editor
Ian Brill - Editor
Dafna Pleban - Editor
Christopher Burns - Editor
Shannon Watters - Assistant Editor
Eric Harburn - Assistant Editor
Adam Staffaroni - Assistant Editor

Brian Latimer - Lead Graphic Designer
Stephanie Gonzaga - Graphic Designer
Phil Barbaro - Operations
Ivan Salazar - Marketing Manager
Devin Funches - Marketing & Sales Assistant

HAPPINESS IS A WARM BLANKET, CHARLIE BROWN — September 2011. Published by KABOOM!, a division of Boom Entertainment, Inc. All contents Copyright © 2011 Peanuts Worldwide LLC. All rights reserved. KABOOM!™ and the KABOOM! logo are trademarks of Boom Entertainment, Inc., registered in various countries and categories. All characters, events, and institutions depicted herein are fictional. Any similarity between any of the names, characters, persons, events, and/or institutions in this publication to actual names, characters, and persons, whether living or dead, events, and/or institutions is unintended and purely coincidental. KABOOM! does not read or accept unsolicited submissions of ideas, stories, or artwork.

A catalog record of this book is available from OCLC and from the KABOOM! website, www.kaboom-studios.com, on the Librarians Page.

BOOM! Studios, 6310 San Vicente Boulevard, Suite 107, Los Angeles, CA 90048-5457. Printed in China. First Printing, Trade Paperback. ISBN: 978-1-60886-681-6

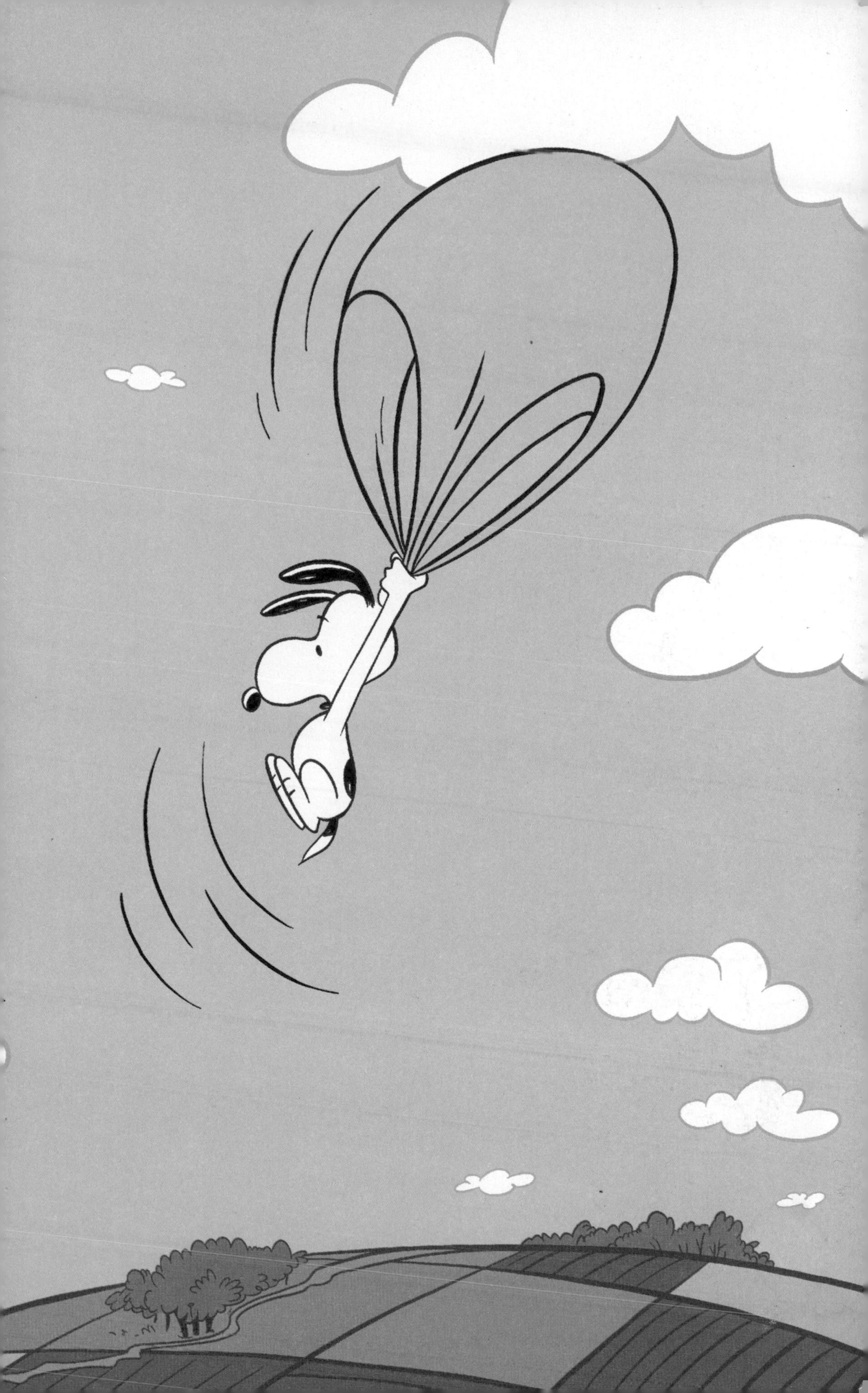

Based on the comic strip by
Charles M. Schulz

ADAPTED BY:

SCRIPT:
Stephan Pastis and Craig Schulz

ART DIRECTION:
Paige Braddock and Andy Beall

LAYOUTS:
Vicki Scott

PENCILS:
Bob Scott and Vicki Scott

INKS:
Ron Zorman

COLORS:
Brian Miller, Hi-Fi Colour Design

COVER:
Bob Scott

EDITORIAL:
Iain R. Morris and Alexis E. Fajardo

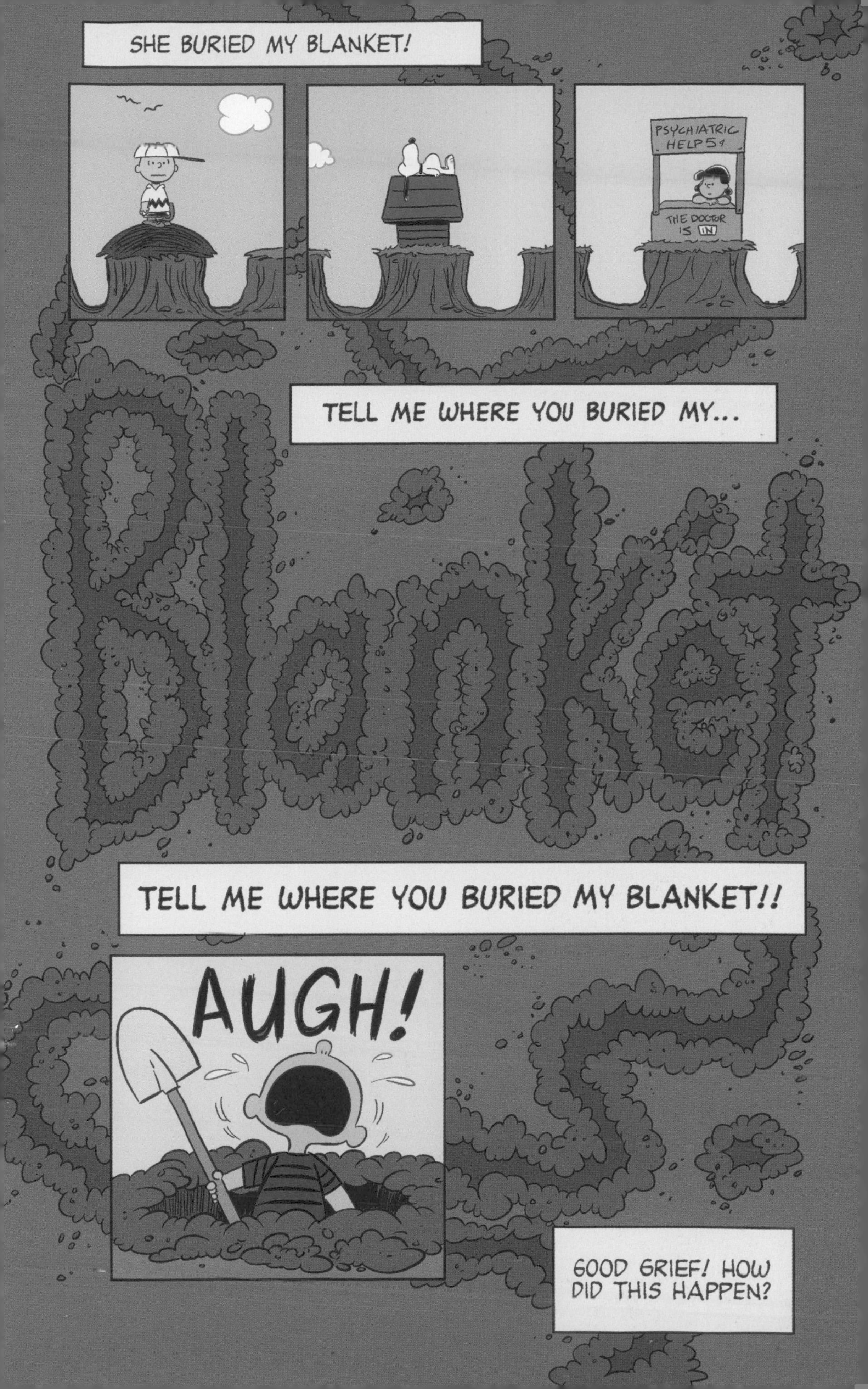
SHE BURIED MY BLANKET!
PSYCHIATRIC HELP 5¢
THE DOCTOR IS IN
TELL ME WHERE YOU BURIED MY...
Blanket
TELL ME WHERE YOU BURIED MY BLANKET!!
AUGH!
GOOD GRIEF! HOW DID THIS HAPPEN?

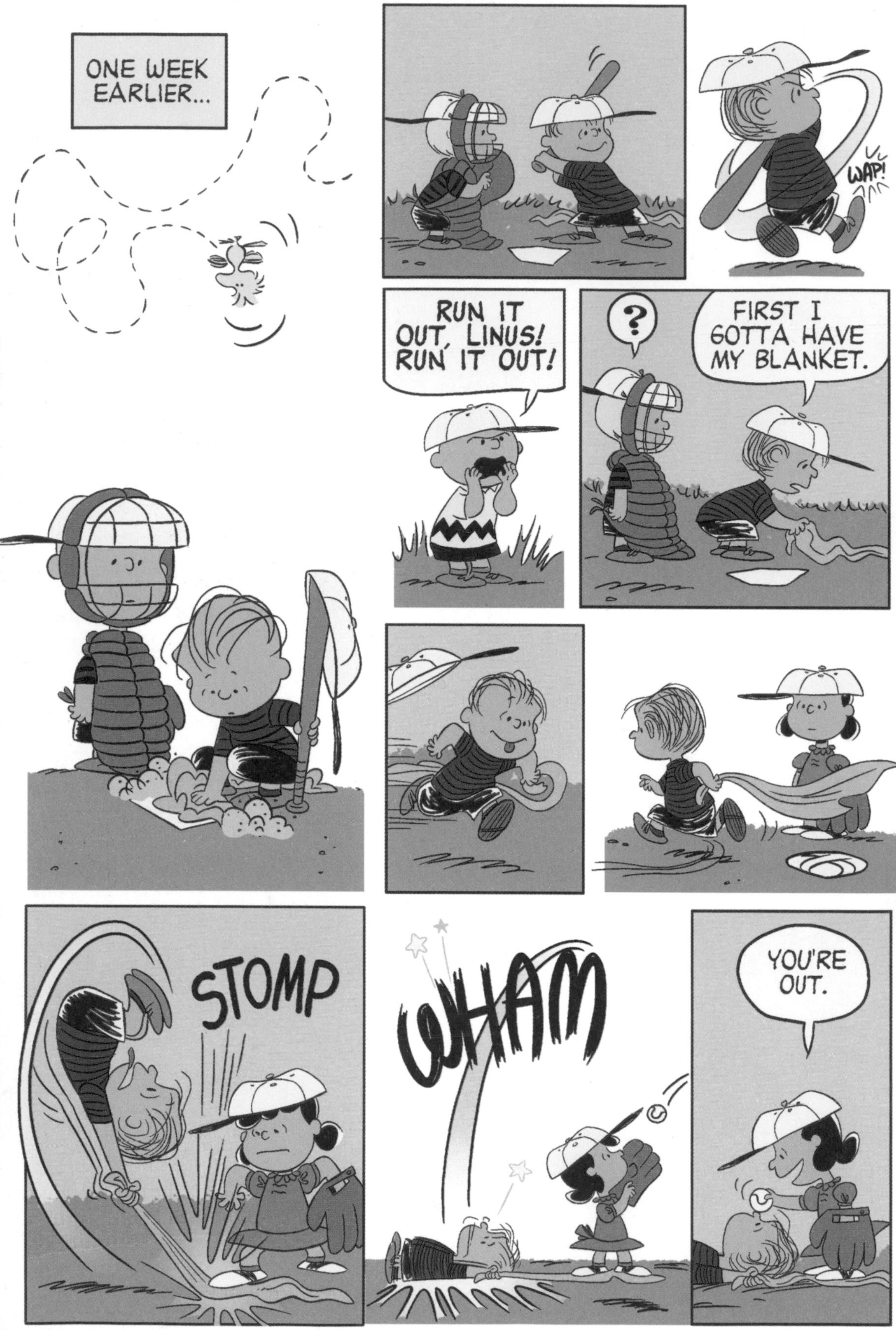
ONE WEEK EARLIER...
WAP!
RUN IT OUT, LINUS! RUN IT OUT!
?
FIRST I GOTTA HAVE MY BLANKET.
STOMP
WHAM
YOU'RE OUT.

IF I WERE YOU, I'D BE AFRAID OF WHAT THE KIDS IN SCHOOL WOULD SAY ABOUT THAT BLANKET.
DO YOU HAVE A PIECE OF CANDY?
!
WHACK!
PING
THEY DON'T SAY VERY MUCH.

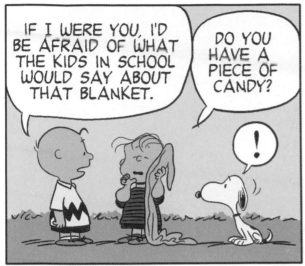

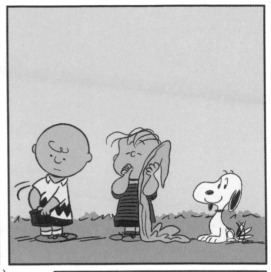

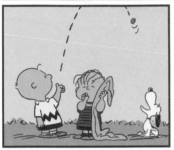

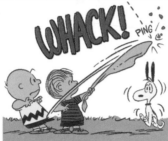

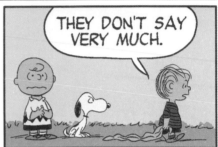

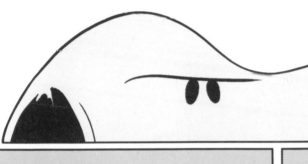

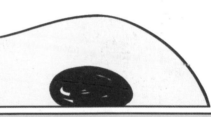

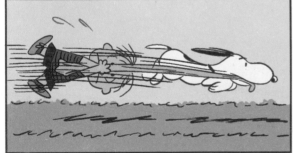

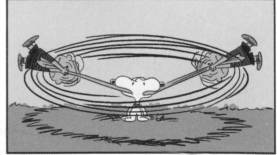

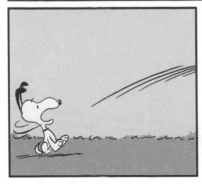

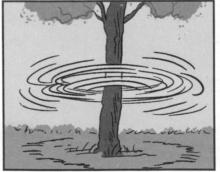

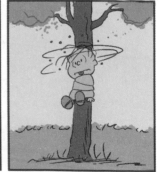

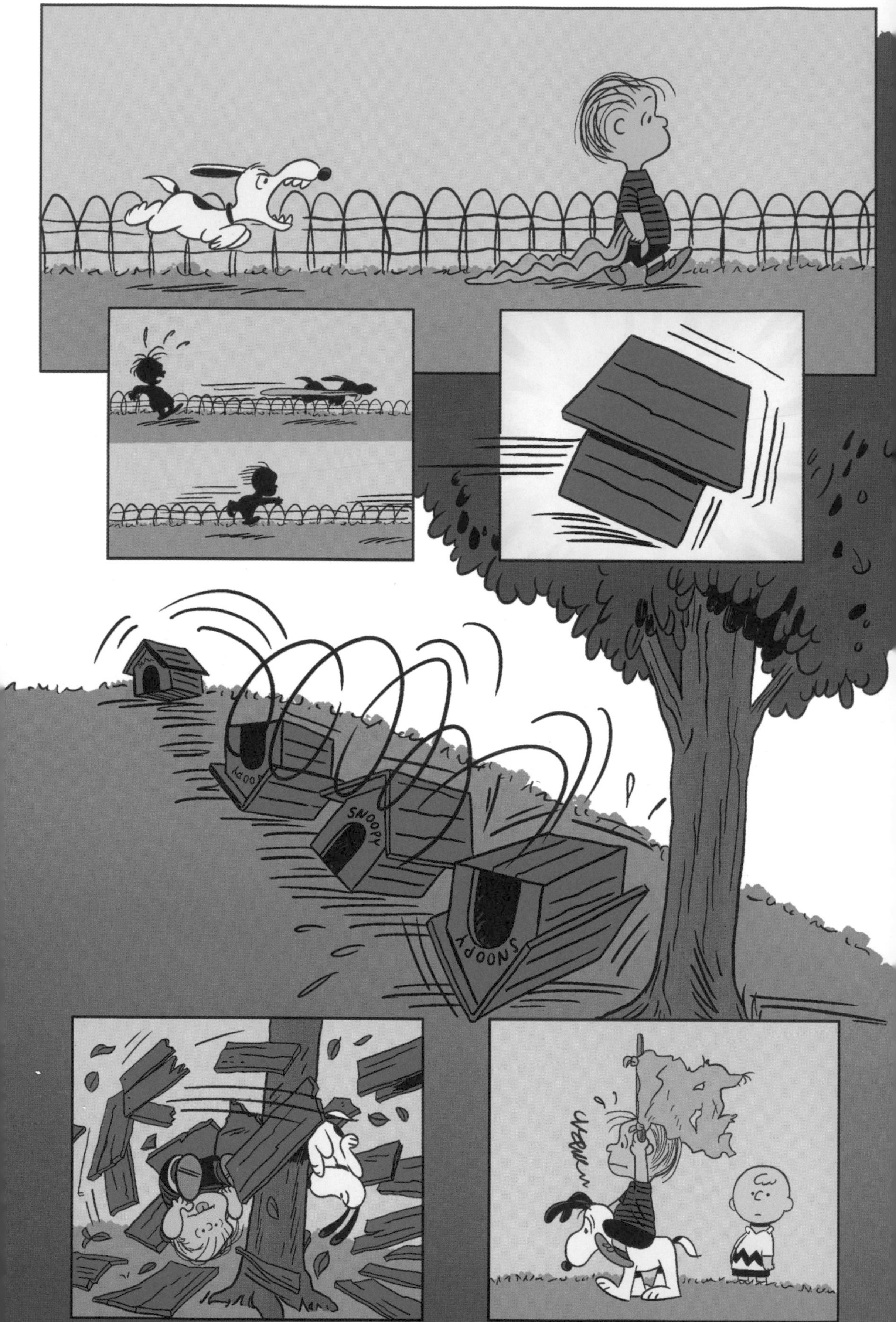
SNOOPY

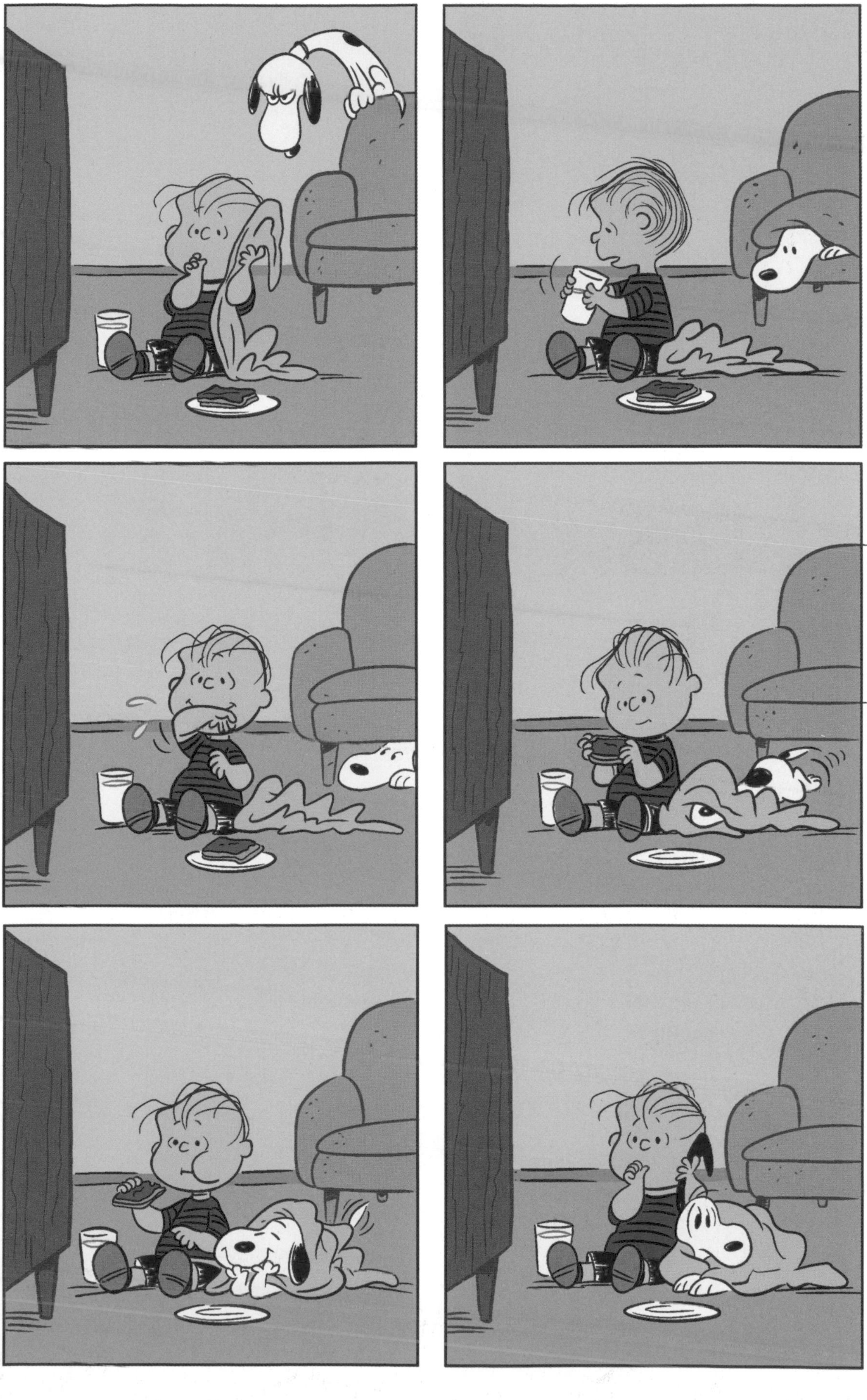

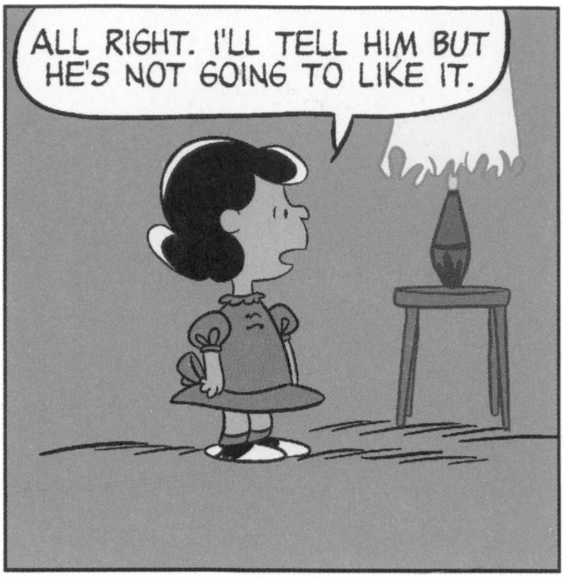
ALL RIGHT. I'LL TELL HIM BUT HE'S NOT GOING TO LIKE IT.

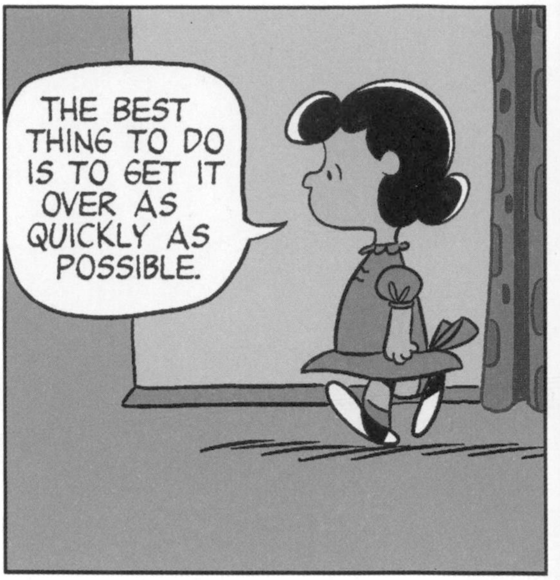
THE BEST THING TO DO IS TO GET IT OVER AS QUICKLY AS POSSIBLE.

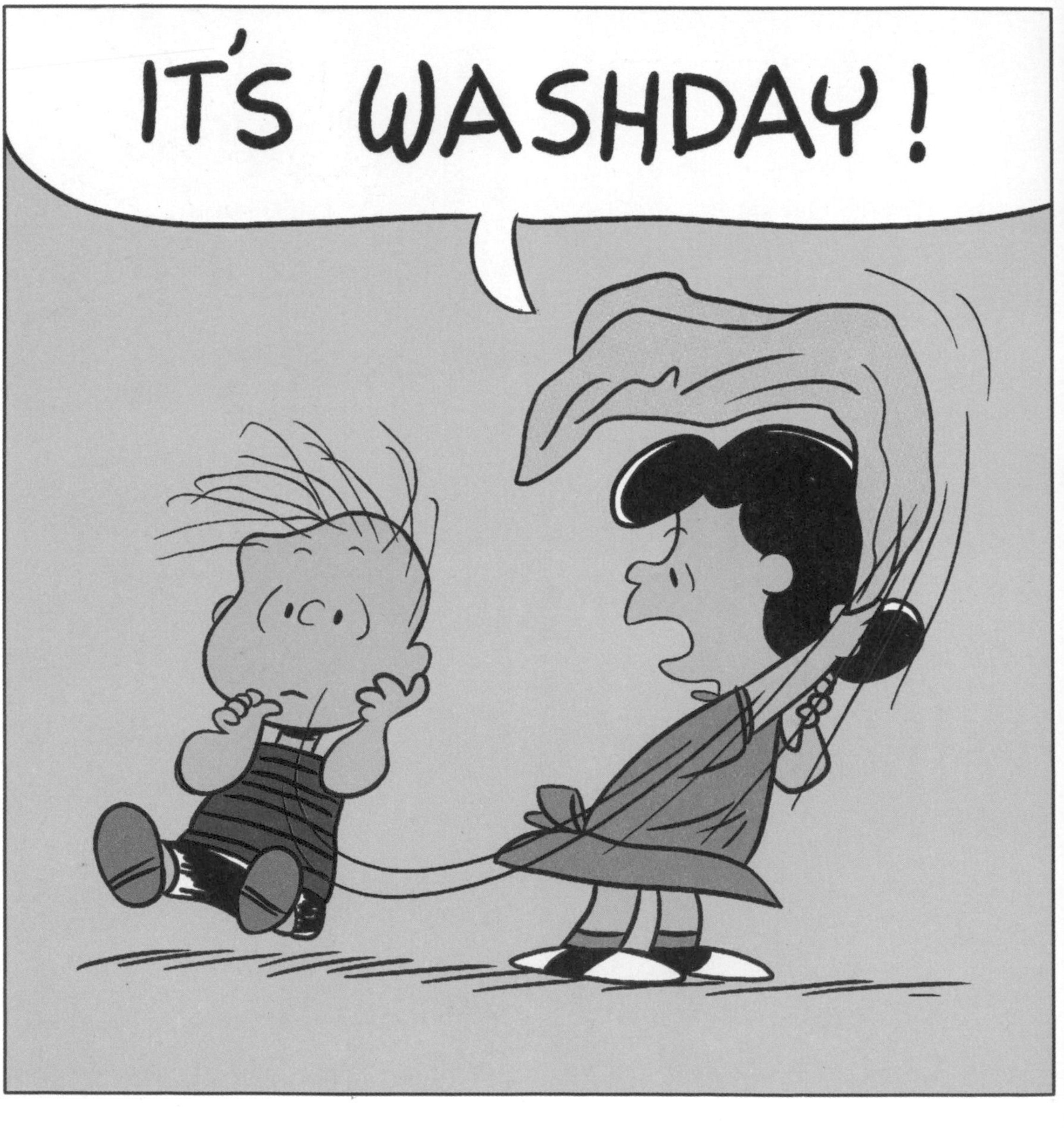
IT'S WASHDAY!

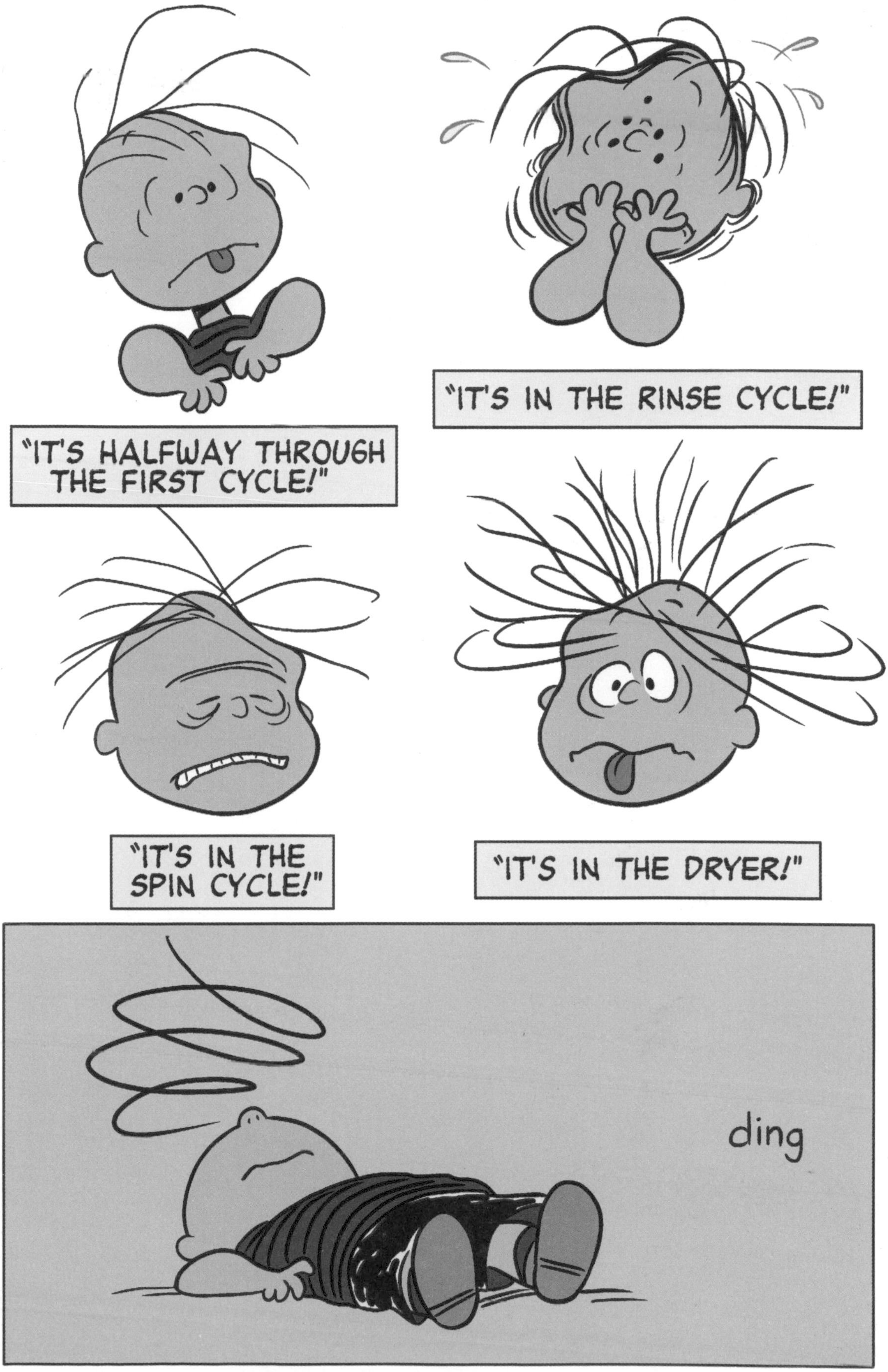
"IT'S HALFWAY THROUGH THE FIRST CYCLE!"
"IT'S IN THE RINSE CYCLE!"
"IT'S IN THE SPIN CYCLE!"
"IT'S IN THE DRYER!"
ding

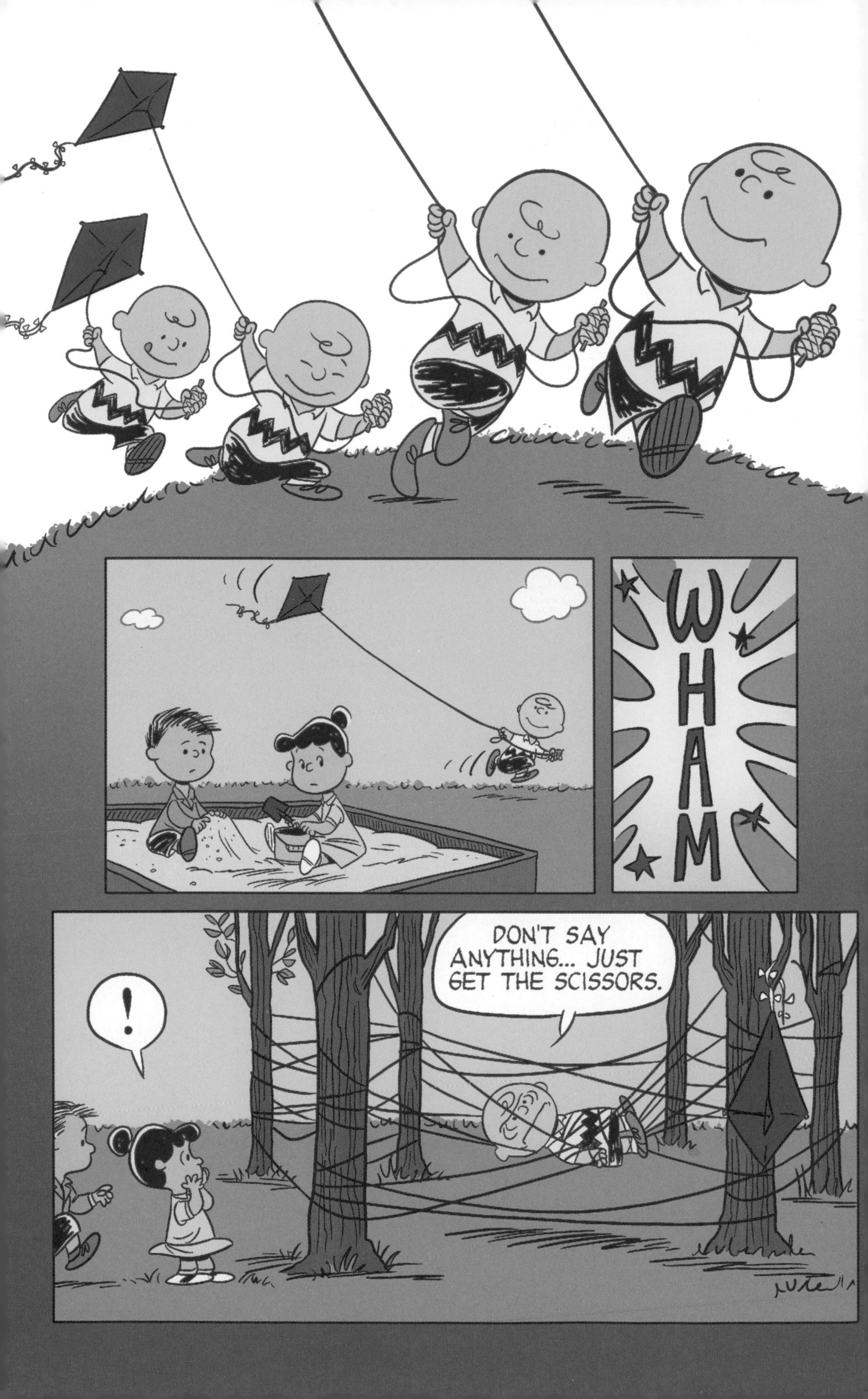
WHAM
!
DON'T SAY ANYTHING... JUST GET THE SCISSORS.

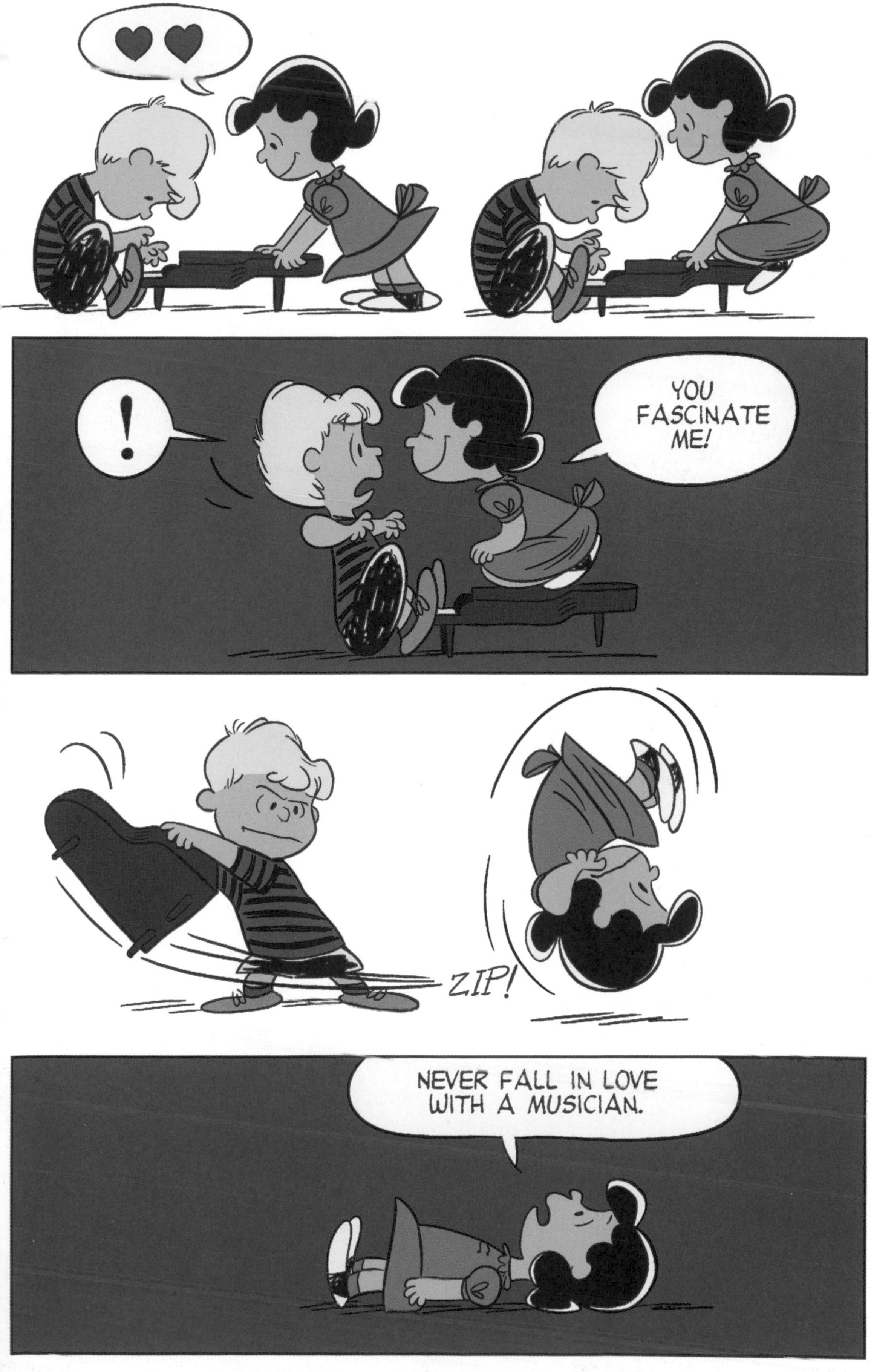
!
YOU FASCINATE ME!
ZIP!
NEVER FALL IN LOVE WITH A MUSICIAN.

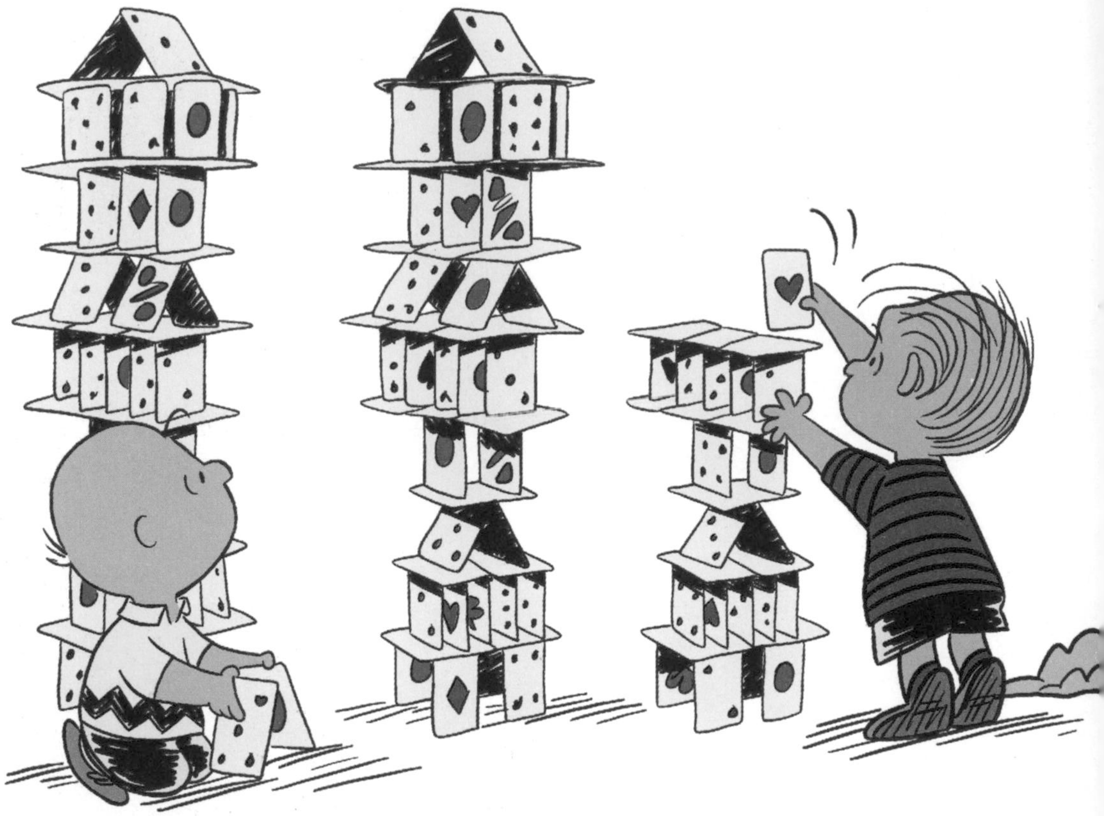

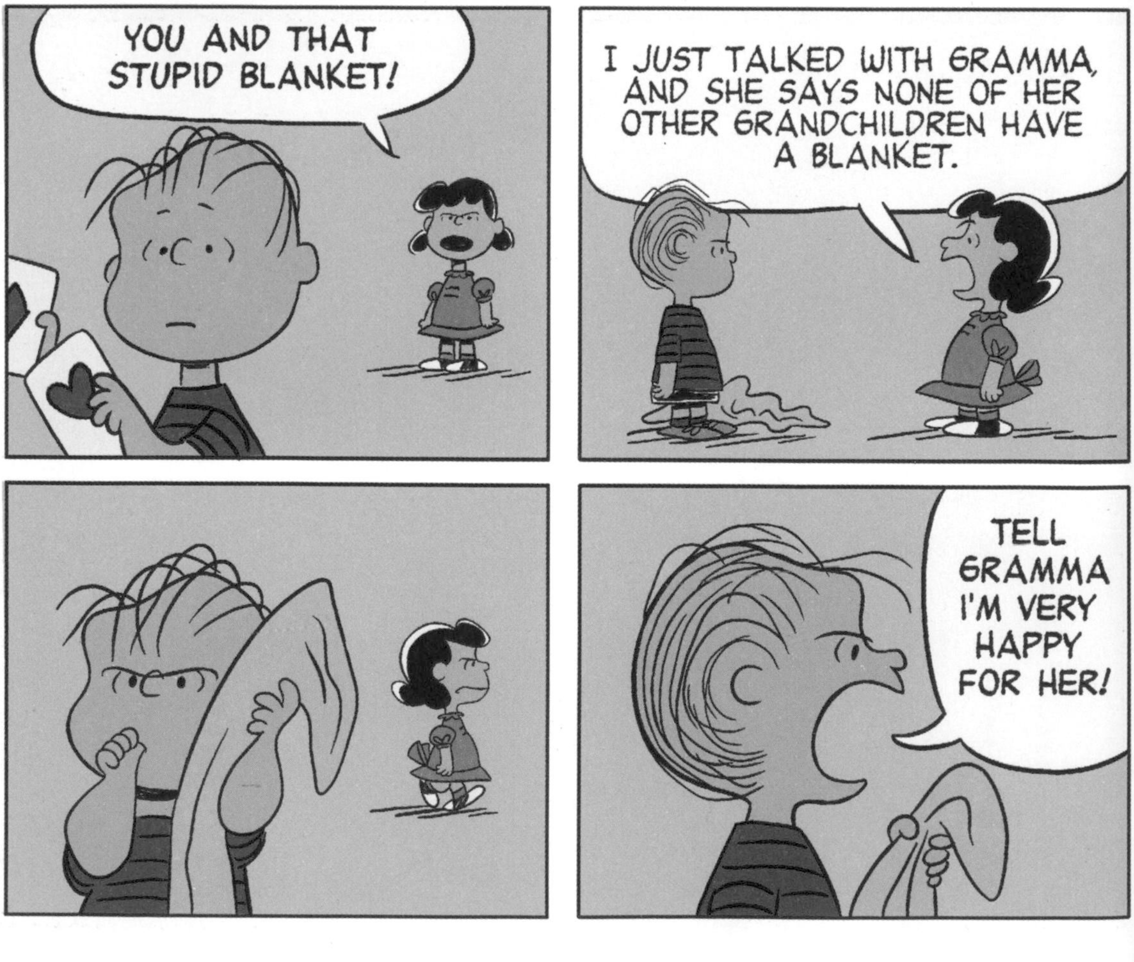
YOU AND THAT STUPID BLANKET!
I JUST TALKED WITH GRAMMA, AND SHE SAYS NONE OF HER OTHER GRANDCHILDREN HAVE A BLANKET.
TELL GRAMMA I'M VERY HAPPY FOR HER!

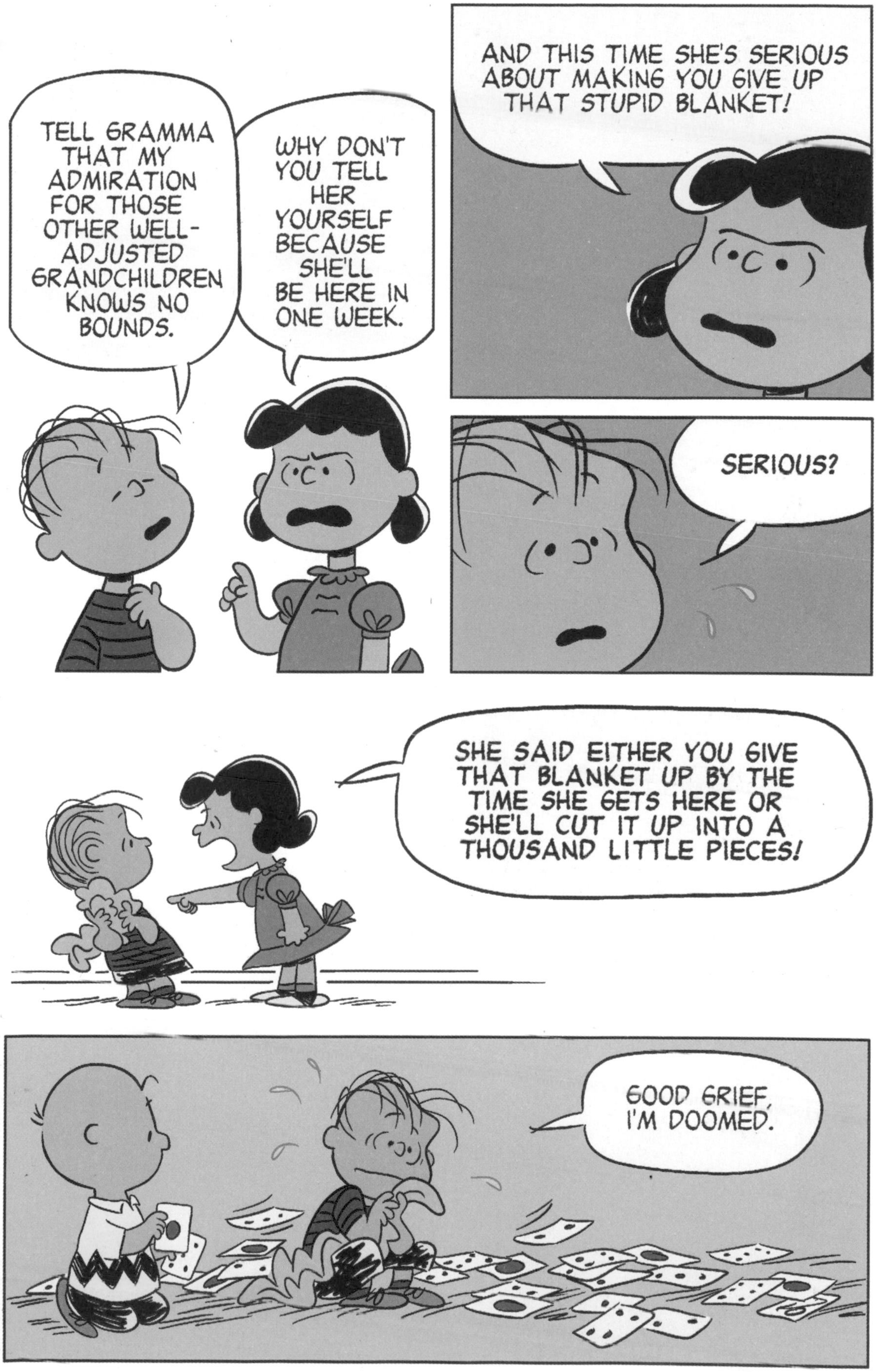
TELL GRAMMA THAT MY ADMIRATION FOR THOSE OTHER WELL-ADJUSTED GRANDCHILDREN KNOWS NO BOUNDS.
WHY DON'T YOU TELL HER YOURSELF BECAUSE SHE'LL BE HERE IN ONE WEEK.
AND THIS TIME SHE'S SERIOUS ABOUT MAKING YOU GIVE UP THAT STUPID BLANKET!
SERIOUS?
SHE SAID EITHER YOU GIVE THAT BLANKET UP BY THE TIME SHE GETS HERE OR SHE'LL CUT IT UP INTO A THOUSAND LITTLE PIECES!
GOOD GRIEF, I'M DOOMED.

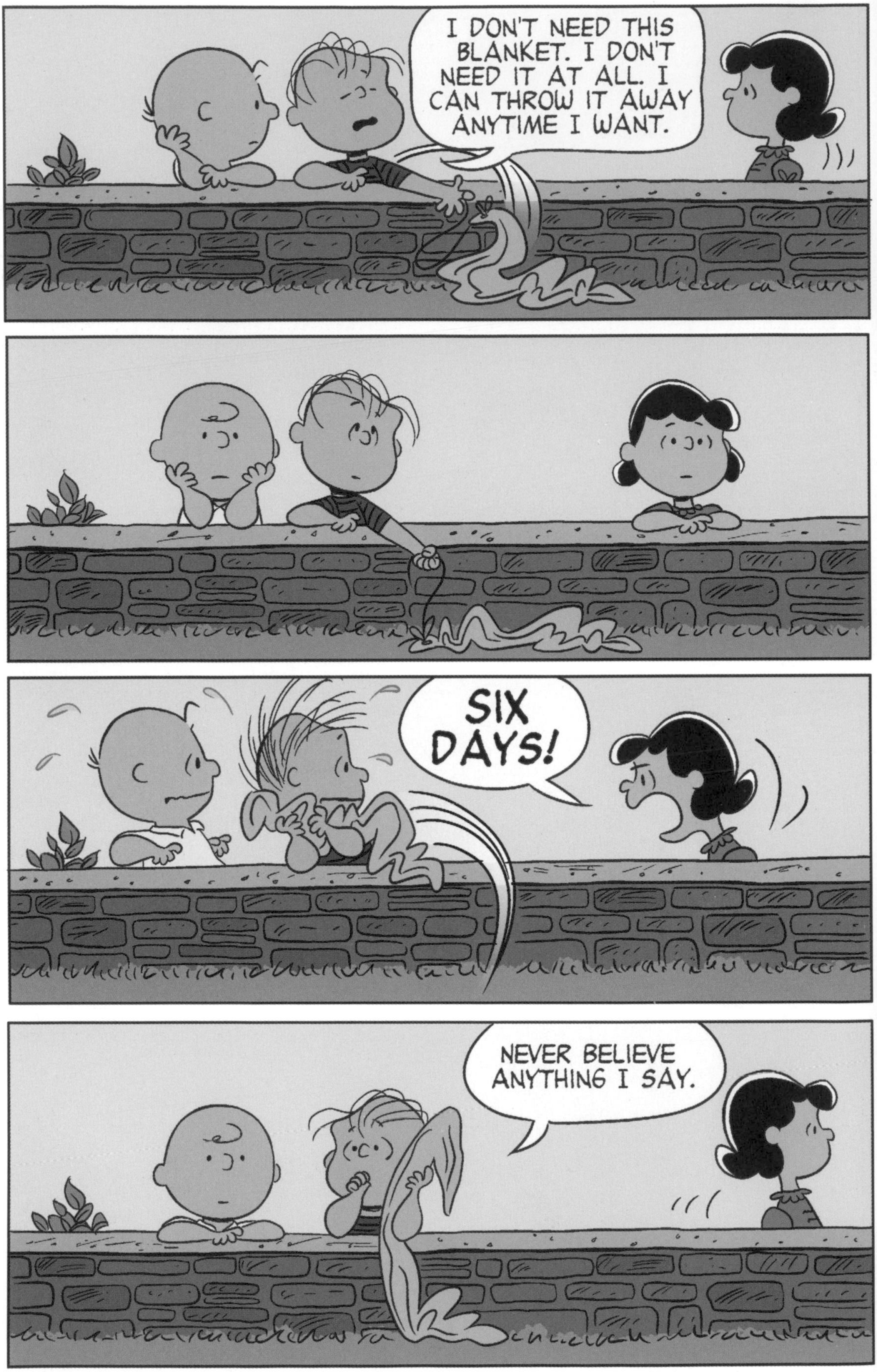
I DON'T NEED THIS BLANKET. I DON'T NEED IT AT ALL. I CAN THROW IT AWAY ANYTIME I WANT.
SIX DAYS!
NEVER BELIEVE ANYTHING I SAY.

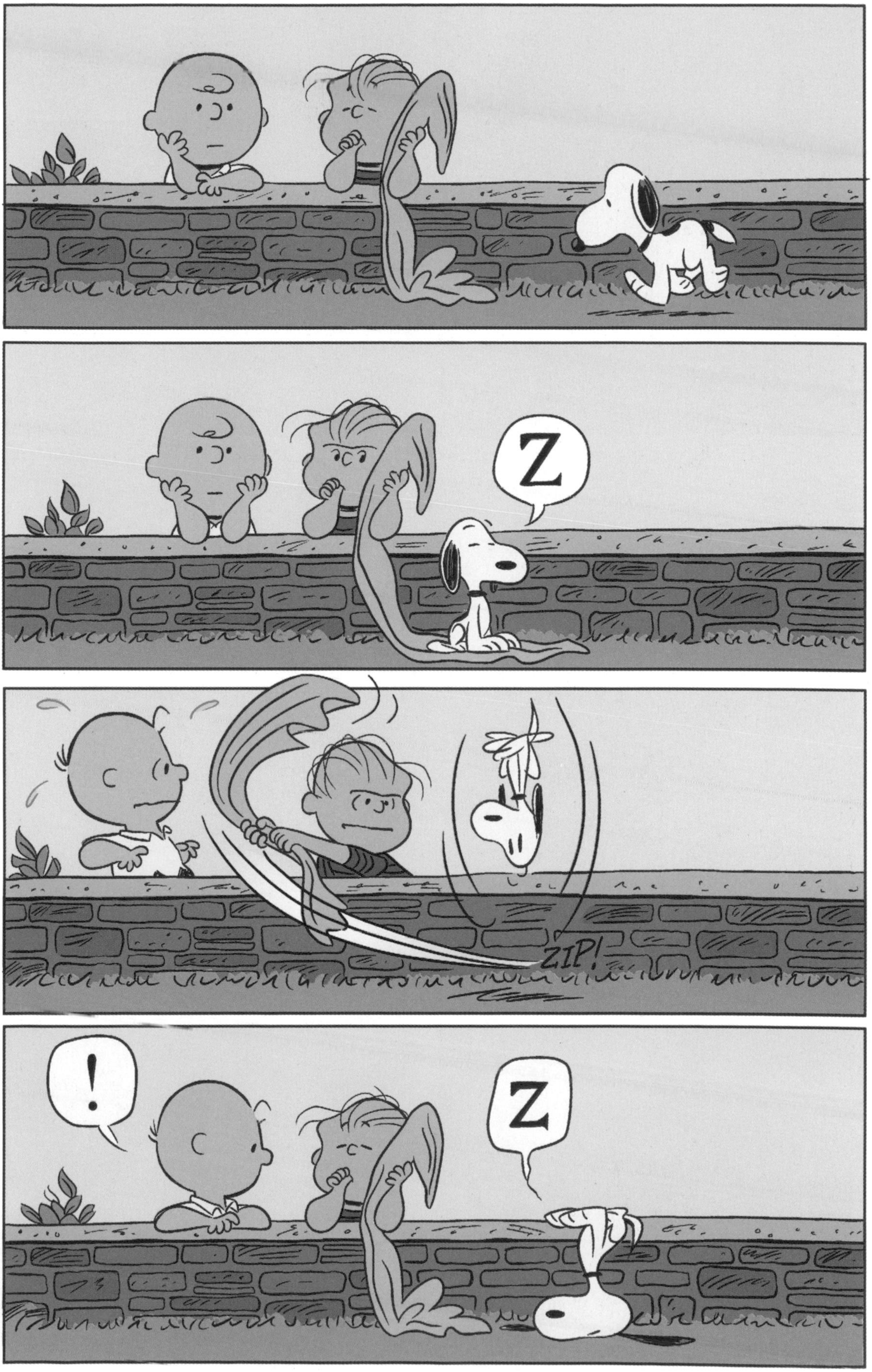
Z
ZIP!
!
Z

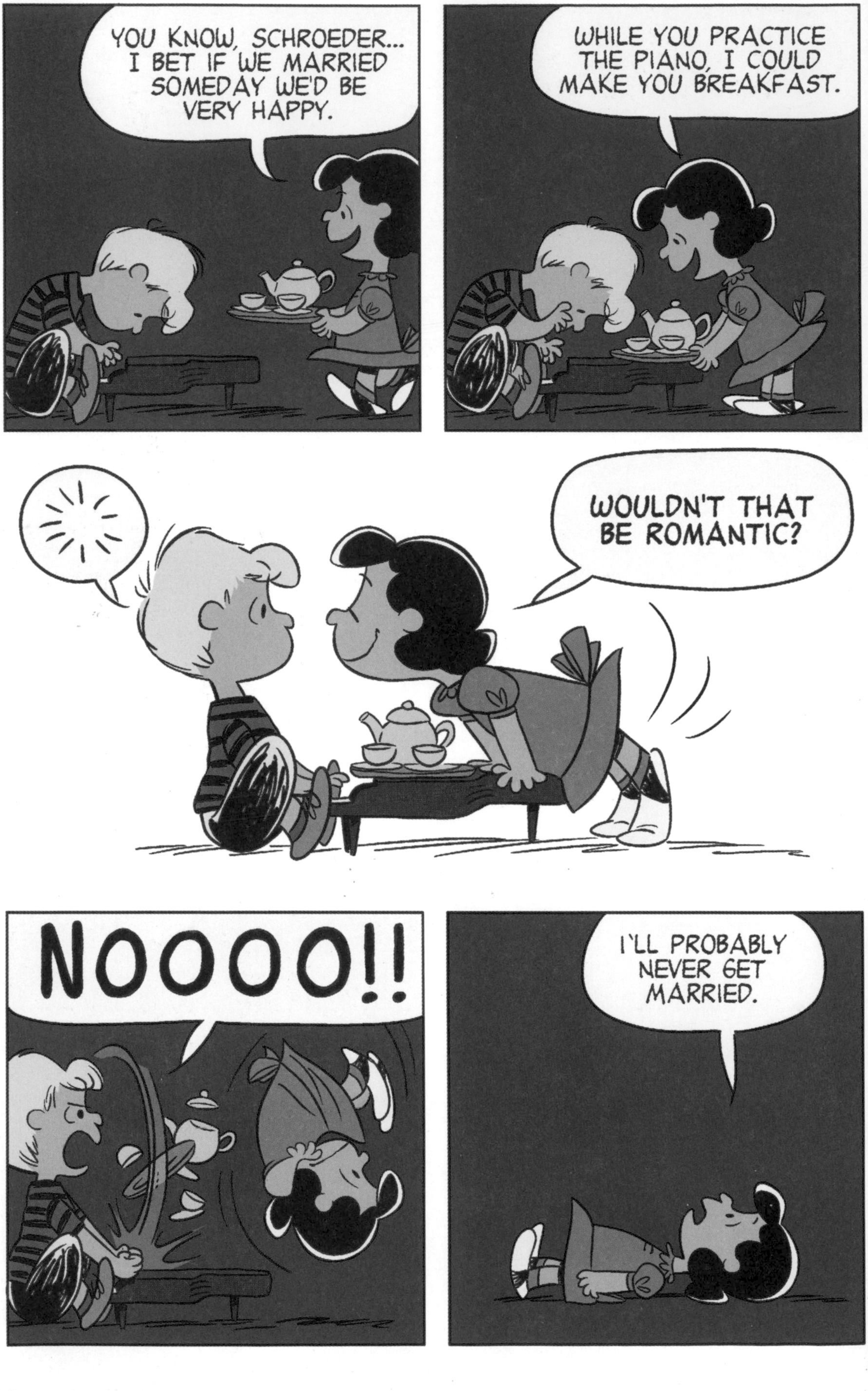
YOU KNOW, SCHROEDER... I BET IF WE MARRIED SOMEDAY WE'D BE VERY HAPPY.
WHILE YOU PRACTICE THE PIANO, I COULD MAKE YOU BREAKFAST.
WOULDN'T THAT BE ROMANTIC?
NOOOO!!
I'LL PROBABLY NEVER GET MARRIED.

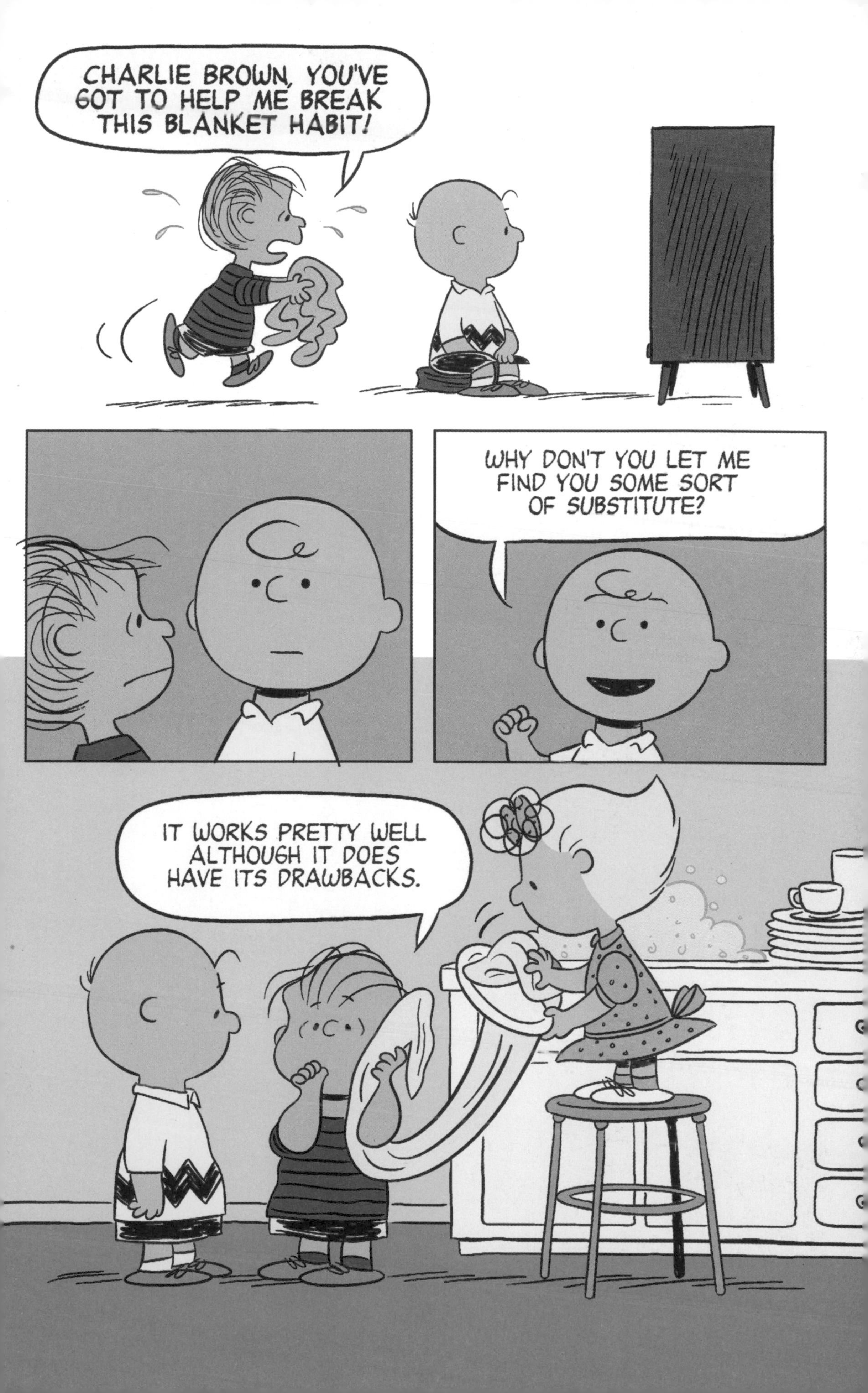
CHARLIE BROWN, YOU'VE GOT TO HELP ME BREAK THIS BLANKET HABIT!
WHY DON'T YOU LET ME FIND YOU SOME SORT OF SUBSTITUTE?
IT WORKS PRETTY WELL ALTHOUGH IT DOES HAVE ITS DRAWBACKS.

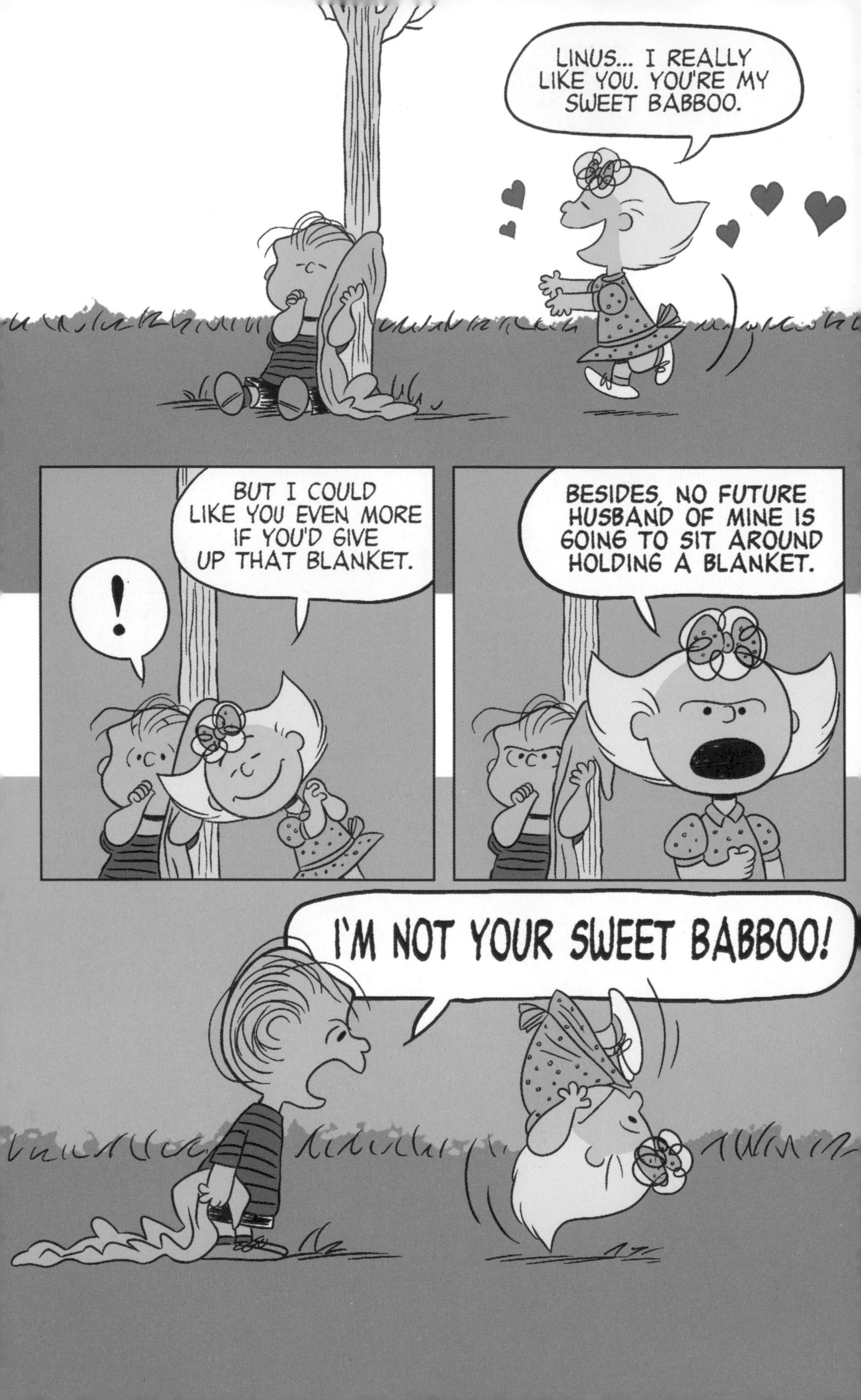

LINUS... I REALLY LIKE YOU. YOU'RE MY SWEET BABBOO.
BUT I COULD LIKE YOU EVEN MORE IF YOU'D GIVE UP THAT BLANKET.
!
BESIDES, NO FUTURE HUSBAND OF MINE IS GOING TO SIT AROUND HOLDING A BLANKET.
I'M NOT YOUR SWEET BABBOO!

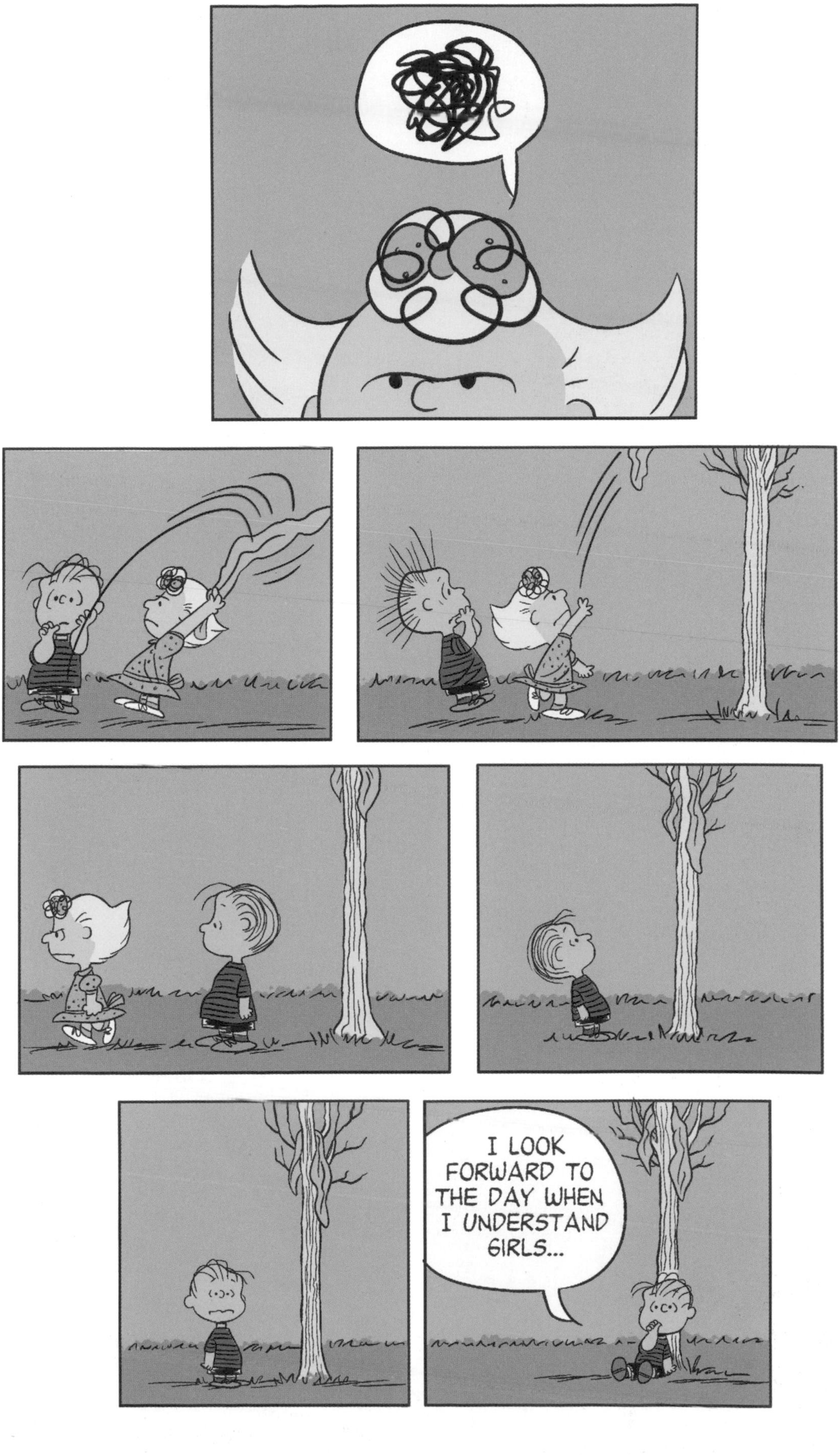
I LOOK FORWARD TO THE DAY WHEN I UNDERSTAND GIRLS...

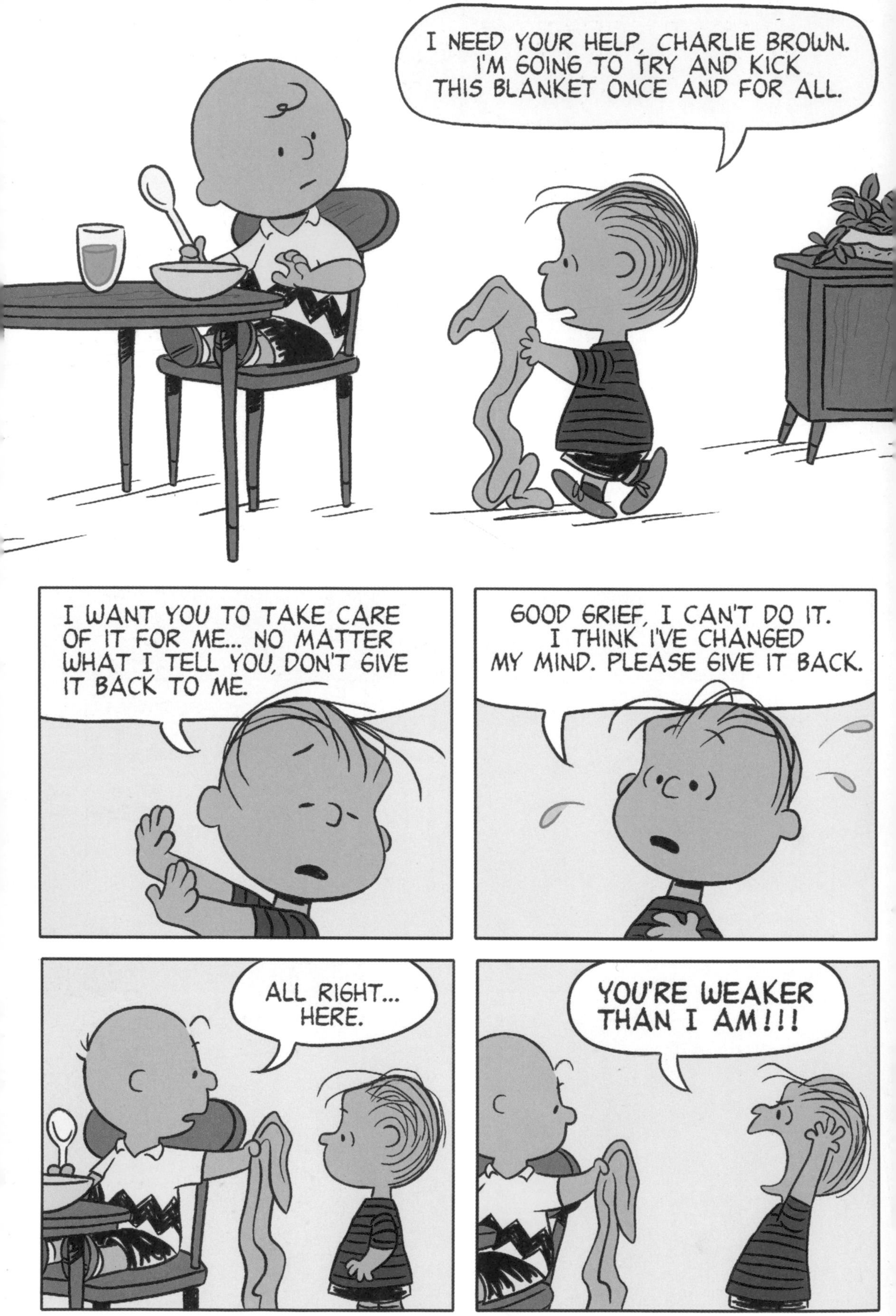
I NEED YOUR HELP, CHARLIE BROWN. I'M GOING TO TRY AND KICK THIS BLANKET ONCE AND FOR ALL.
I WANT YOU TO TAKE CARE OF IT FOR ME... NO MATTER WHAT I TELL YOU, DON'T GIVE IT BACK TO ME.
GOOD GRIEF, I CAN'T DO IT. I THINK I'VE CHANGED MY MIND. PLEASE GIVE IT BACK.
ALL RIGHT... HERE.
YOU'RE WEAKER THAN I AM!!!

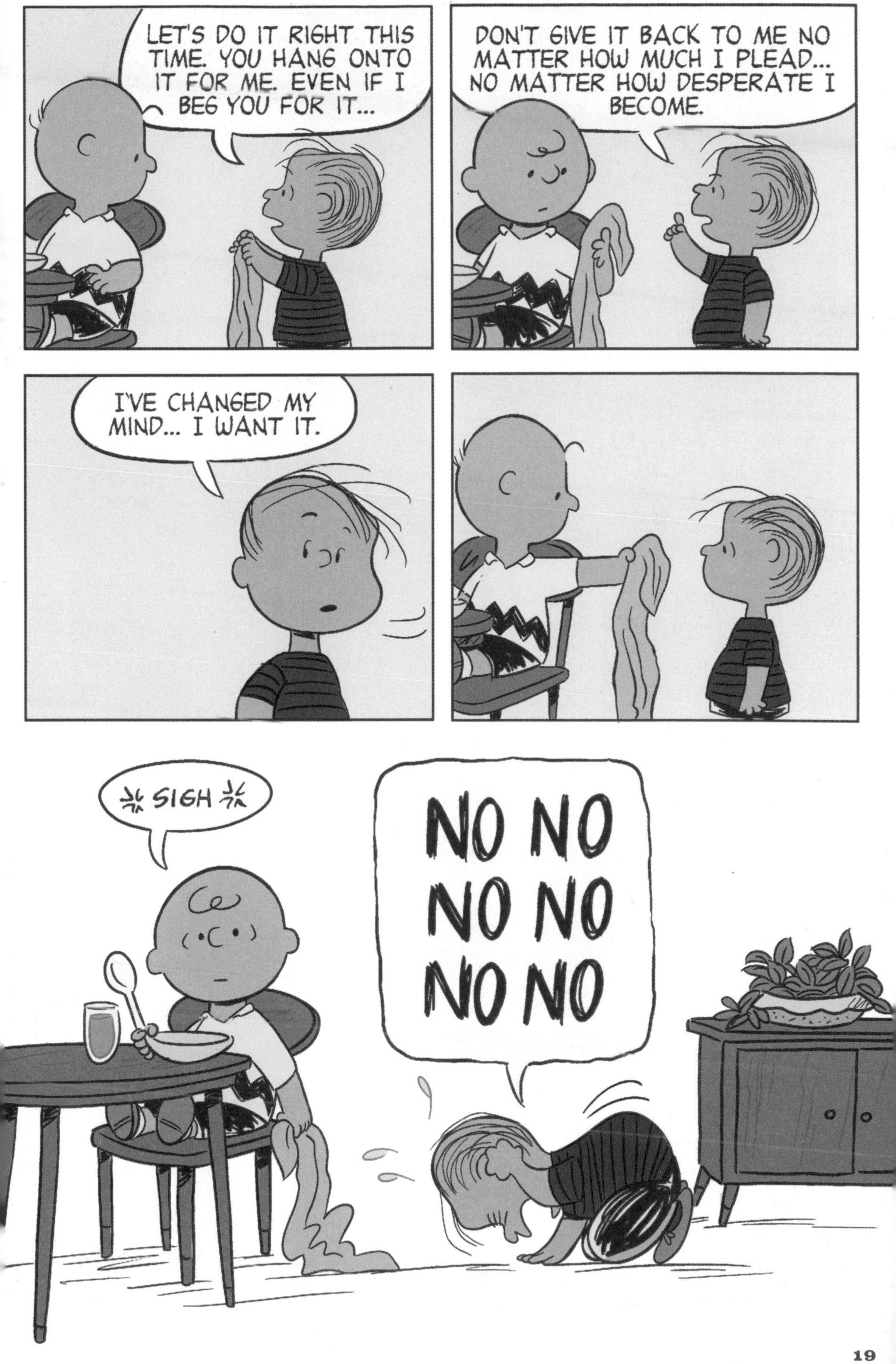
LET'S DO IT RIGHT THIS TIME. YOU HANG ONTO IT FOR ME. EVEN IF I BEG YOU FOR IT...
DON'T GIVE IT BACK TO ME NO MATTER HOW MUCH I PLEAD... NO MATTER HOW DESPERATE I BECOME.
I'VE CHANGED MY MIND... I WANT IT.
SIGH
NO NO NO NO NO NO

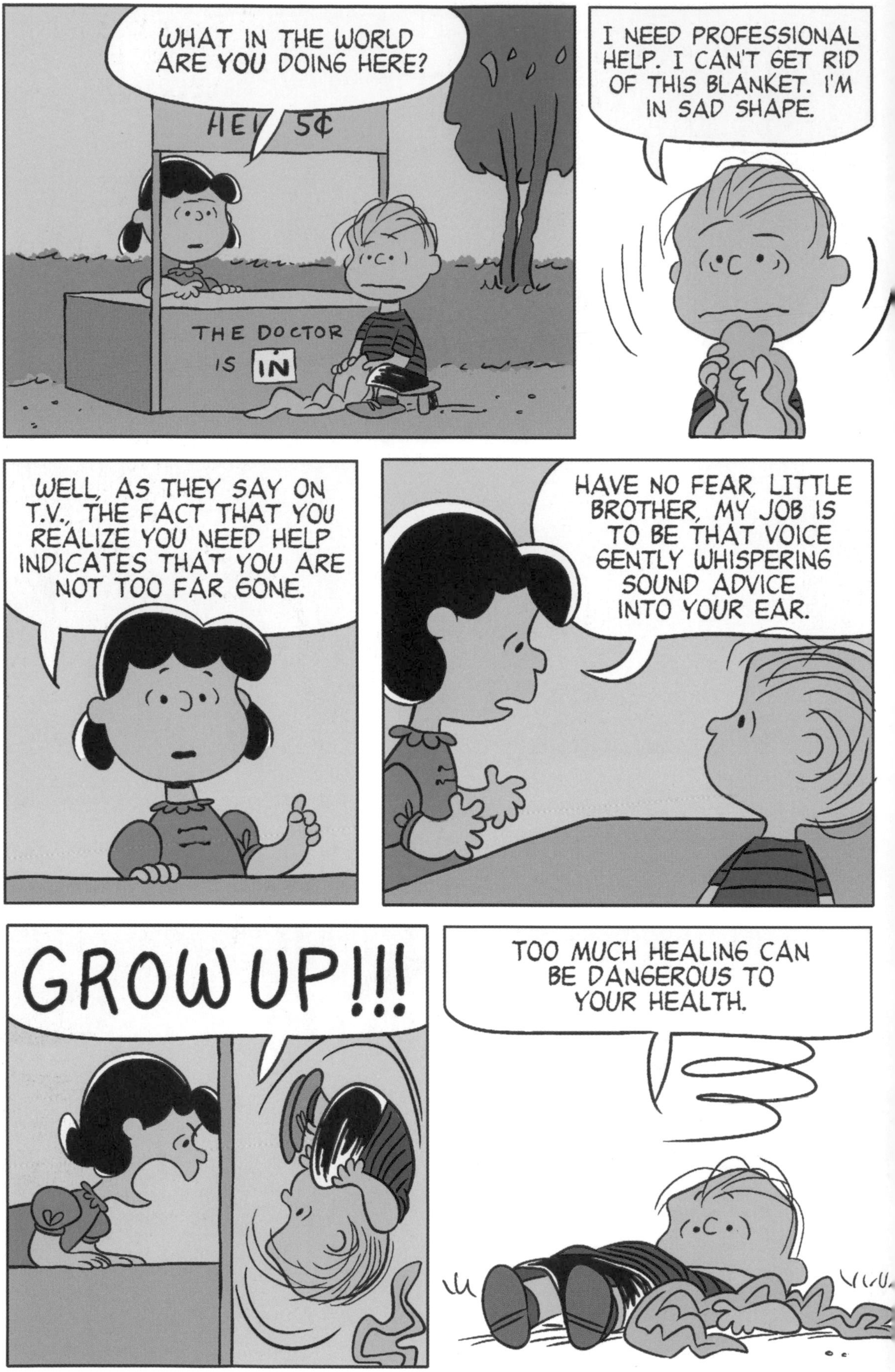
WHAT IN THE WORLD ARE YOU DOING HERE?
HEL 5¢
THE DOCTOR IS IN
I NEED PROFESSIONAL HELP. I CAN'T GET RID OF THIS BLANKET. I'M IN SAD SHAPE.
WELL, AS THEY SAY ON T.V., THE FACT THAT YOU REALIZE YOU NEED HELP INDICATES THAT YOU ARE NOT TOO FAR GONE.
HAVE NO FEAR, LITTLE BROTHER, MY JOB IS TO BE THAT VOICE GENTLY WHISPERING SOUND ADVICE INTO YOUR EAR.
GROW UP!!!
TOO MUCH HEALING CAN BE DANGEROUS TO YOUR HEALTH.

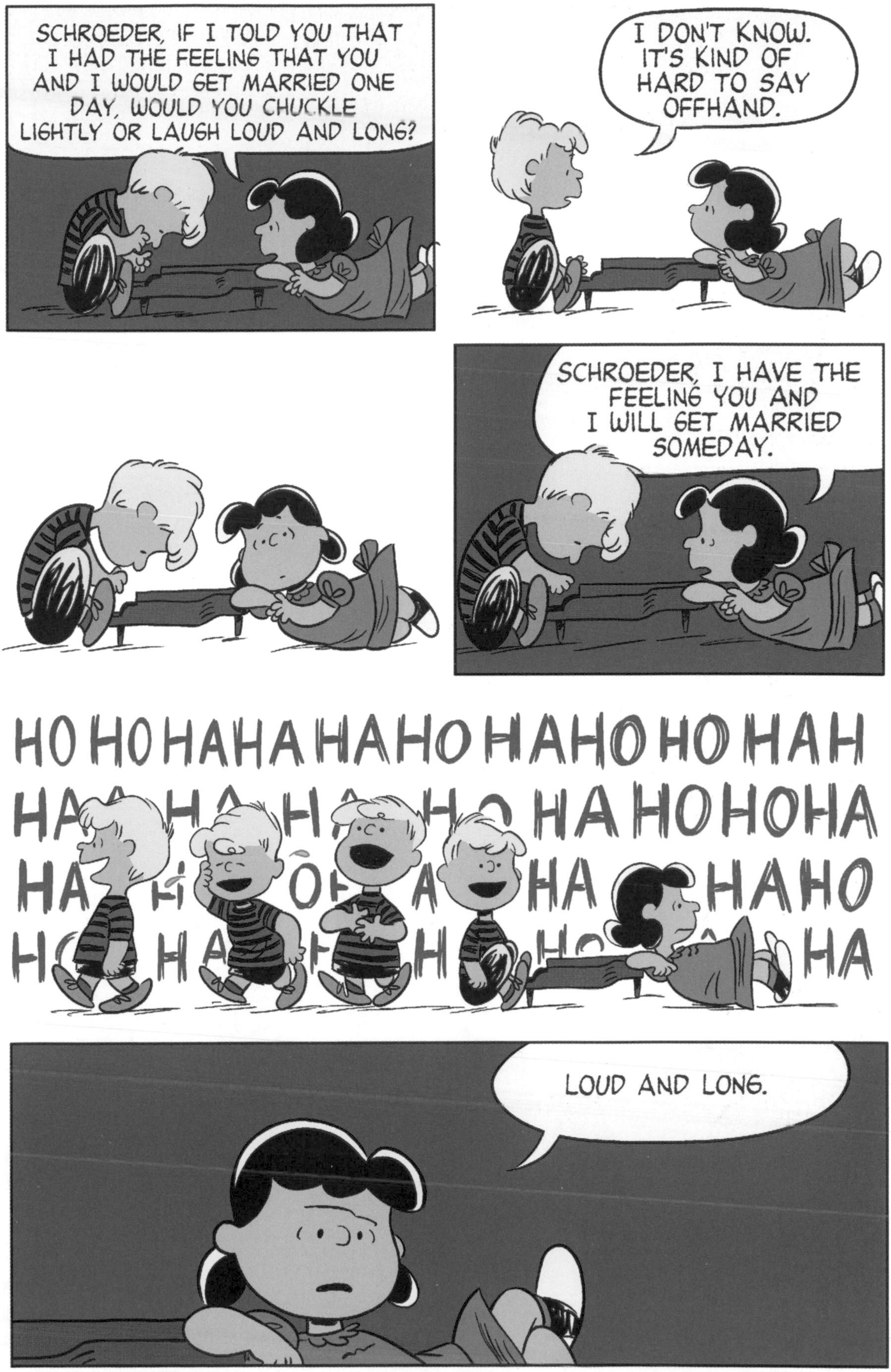
SCHROEDER, IF I TOLD YOU THAT I HAD THE FEELING THAT YOU AND I WOULD GET MARRIED ONE DAY, WOULD YOU CHUCKLE LIGHTLY OR LAUGH LOUD AND LONG?
I DON'T KNOW. IT'S KIND OF HARD TO SAY OFFHAND.
SCHROEDER, I HAVE THE FEELING YOU AND I WILL GET MARRIED SOMEDAY.
HO HO HA HA HA HO HA HO HO HAH
HA HO HO HA
HA HA HO
HA
LOUD AND LONG.

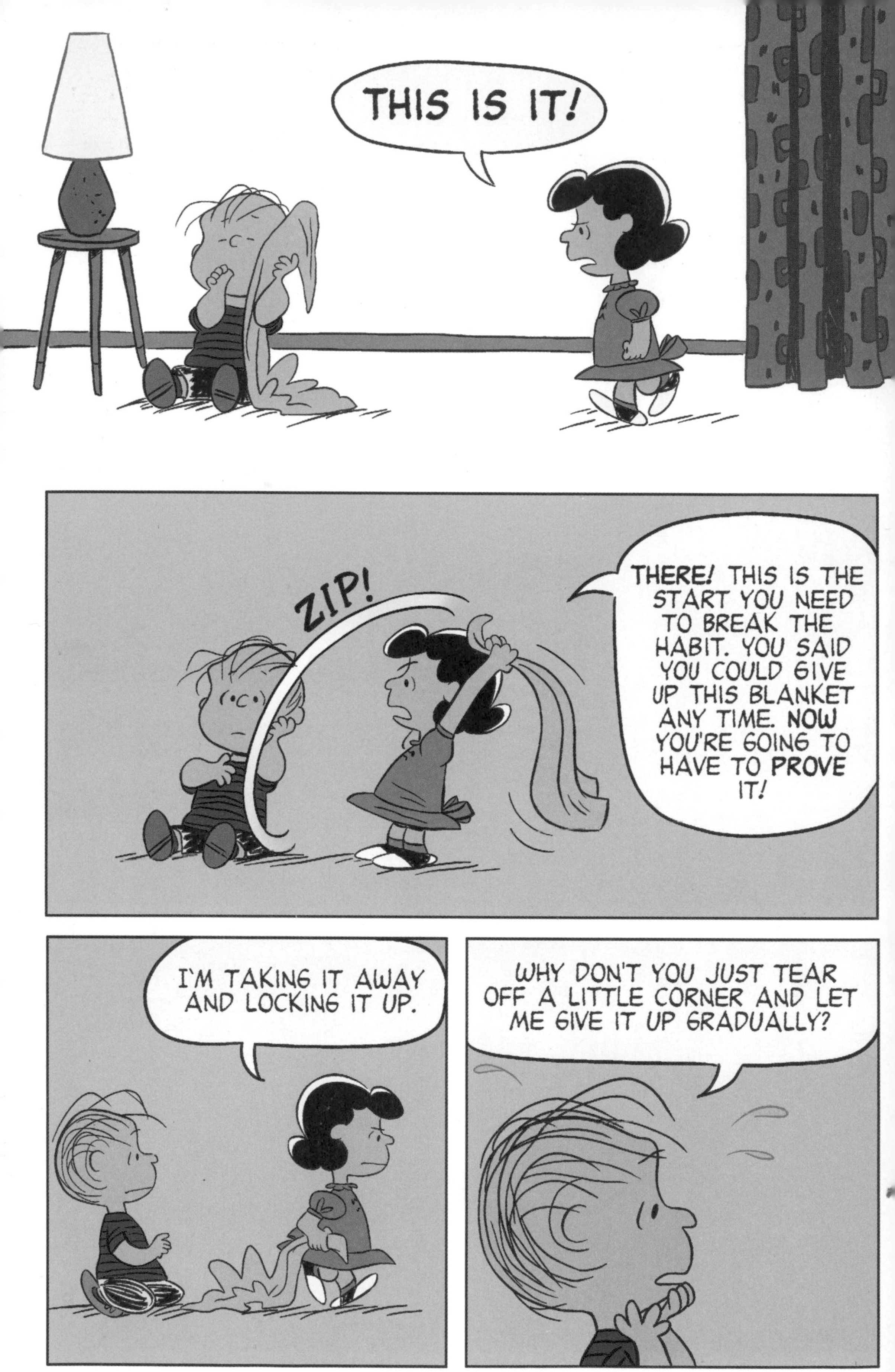
THIS IS IT!
ZIP!
THERE! THIS IS THE START YOU NEED TO BREAK THE HABIT. YOU SAID YOU COULD GIVE UP THIS BLANKET ANY TIME. NOW YOU'RE GOING TO HAVE TO PROVE IT!
I'M TAKING IT AWAY AND LOCKING IT UP.
WHY DON'T YOU JUST TEAR OFF A LITTLE CORNER AND LET ME GIVE IT UP GRADUALLY?

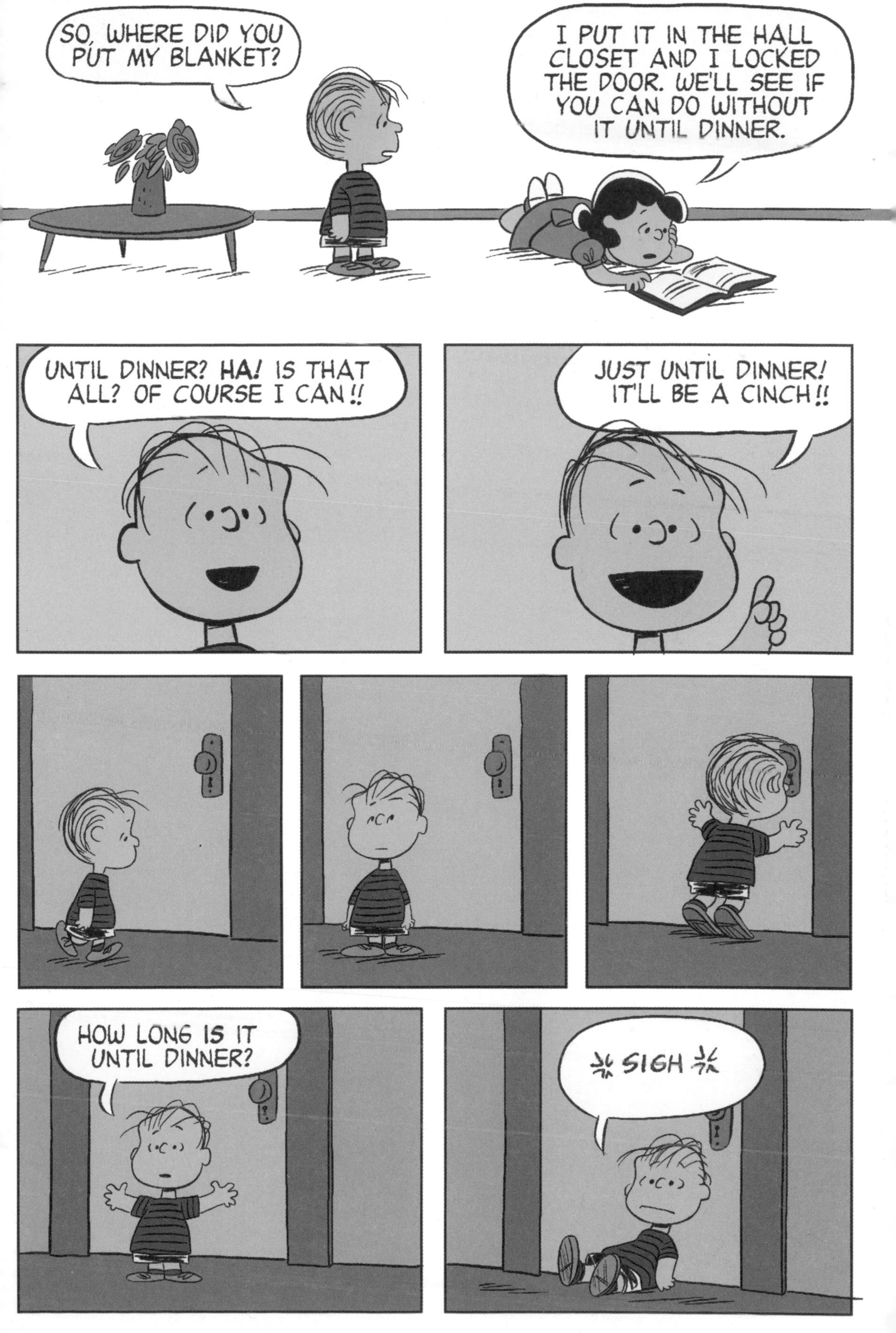
SO, WHERE DID YOU PUT MY BLANKET?
I PUT IT IN THE HALL CLOSET AND I LOCKED THE DOOR. WE'LL SEE IF YOU CAN DO WITHOUT IT UNTIL DINNER.
UNTIL DINNER? HA! IS THAT ALL? OF COURSE I CAN!!
JUST UNTIL DINNER! IT'LL BE A CINCH!!
HOW LONG IS IT UNTIL DINNER?
SIGH

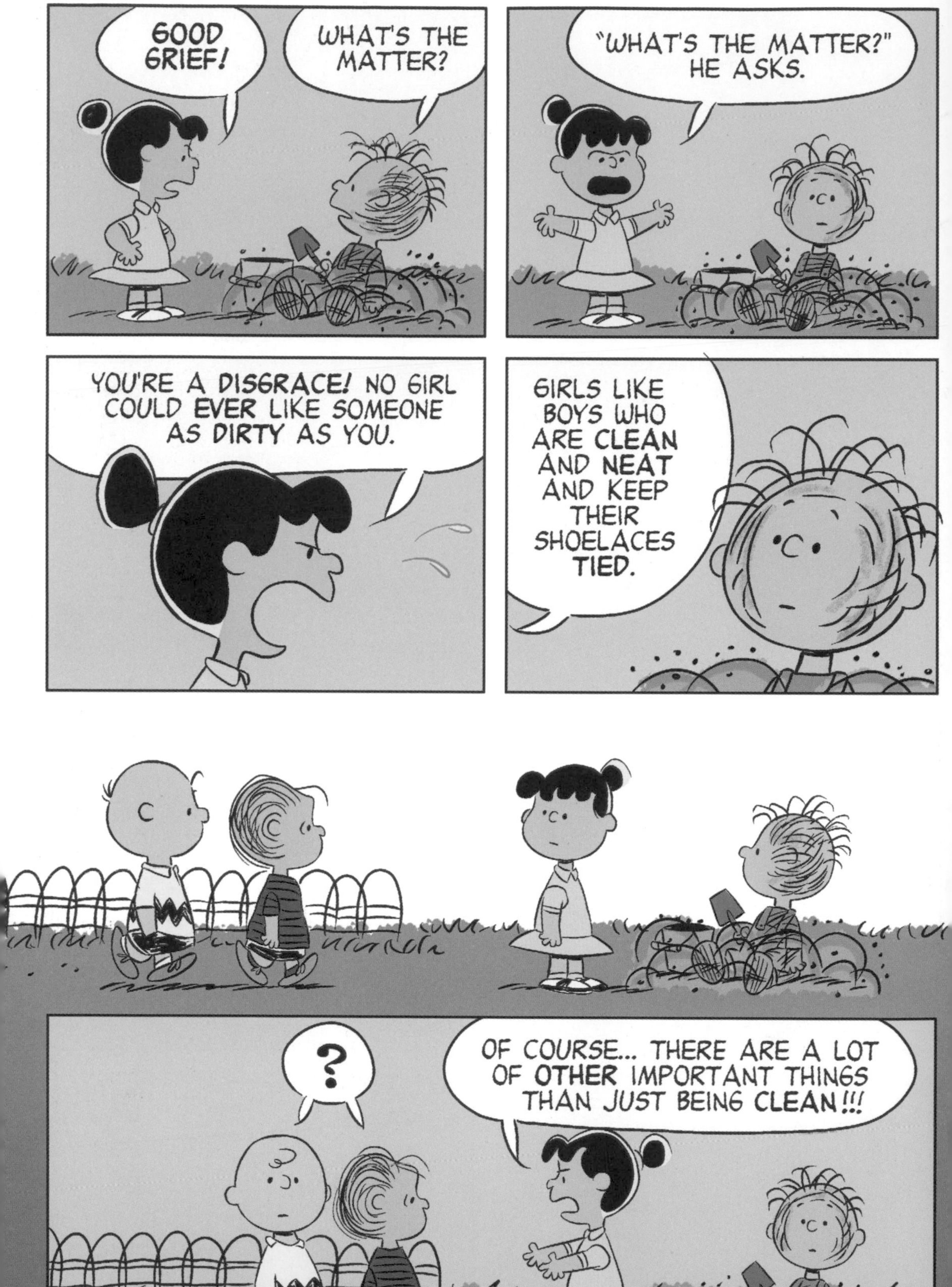
GOOD GRIEF!
WHAT'S THE MATTER?
"WHAT'S THE MATTER?" HE ASKS.
YOU'RE A DISGRACE! NO GIRL COULD EVER LIKE SOMEONE AS DIRTY AS YOU.
GIRLS LIKE BOYS WHO ARE CLEAN AND NEAT AND KEEP THEIR SHOELACES TIED.
?
OF COURSE... THERE ARE A LOT OF OTHER IMPORTANT THINGS THAN JUST BEING CLEAN!!!

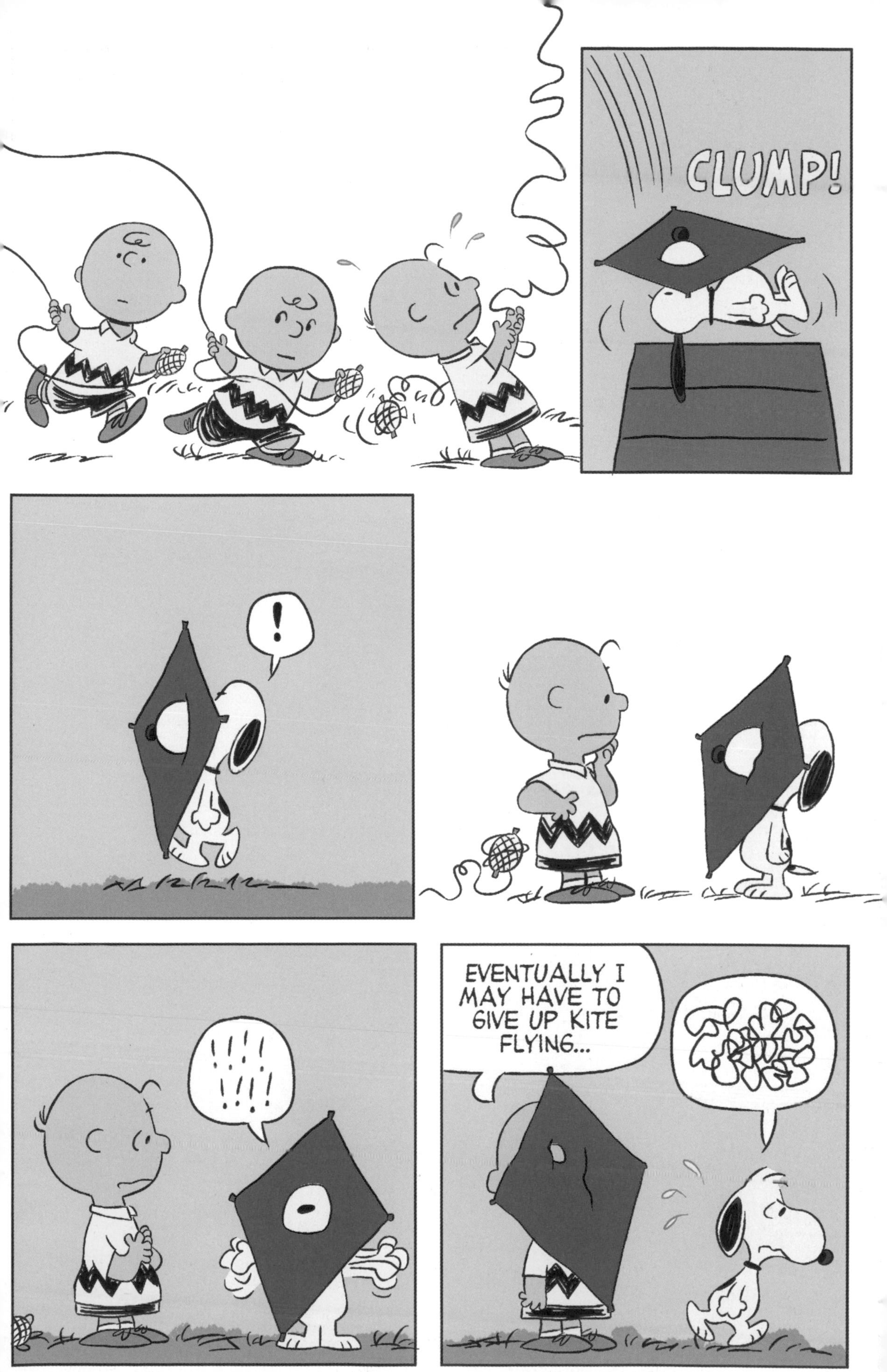
CLUMP!
!
!!!
!!!!
EVENTUALLY I MAY HAVE TO GIVE UP KITE FLYING...

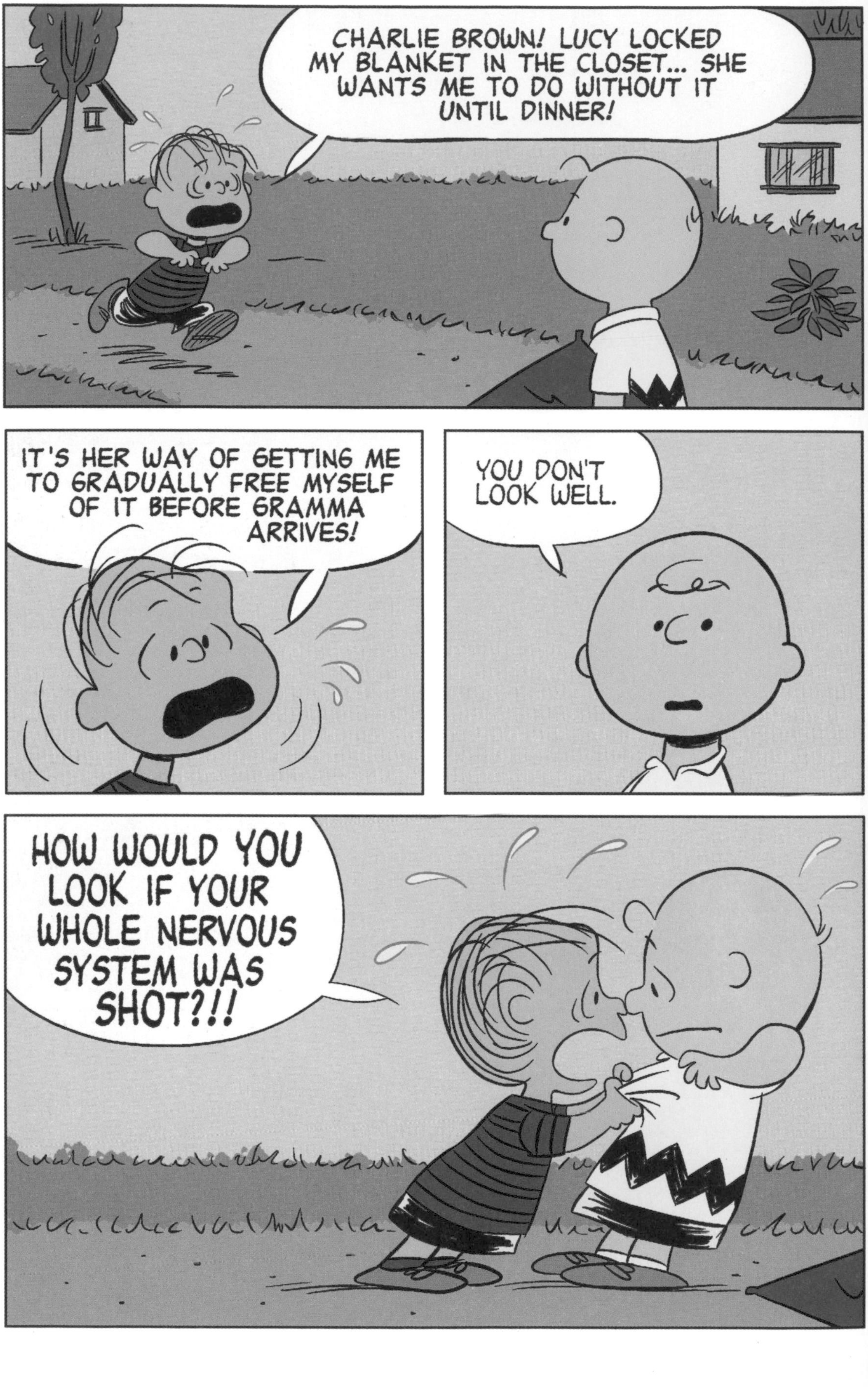

CHARLIE BROWN! LUCY LOCKED MY BLANKET IN THE CLOSET... SHE WANTS ME TO DO WITHOUT IT UNTIL DINNER!
IT'S HER WAY OF GETTING ME TO GRADUALLY FREE MYSELF OF IT BEFORE GRAMMA ARRIVES!
YOU DON'T LOOK WELL.
HOW WOULD YOU LOOK IF YOUR WHOLE NERVOUS SYSTEM WAS SHOT?!!

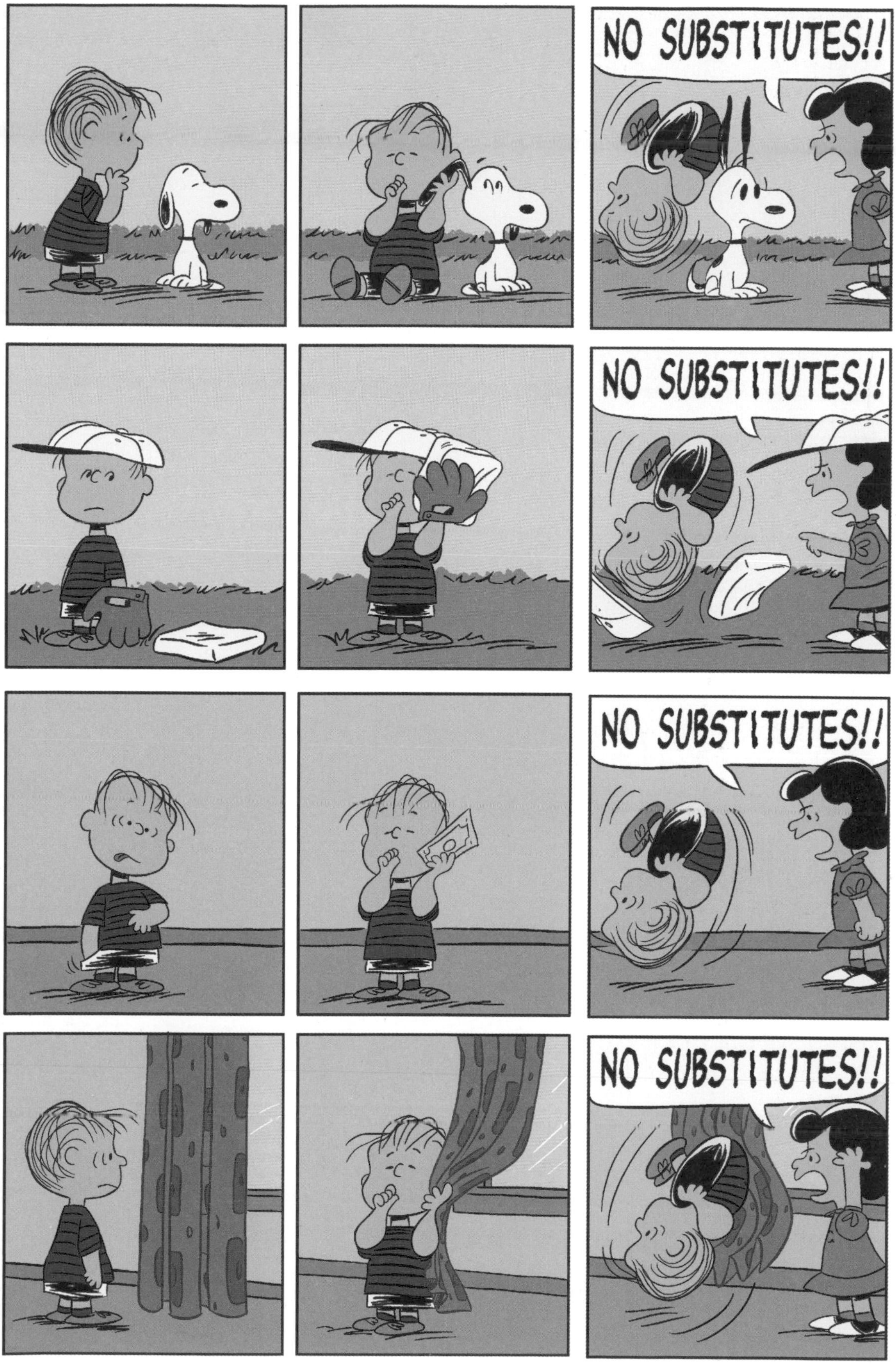
NO SUBSTITUTES!!
NO SUBSTITUTES!!
NO SUBSTITUTES!!
NO SUBSTITUTES!!

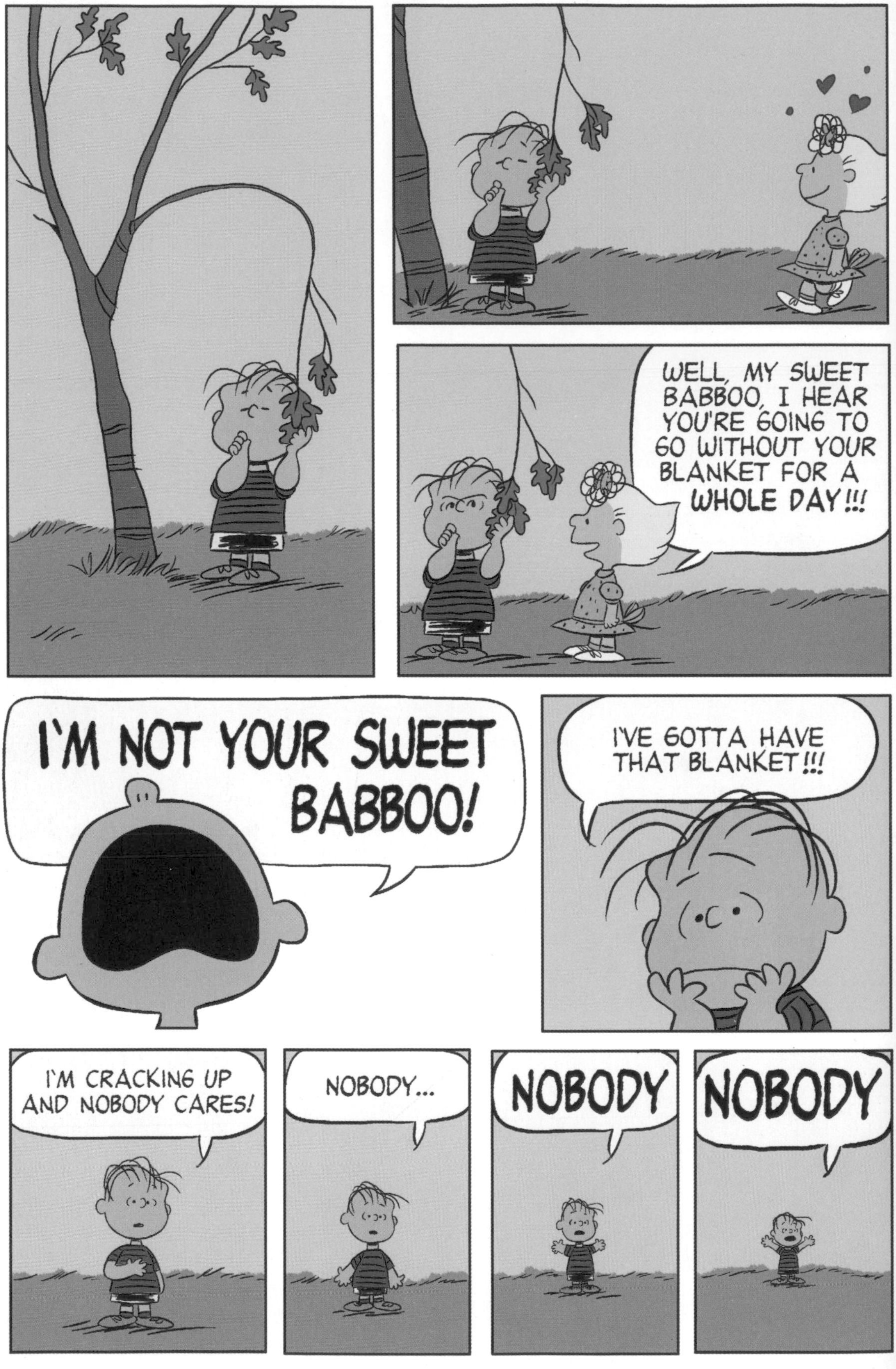

WELL, MY SWEET BABBOO, I HEAR YOU'RE GOING TO GO WITHOUT YOUR BLANKET FOR A WHOLE DAY!!!
I'M NOT YOUR SWEET BABBOO!
I'VE GOTTA HAVE THAT BLANKET!!!
I'M CRACKING UP AND NOBODY CARES!
NOBODY...
NOBODY
NOBODY

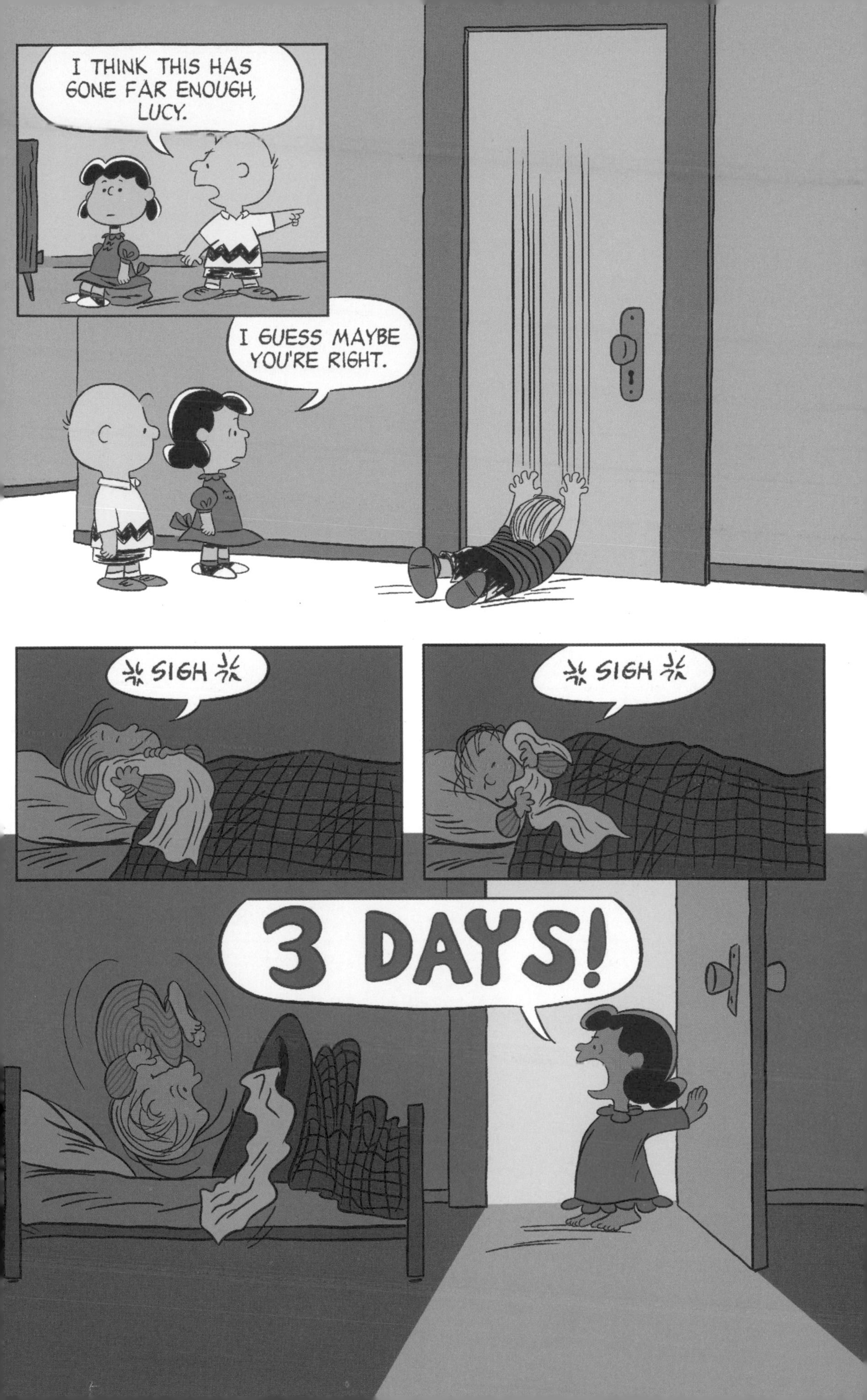
I THINK THIS HAS GONE FAR ENOUGH, LUCY.
I GUESS MAYBE YOU'RE RIGHT.
SIGH
SIGH
3 DAYS!

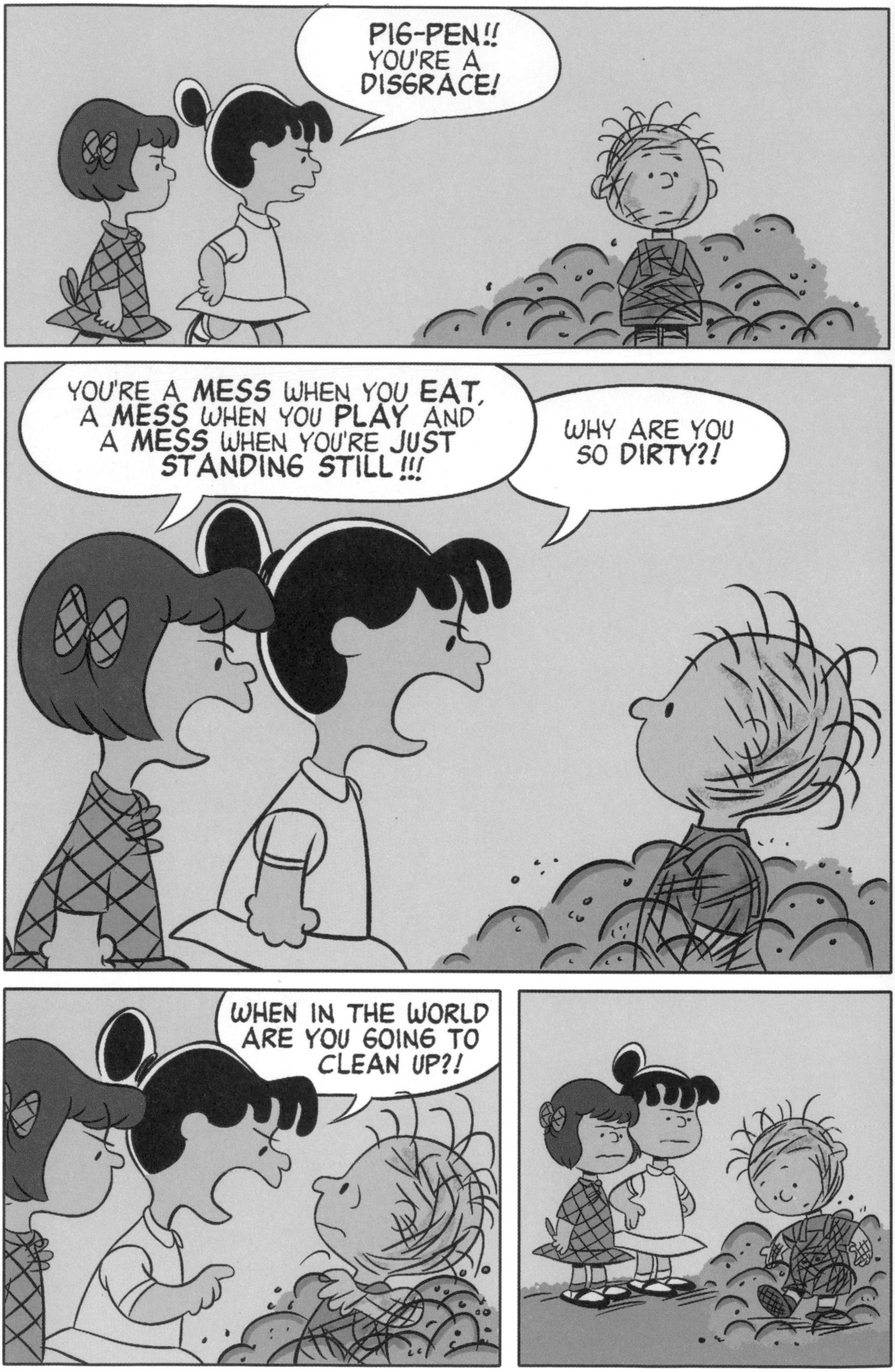
PIG-PEN!! YOU'RE A DISGRACE!
YOU'RE A MESS WHEN YOU EAT, A MESS WHEN YOU PLAY AND A MESS WHEN YOU'RE JUST STANDING STILL!!!
WHY ARE YOU SO DIRTY?!
WHEN IN THE WORLD ARE YOU GOING TO CLEAN UP?!

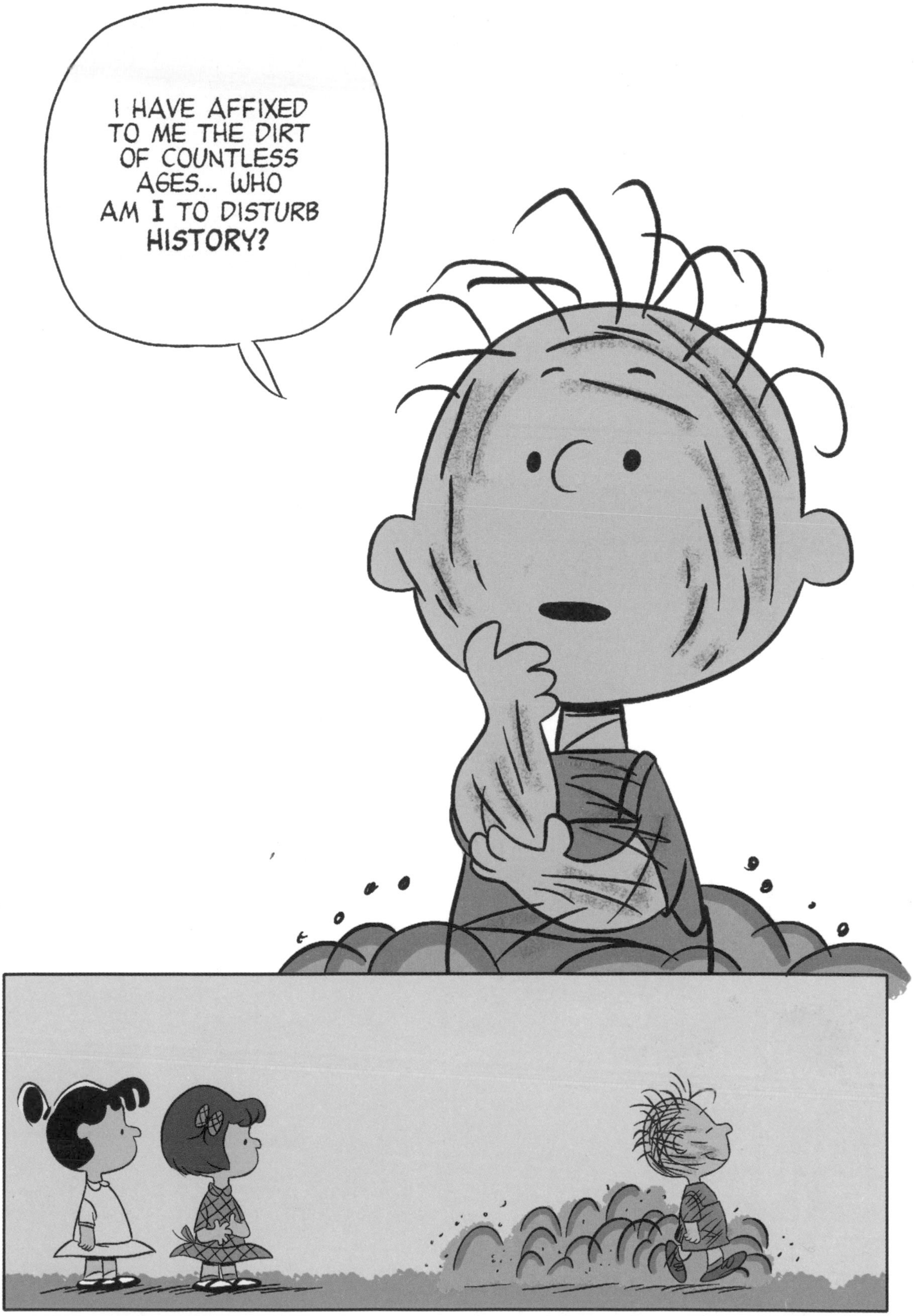
I HAVE AFFIXED TO ME THE DIRT OF COUNTLESS AGES... WHO AM I TO DISTURB HISTORY?

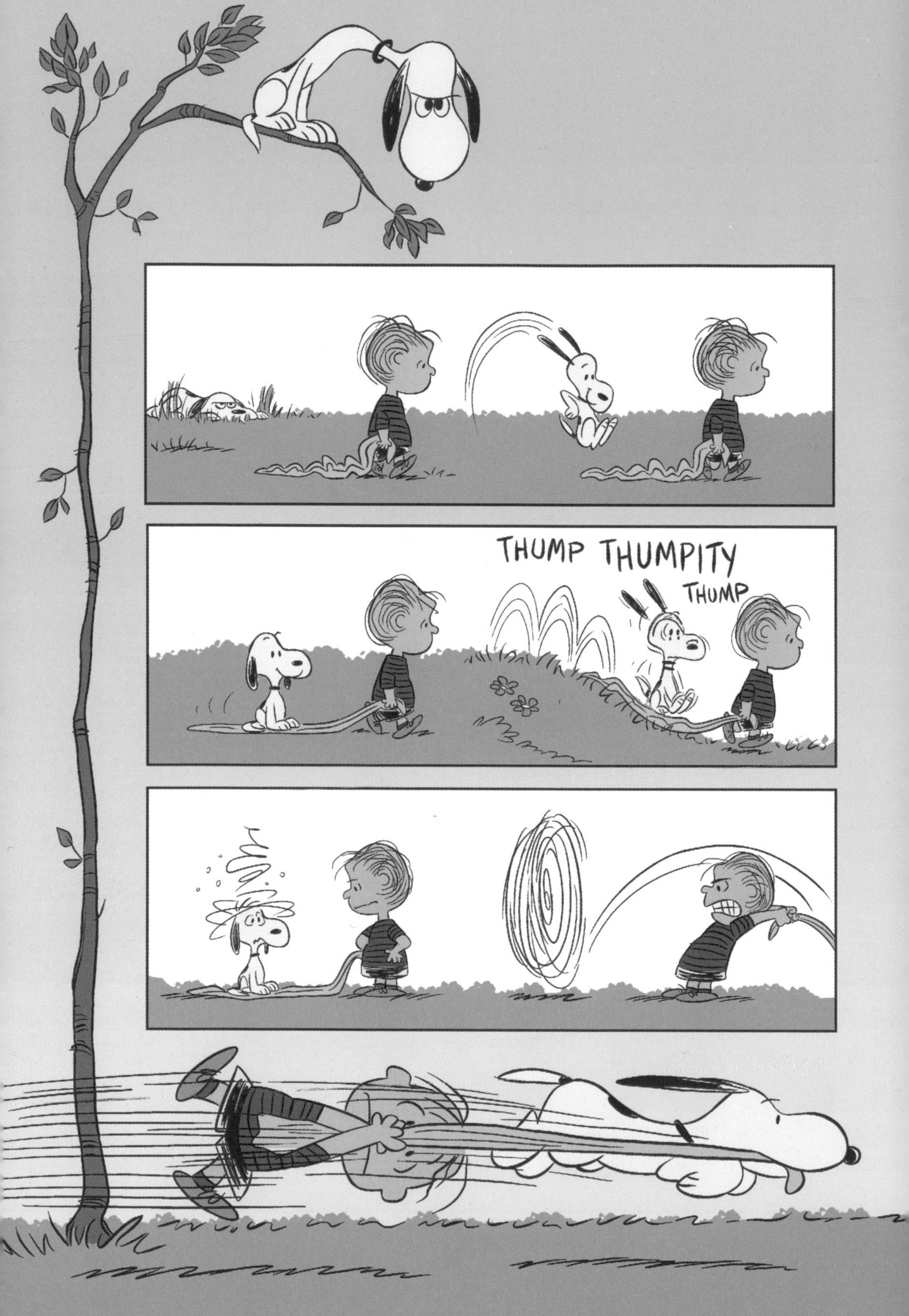
THUMP THUMPITY
THUMP

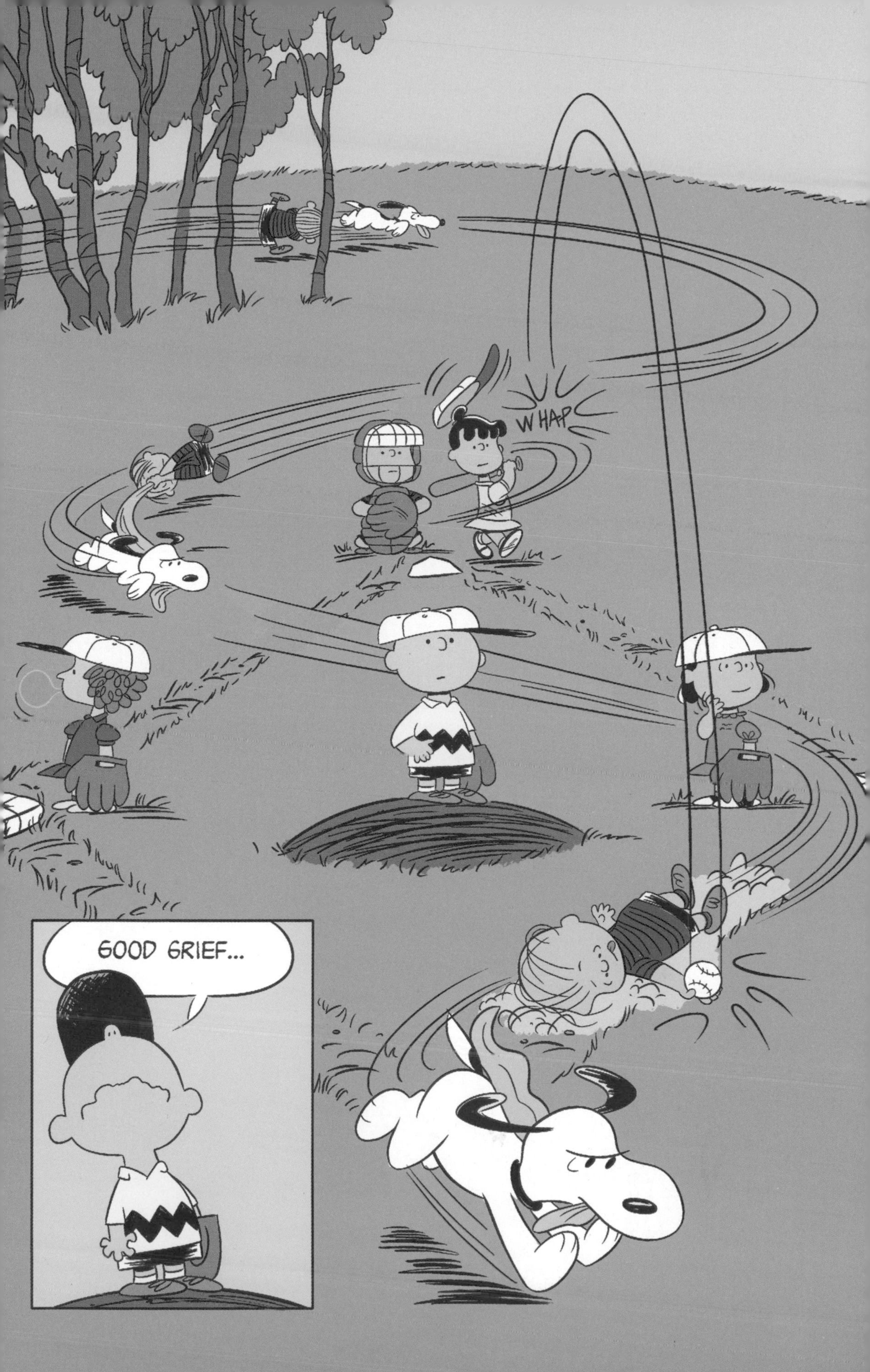
WHAP
GOOD GRIEF...

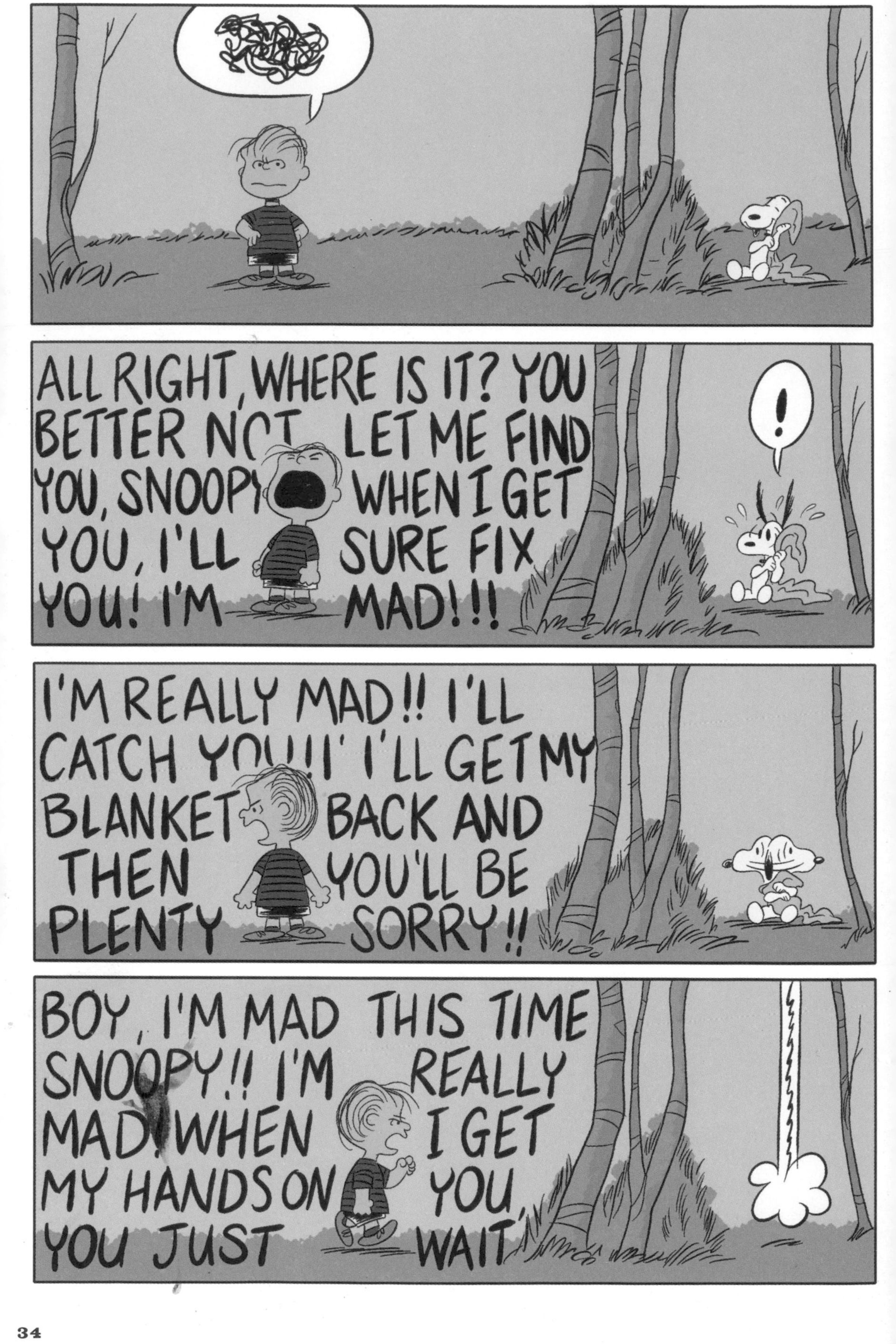
ALL RIGHT, WHERE IS IT? YOU BETTER NOT LET ME FIND YOU, SNOOPY! WHEN I GET YOU, I'LL SURE FIX YOU! I'M MAD!!!
!
I'M REALLY MAD!! I'LL CATCH YOU!! I'LL GET MY BLANKET BACK AND THEN YOU'LL BE PLENTY SORRY!!
BOY, I'M MAD THIS TIME SNOOPY!! I'M REALLY MAD! WHEN I GET MY HANDS ON YOU, YOU JUST WAIT!

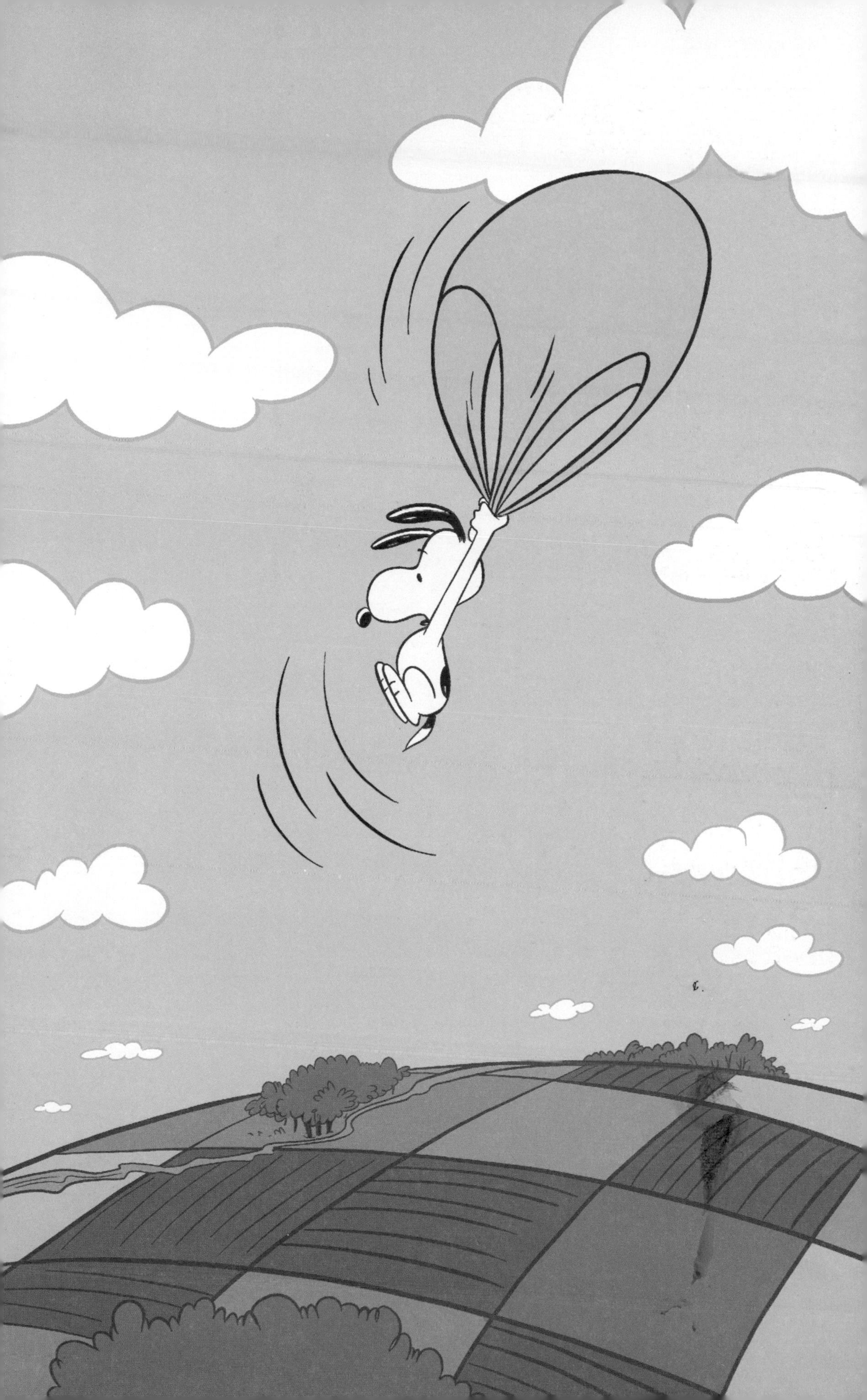

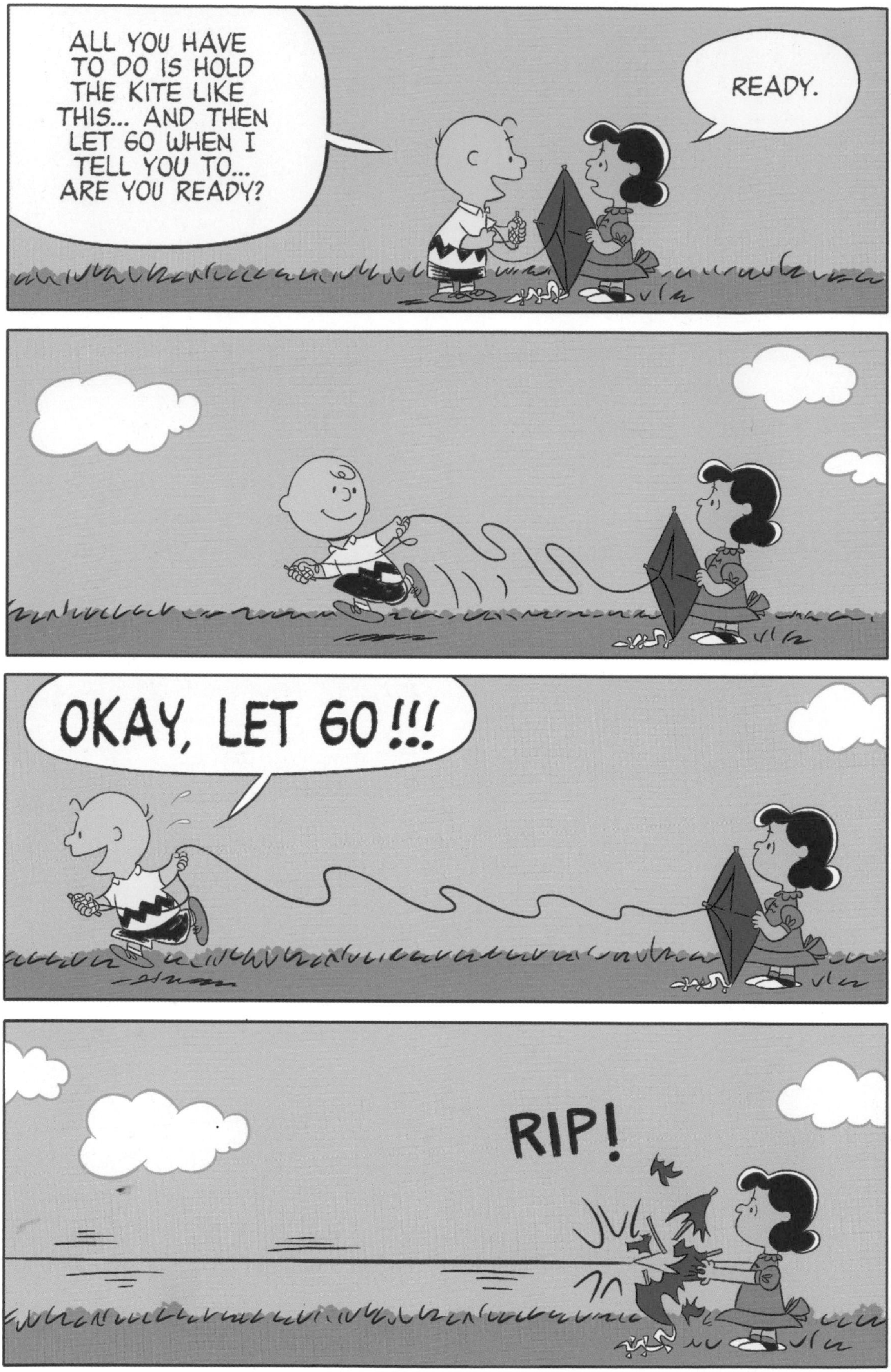
ALL YOU HAVE TO DO IS HOLD THE KITE LIKE THIS... AND THEN LET GO WHEN I TELL YOU TO... ARE YOU READY?
READY.
OKAY, LET GO!!!
RIP!

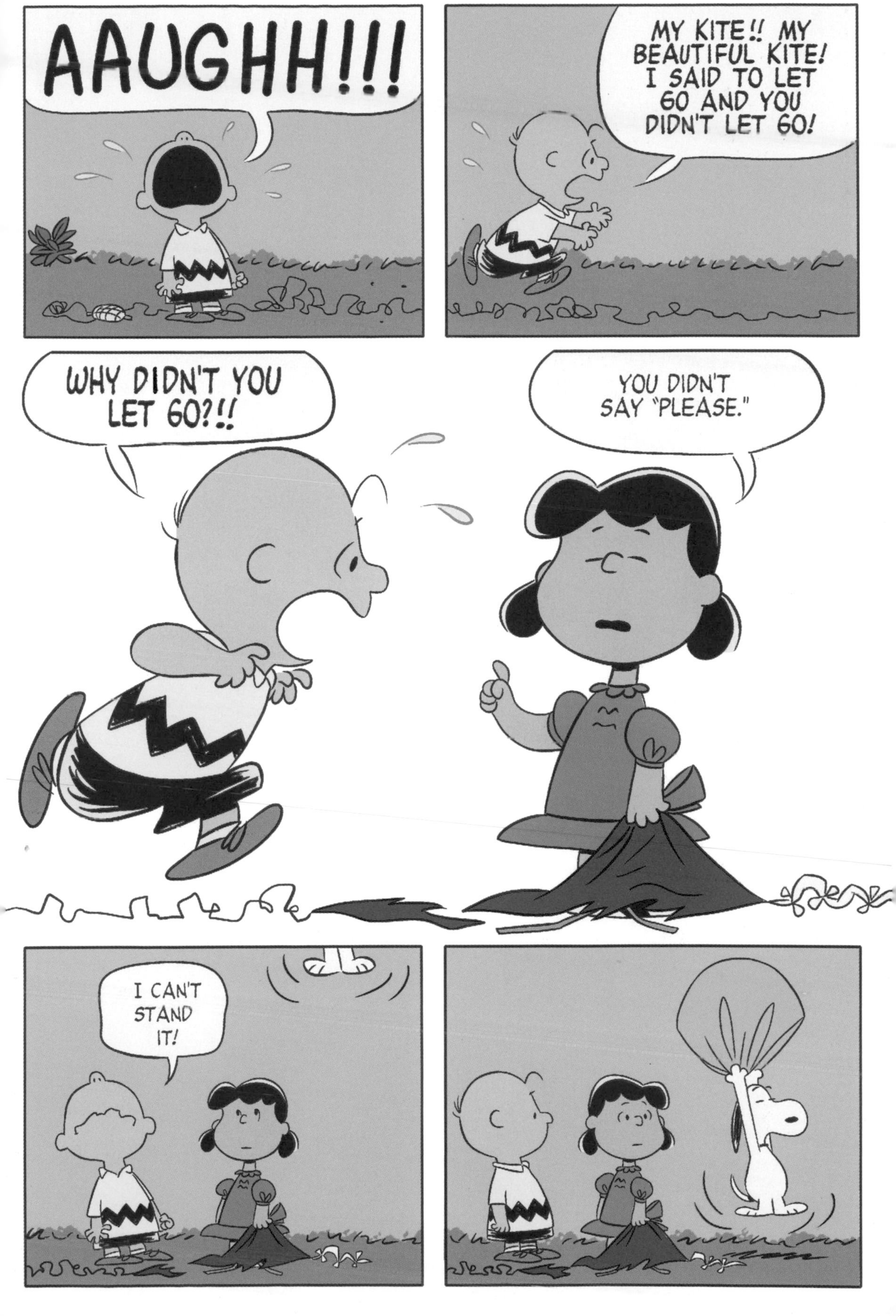
AAUGHH!!!
MY KITE!! MY BEAUTIFUL KITE! I SAID TO LET GO AND YOU DIDN'T LET GO!
WHY DIDN'T YOU LET GO?!!
YOU DIDN'T SAY "PLEASE."
I CAN'T STAND IT!

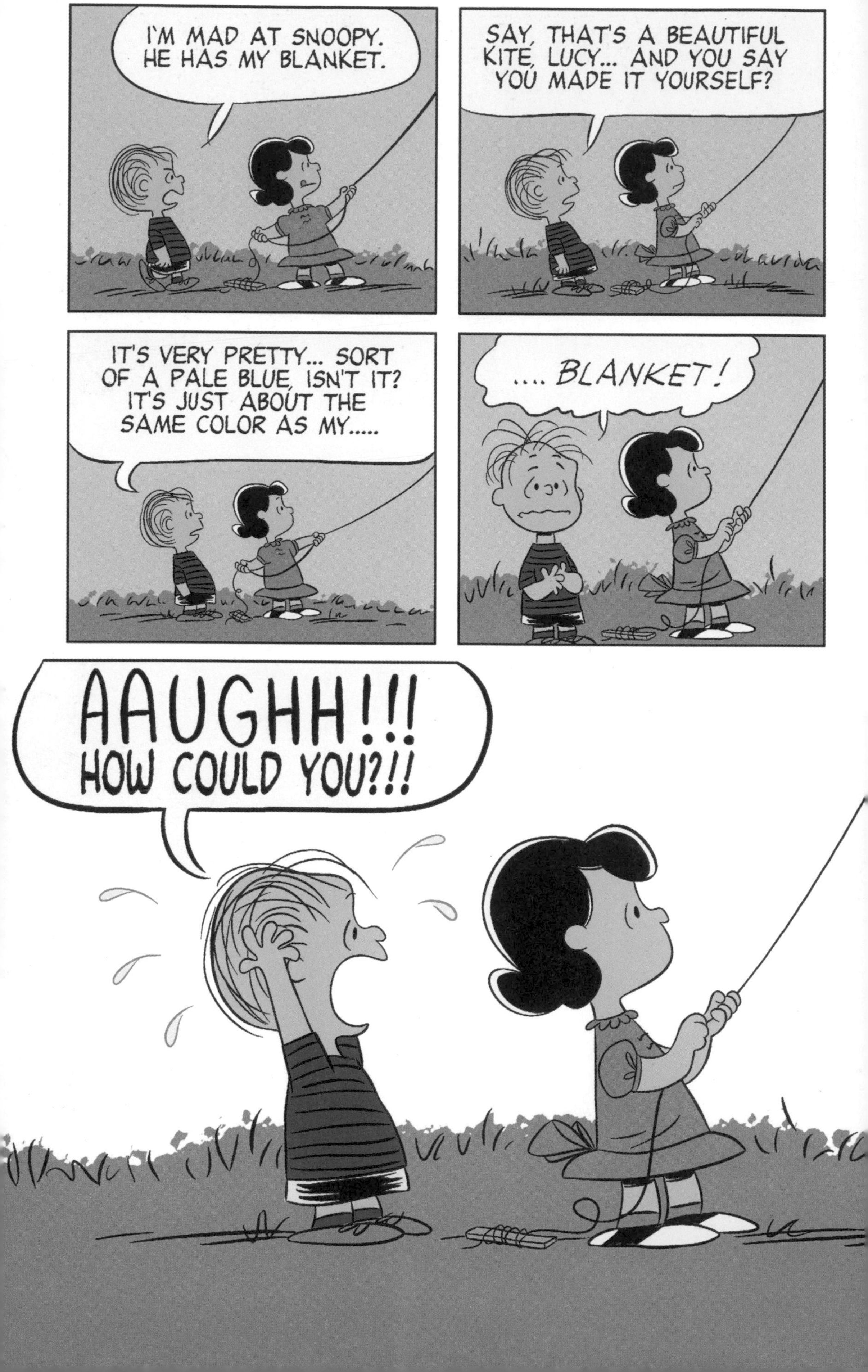
I'M MAD AT SNOOPY. HE HAS MY BLANKET.
SAY, THAT'S A BEAUTIFUL KITE, LUCY... AND YOU SAY YOU MADE IT YOURSELF?
IT'S VERY PRETTY... SORT OF A PALE BLUE, ISN'T IT? IT'S JUST ABOUT THE SAME COLOR AS MY.....
.... BLANKET!
AAUGHH!!! HOW COULD YOU?!!

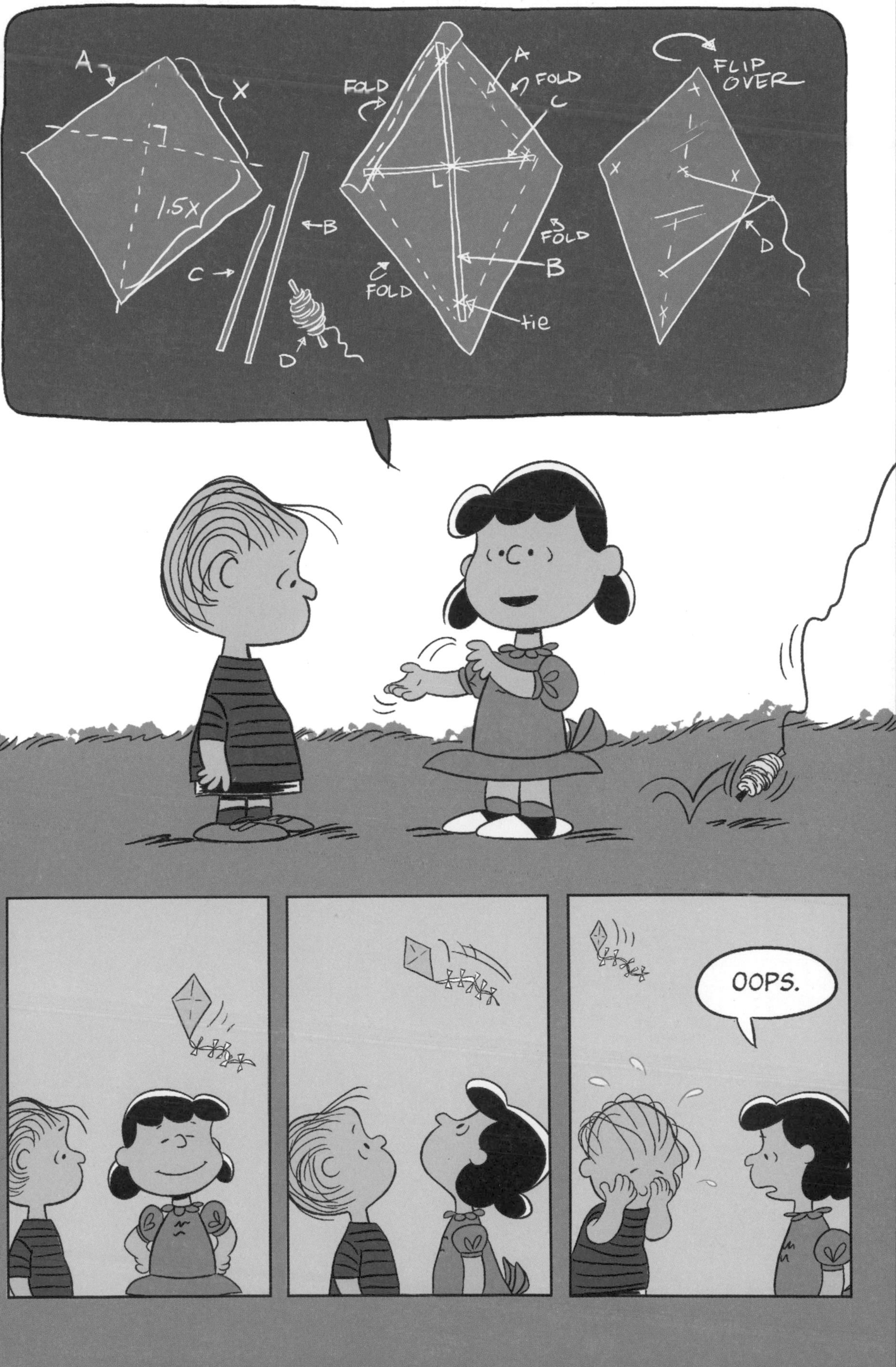
A
X
1.5X
B
C
D
FOLD
A
FOLD
C
L
B
FOLD
FOLD
tie
FLIP OVER
D
OOPS.

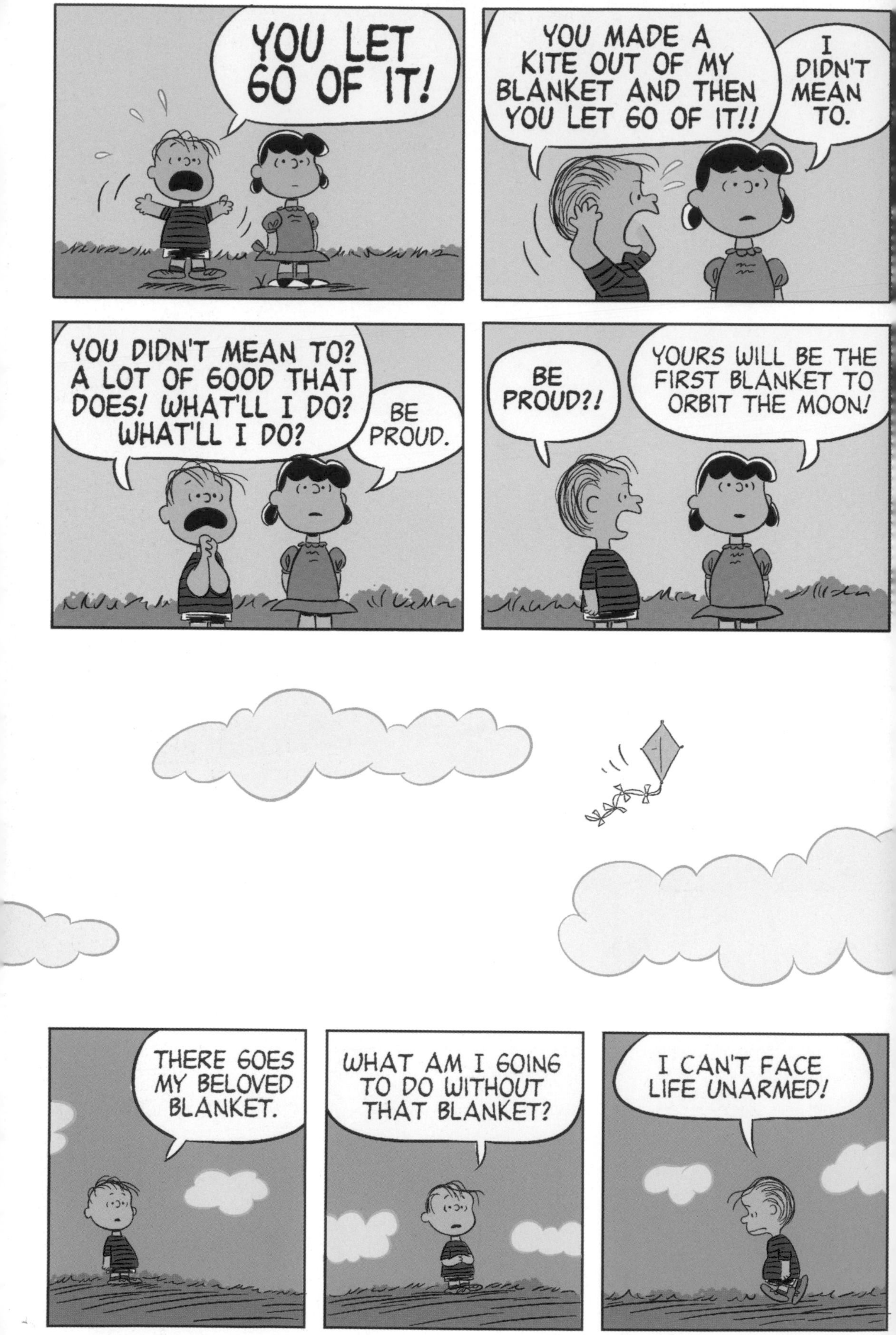
YOU LET GO OF IT!
YOU MADE A KITE OUT OF MY BLANKET AND THEN YOU LET GO OF IT!!
I DIDN'T MEAN TO.
YOU DIDN'T MEAN TO? A LOT OF GOOD THAT DOES! WHAT'LL I DO? WHAT'LL I DO?
BE PROUD.
BE PROUD?!
YOURS WILL BE THE FIRST BLANKET TO ORBIT THE MOON!
THERE GOES MY BELOVED BLANKET.
WHAT AM I GOING TO DO WITHOUT THAT BLANKET?
I CAN'T FACE LIFE UNARMED!

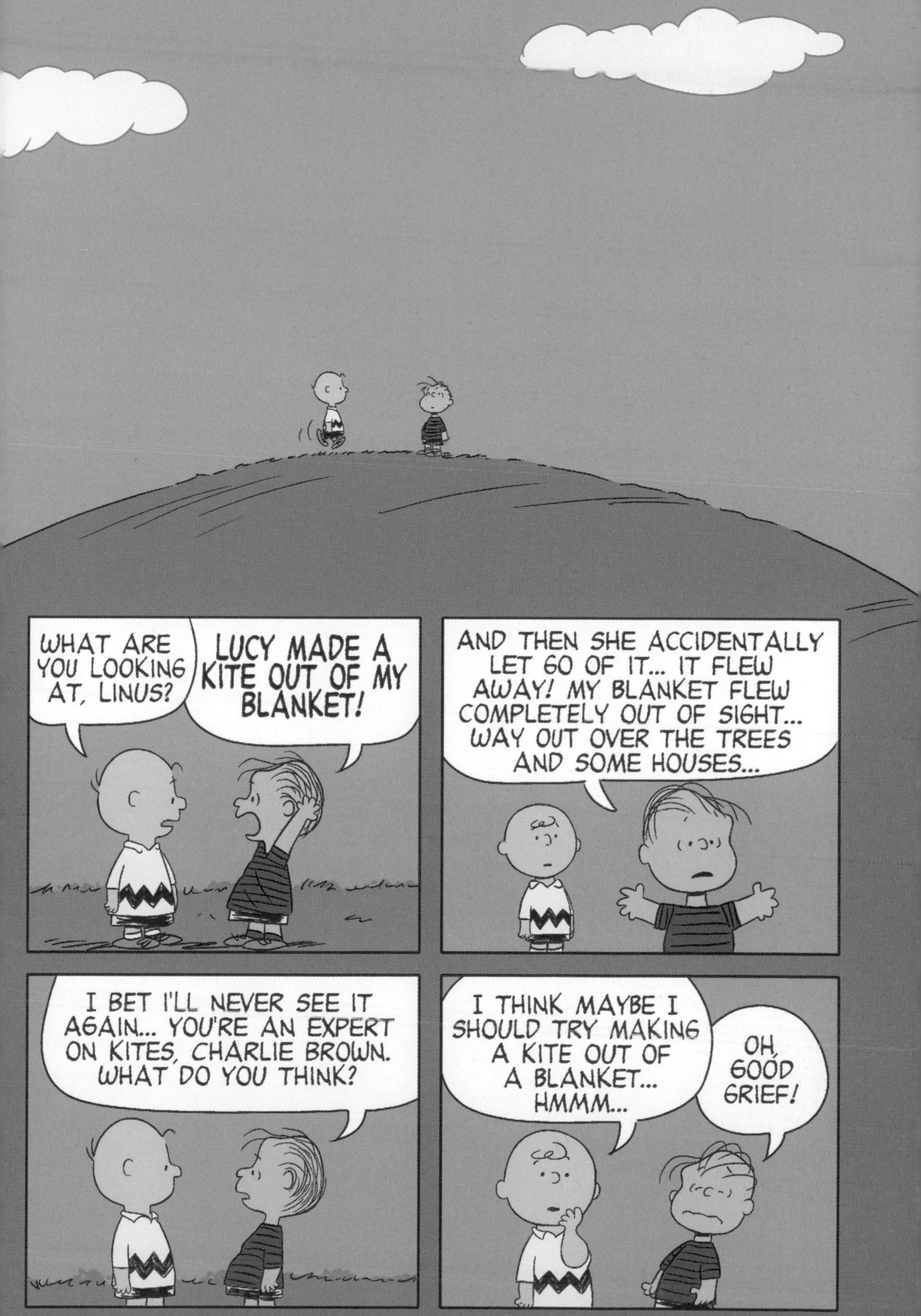

WHAT ARE YOU LOOKING AT, LINUS?
LUCY MADE A KITE OUT OF MY BLANKET!
AND THEN SHE ACCIDENTALLY LET GO OF IT... IT FLEW AWAY! MY BLANKET FLEW COMPLETELY OUT OF SIGHT... WAY OUT OVER THE TREES AND SOME HOUSES...
I BET I'LL NEVER SEE IT AGAIN... YOU'RE AN EXPERT ON KITES, CHARLIE BROWN. WHAT DO YOU THINK?
I THINK MAYBE I SHOULD TRY MAKING A KITE OUT OF A BLANKET... HMMM...
OH, GOOD GRIEF!

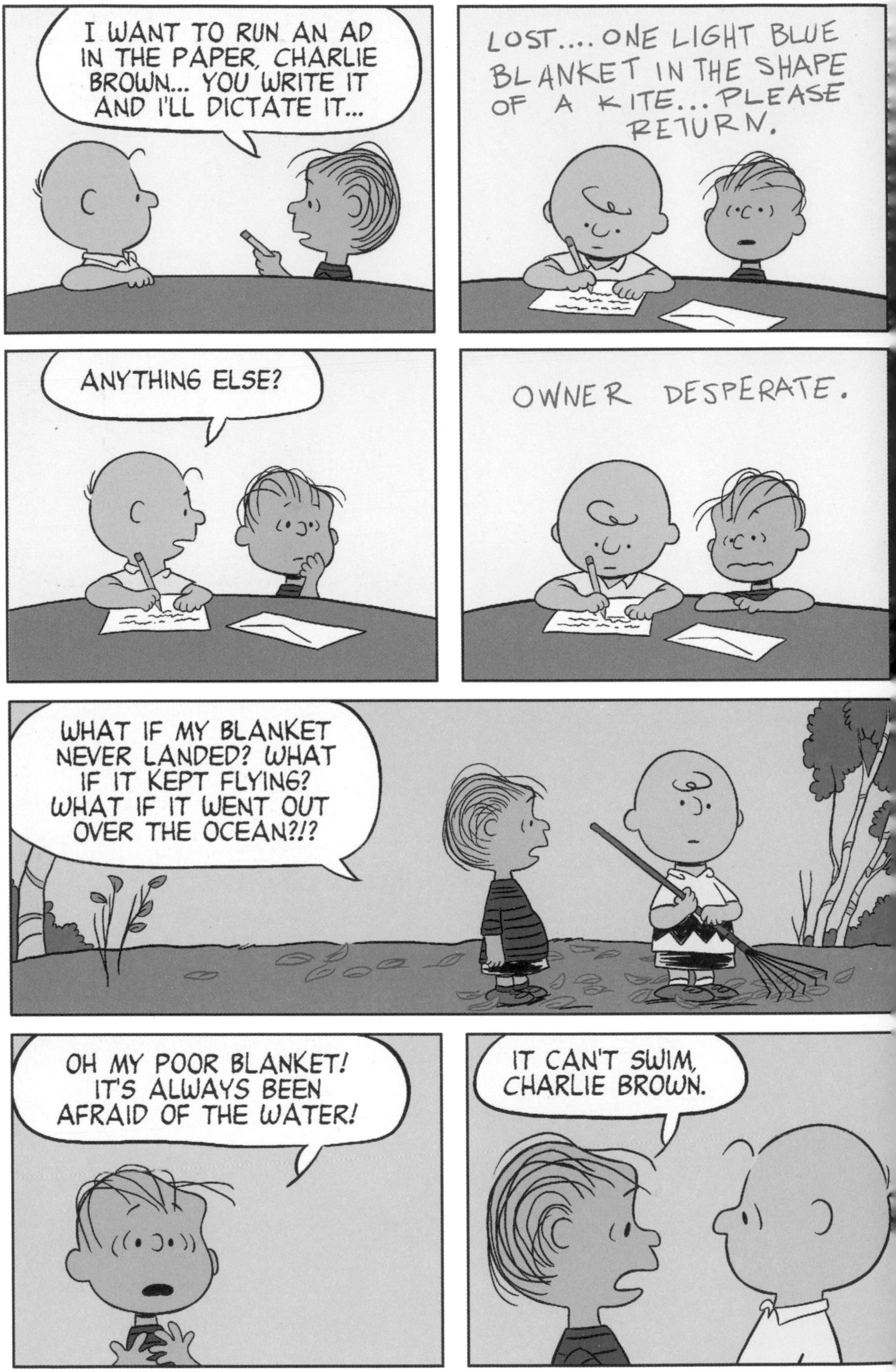
I WANT TO RUN AN AD IN THE PAPER, CHARLIE BROWN... YOU WRITE IT AND I'LL DICTATE IT...
LOST.... ONE LIGHT BLUE BLANKET IN THE SHAPE OF A KITE... PLEASE RETURN.
ANYTHING ELSE?
OWNER DESPERATE.
WHAT IF MY BLANKET NEVER LANDED? WHAT IF IT KEPT FLYING? WHAT IF IT WENT OUT OVER THE OCEAN?!?
OH MY POOR BLANKET! IT'S ALWAYS BEEN AFRAID OF THE WATER!
IT CAN'T SWIM, CHARLIE BROWN.

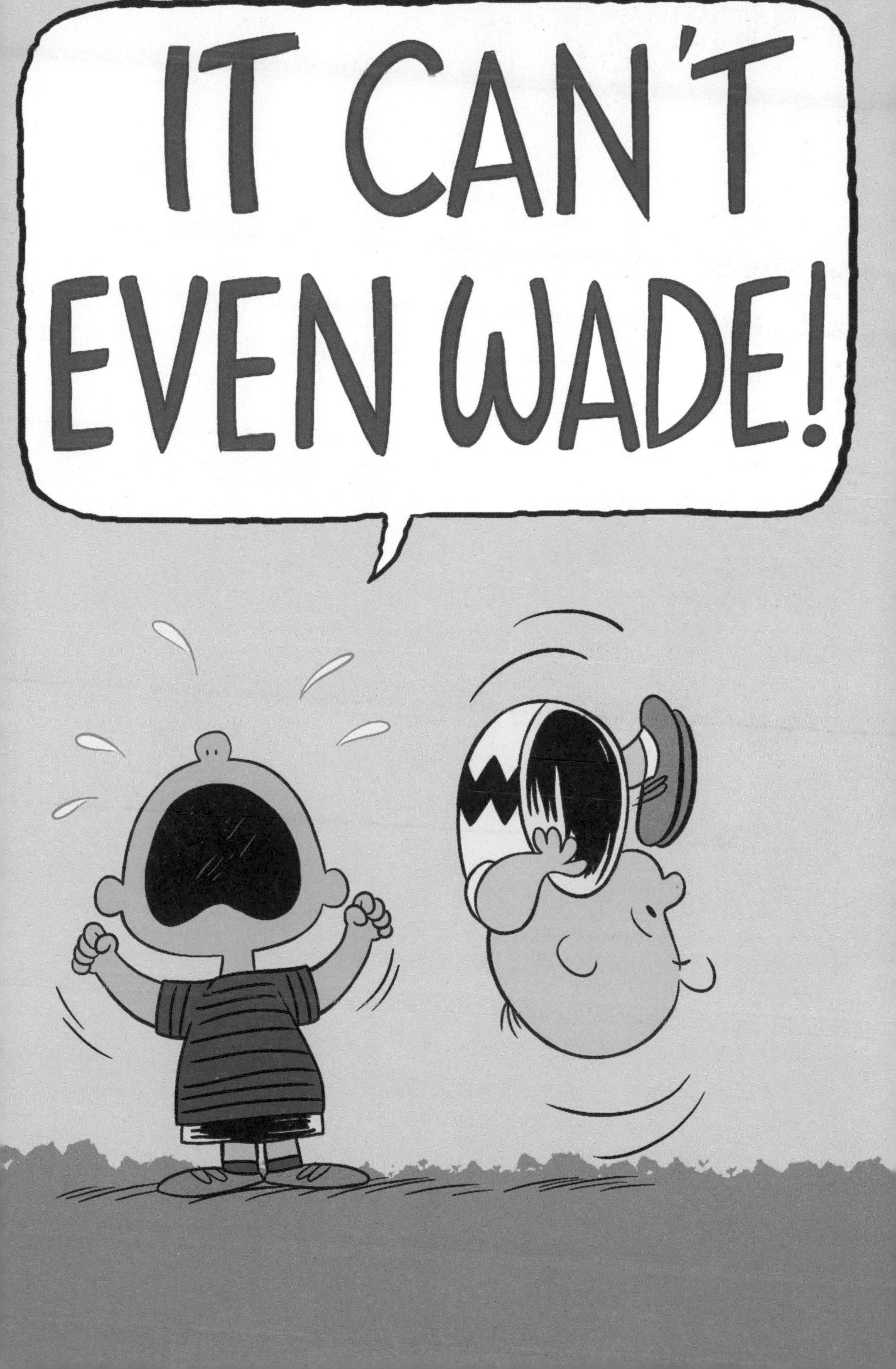
IT CAN'T EVEN WADE!

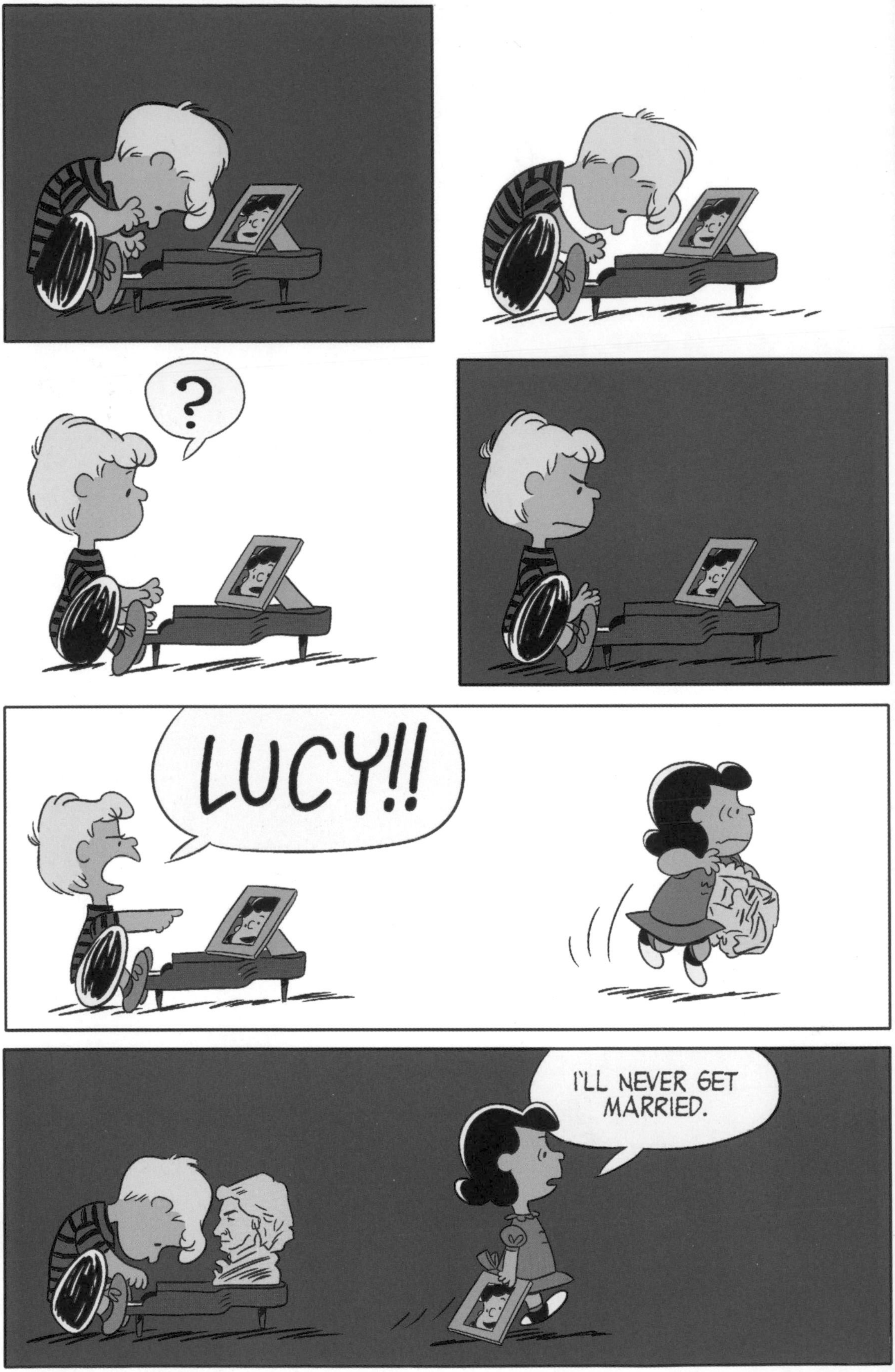
?
LUCY!!
I'LL NEVER GET MARRIED.

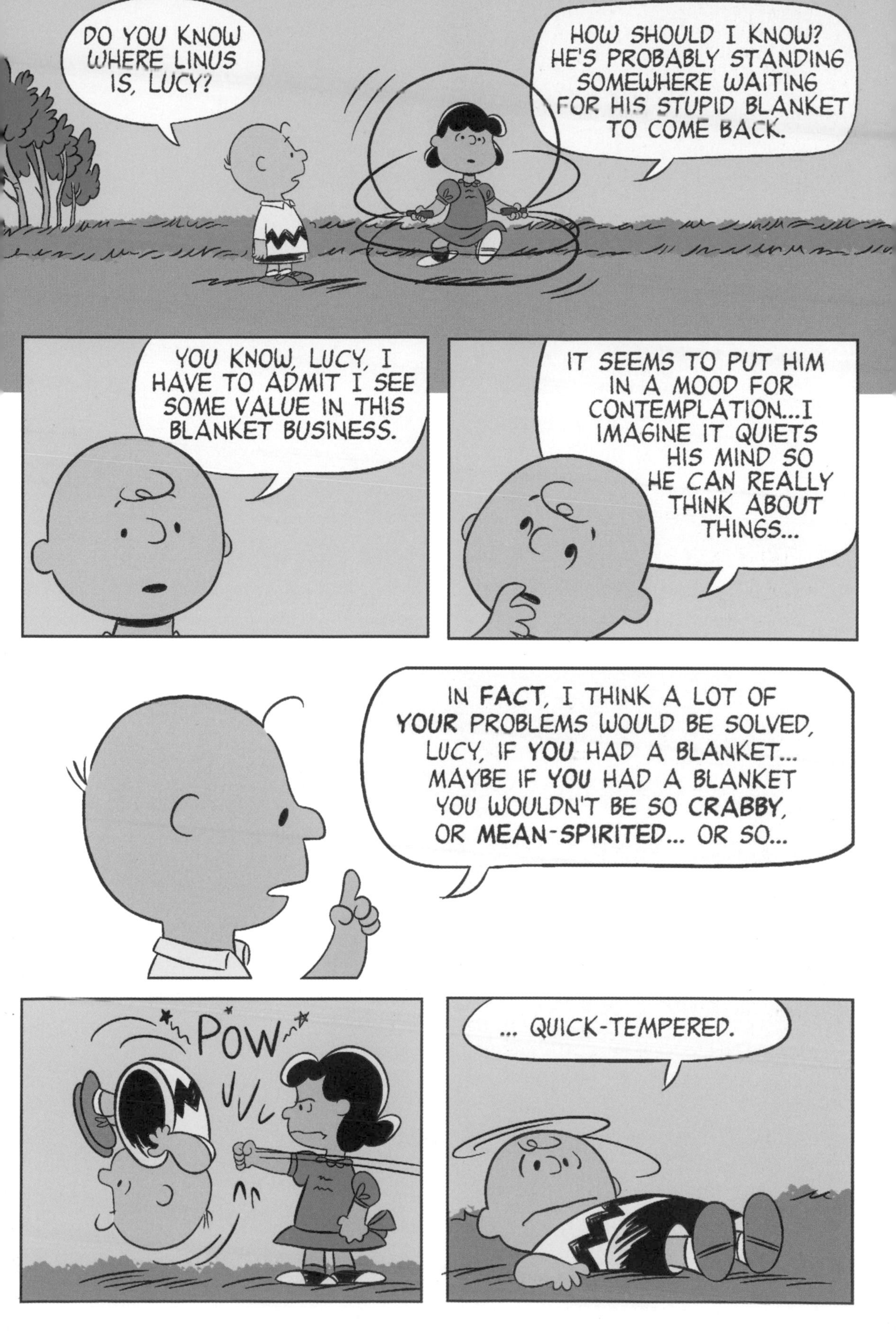
DO YOU KNOW WHERE LINUS IS, LUCY?
HOW SHOULD I KNOW? HE'S PROBABLY STANDING SOMEWHERE WAITING FOR HIS STUPID BLANKET TO COME BACK.
YOU KNOW, LUCY, I HAVE TO ADMIT I SEE SOME VALUE IN THIS BLANKET BUSINESS.
IT SEEMS TO PUT HIM IN A MOOD FOR CONTEMPLATION...I IMAGINE IT QUIETS HIS MIND SO HE CAN REALLY THINK ABOUT THINGS...
IN FACT, I THINK A LOT OF YOUR PROBLEMS WOULD BE SOLVED, LUCY, IF YOU HAD A BLANKET... MAYBE IF YOU HAD A BLANKET YOU WOULDN'T BE SO CRABBY, OR MEAN-SPIRITED... OR SO...
POW
... QUICK-TEMPERED.

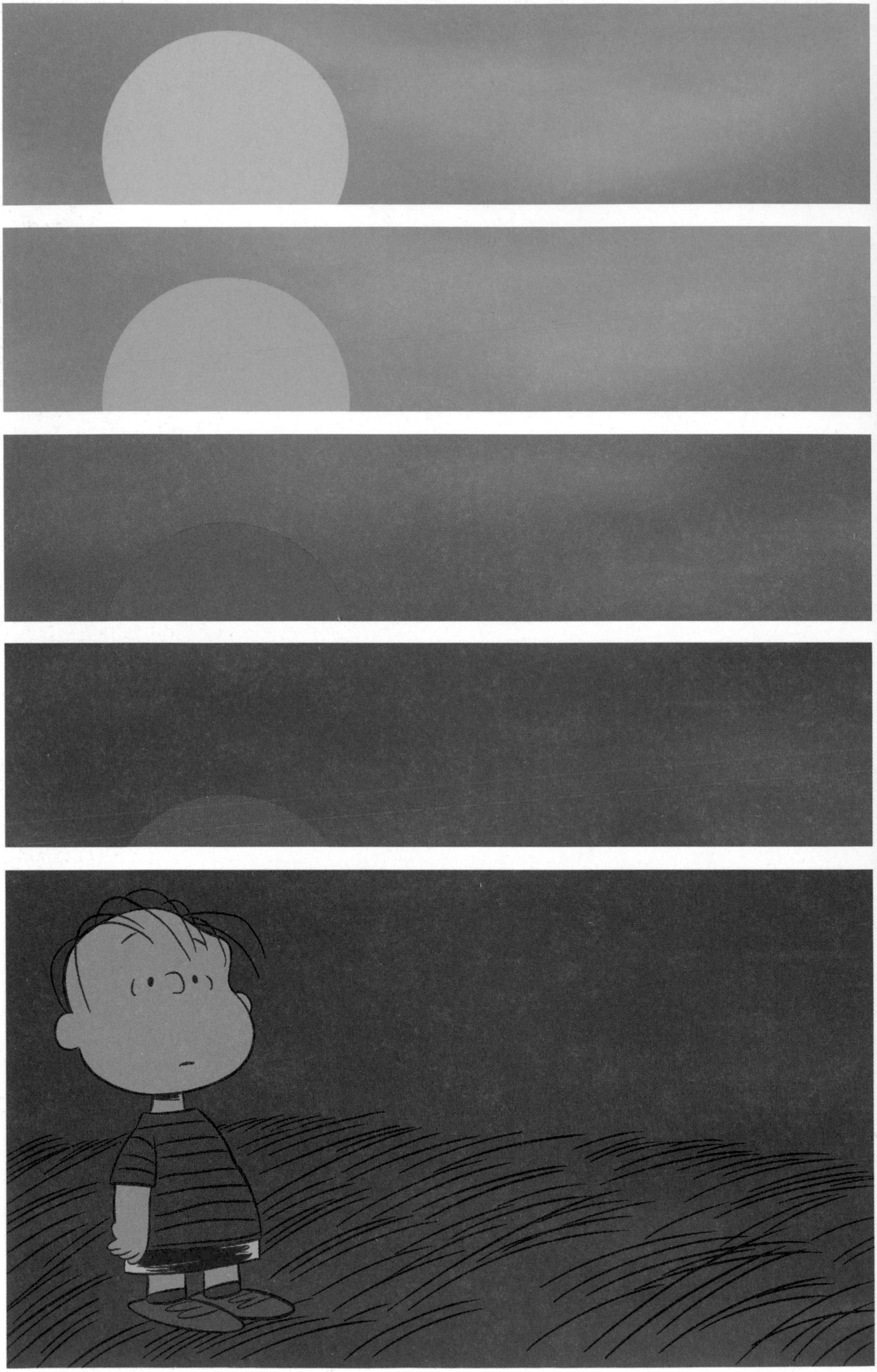

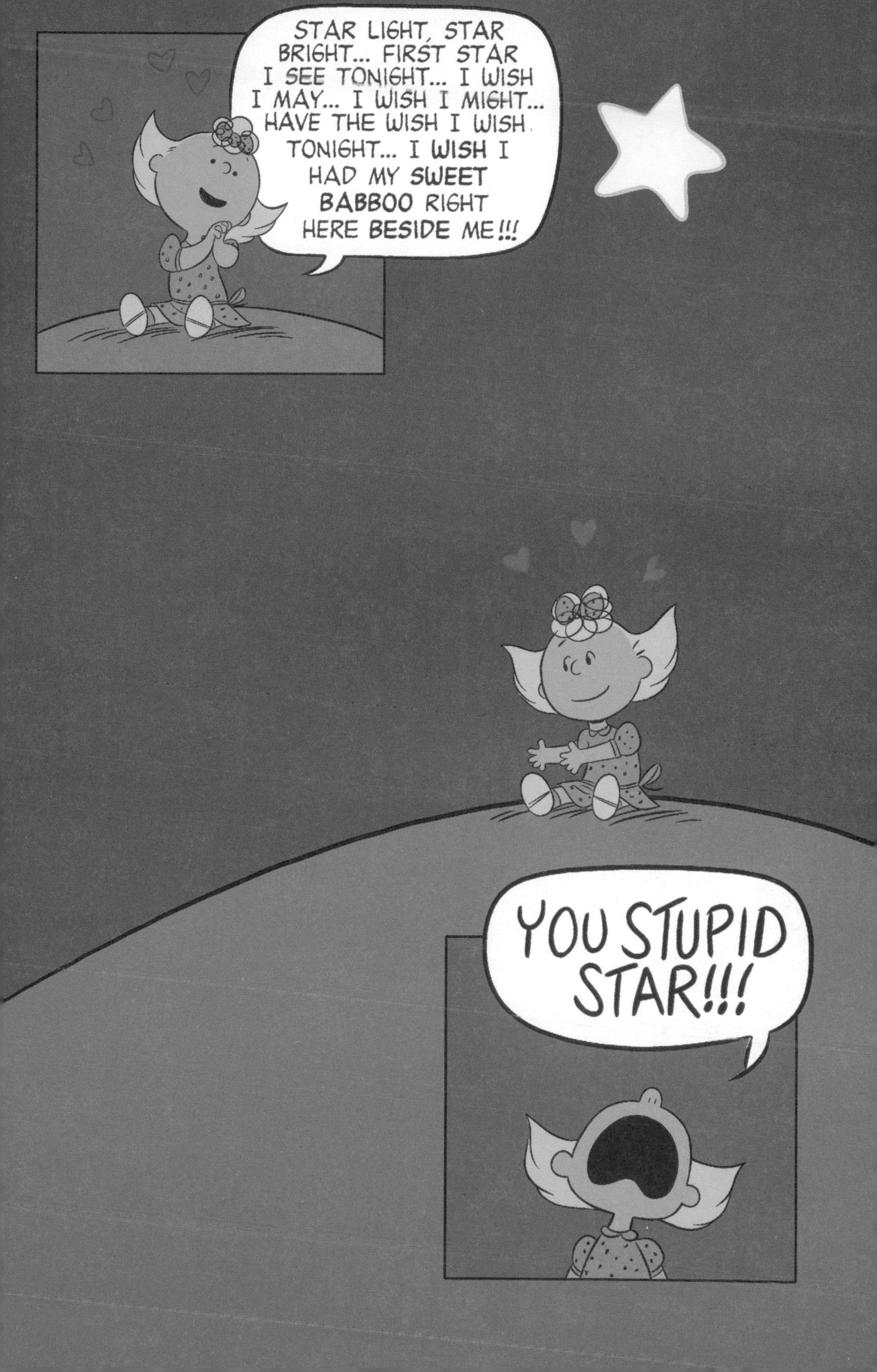
STAR LIGHT, STAR BRIGHT... FIRST STAR I SEE TONIGHT... I WISH I MAY... I WISH I MIGHT... HAVE THE WISH I WISH TONIGHT... I WISH I HAD MY SWEET BABBOO RIGHT HERE BESIDE ME!!!
YOU STUPID STAR!!!

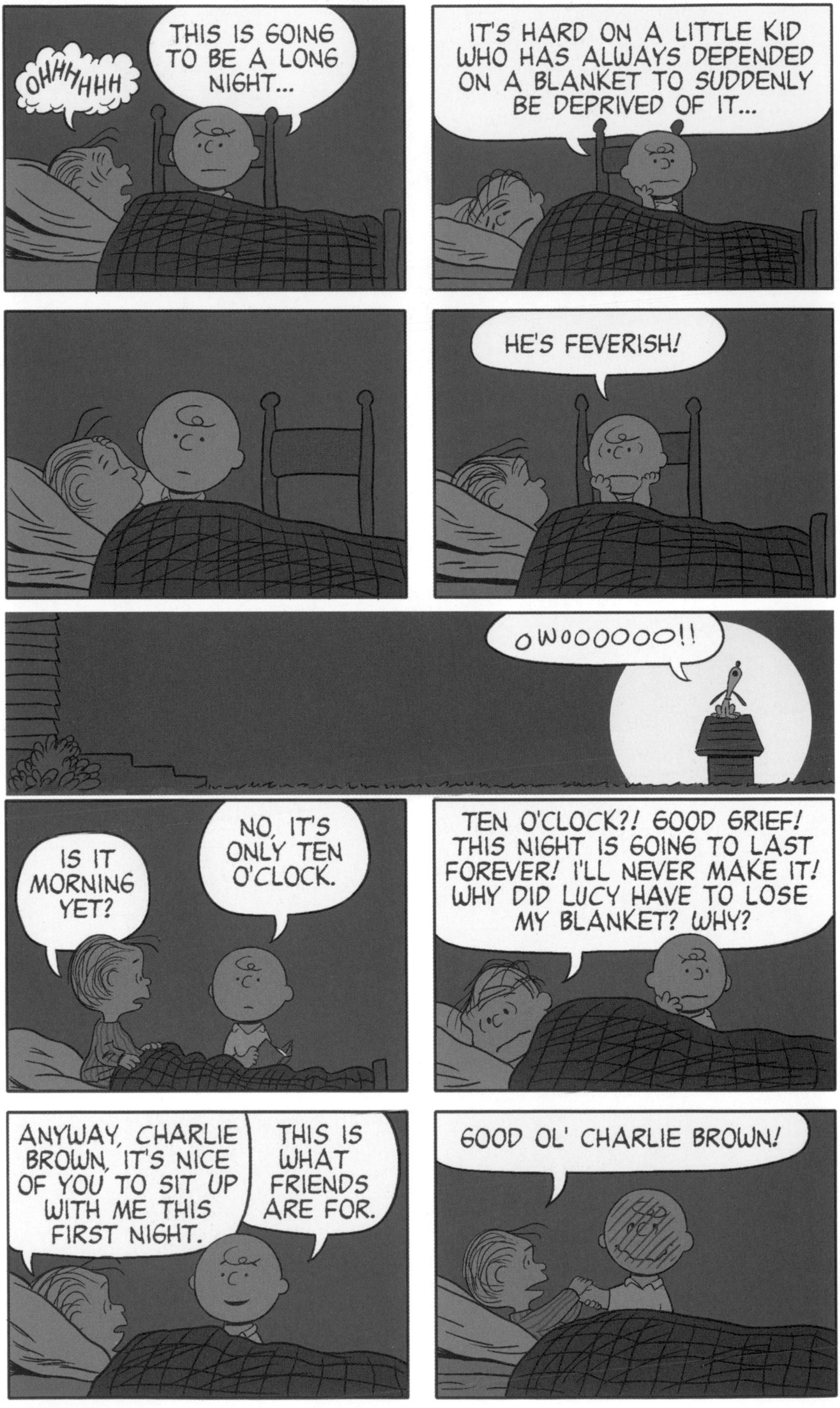
OHHHHHH
THIS IS GOING TO BE A LONG NIGHT...
IT'S HARD ON A LITTLE KID WHO HAS ALWAYS DEPENDED ON A BLANKET TO SUDDENLY BE DEPRIVED OF IT...
HE'S FEVERISH!
OWOOOOOO!!
IS IT MORNING YET?
NO, IT'S ONLY TEN O'CLOCK.
TEN O'CLOCK?! GOOD GRIEF! THIS NIGHT IS GOING TO LAST FOREVER! I'LL NEVER MAKE IT! WHY DID LUCY HAVE TO LOSE MY BLANKET? WHY?
ANYWAY, CHARLIE BROWN, IT'S NICE OF YOU TO SIT UP WITH ME THIS FIRST NIGHT.
THIS IS WHAT FRIENDS ARE FOR.
GOOD OL' CHARLIE BROWN!

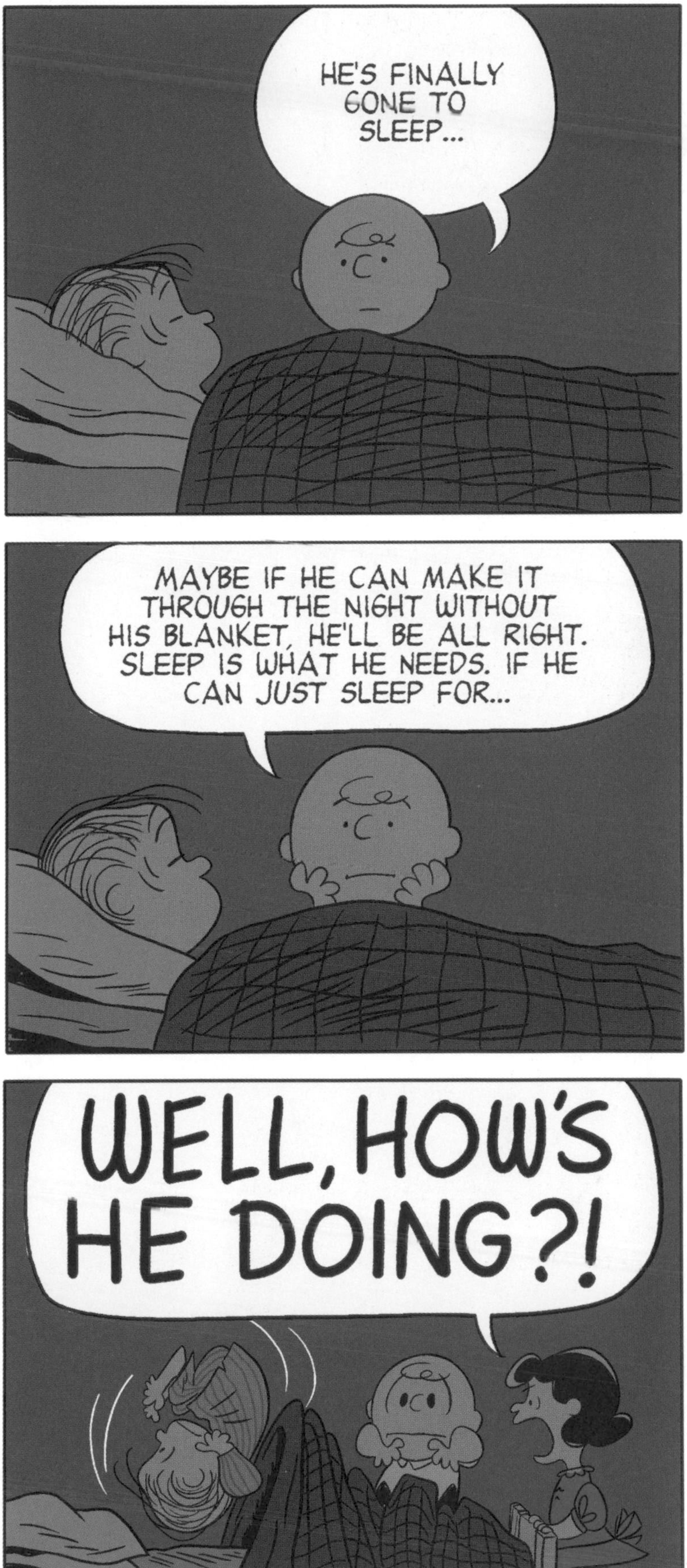
HE'S FINALLY GONE TO SLEEP...
MAYBE IF HE CAN MAKE IT THROUGH THE NIGHT WITHOUT HIS BLANKET, HE'LL BE ALL RIGHT. SLEEP IS WHAT HE NEEDS. IF HE CAN JUST SLEEP FOR...
WELL, HOW'S HE DOING?!

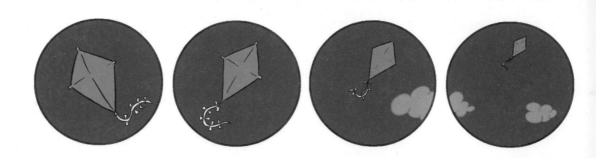

**BAM
BAM
BAM**

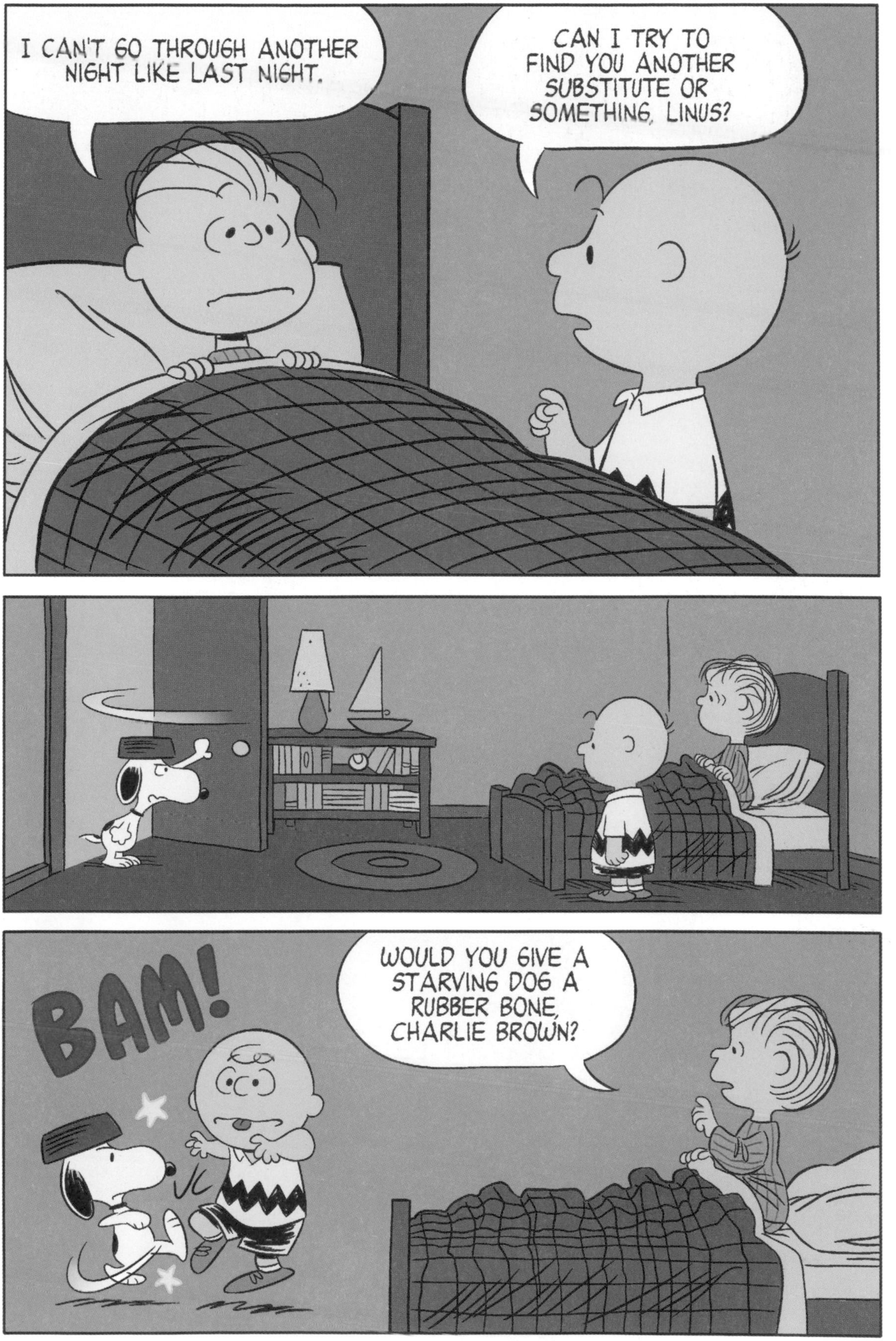
I CAN'T GO THROUGH ANOTHER NIGHT LIKE LAST NIGHT.
CAN I TRY TO FIND YOU ANOTHER SUBSTITUTE OR SOMETHING, LINUS?
BAM!
WOULD YOU GIVE A STARVING DOG A RUBBER BONE, CHARLIE BROWN?

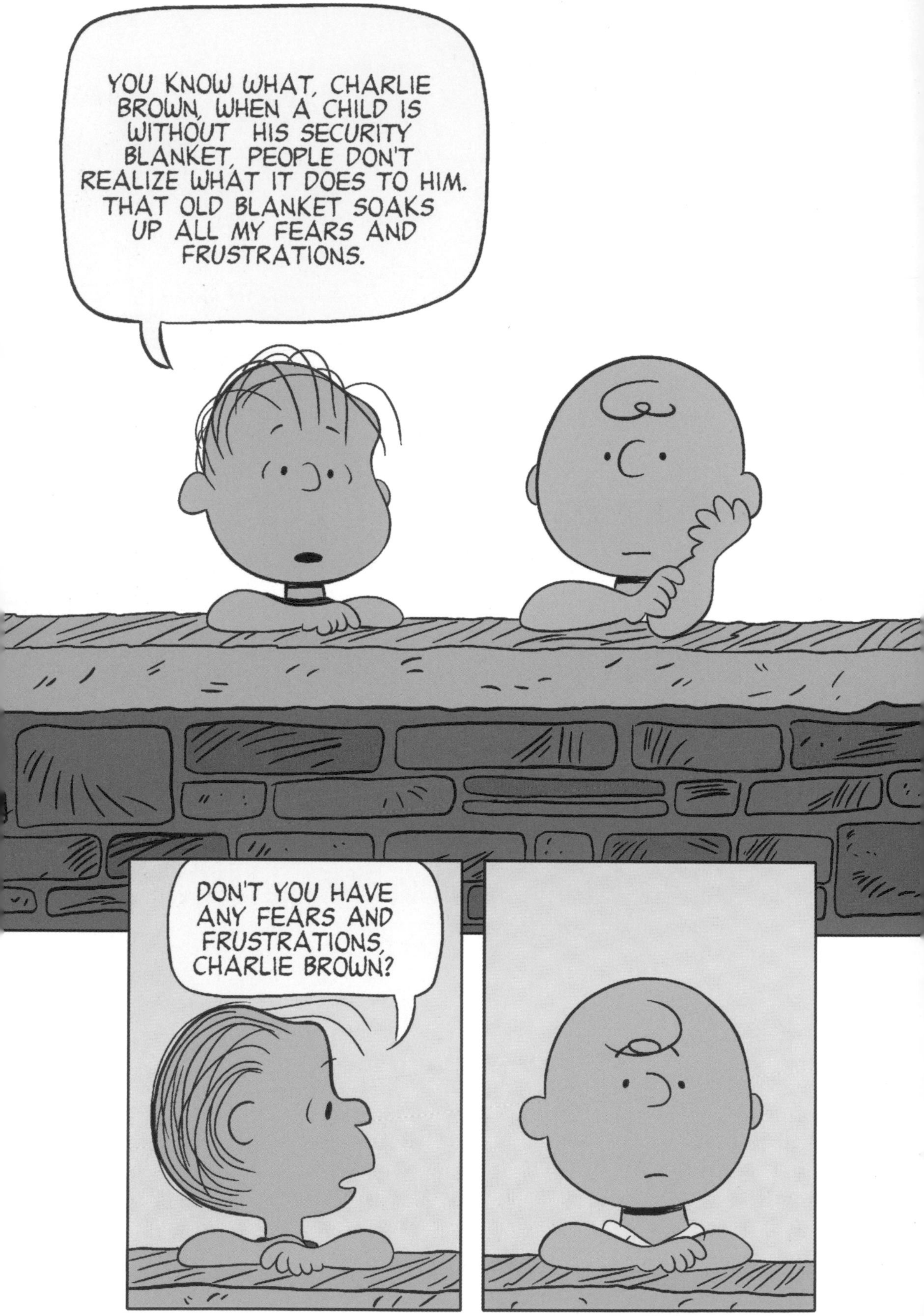
YOU KNOW WHAT, CHARLIE BROWN, WHEN A CHILD IS WITHOUT HIS SECURITY BLANKET, PEOPLE DON'T REALIZE WHAT IT DOES TO HIM. THAT OLD BLANKET SOAKS UP ALL MY FEARS AND FRUSTRATIONS.
DON'T YOU HAVE ANY FEARS AND FRUSTRATIONS, CHARLIE BROWN?

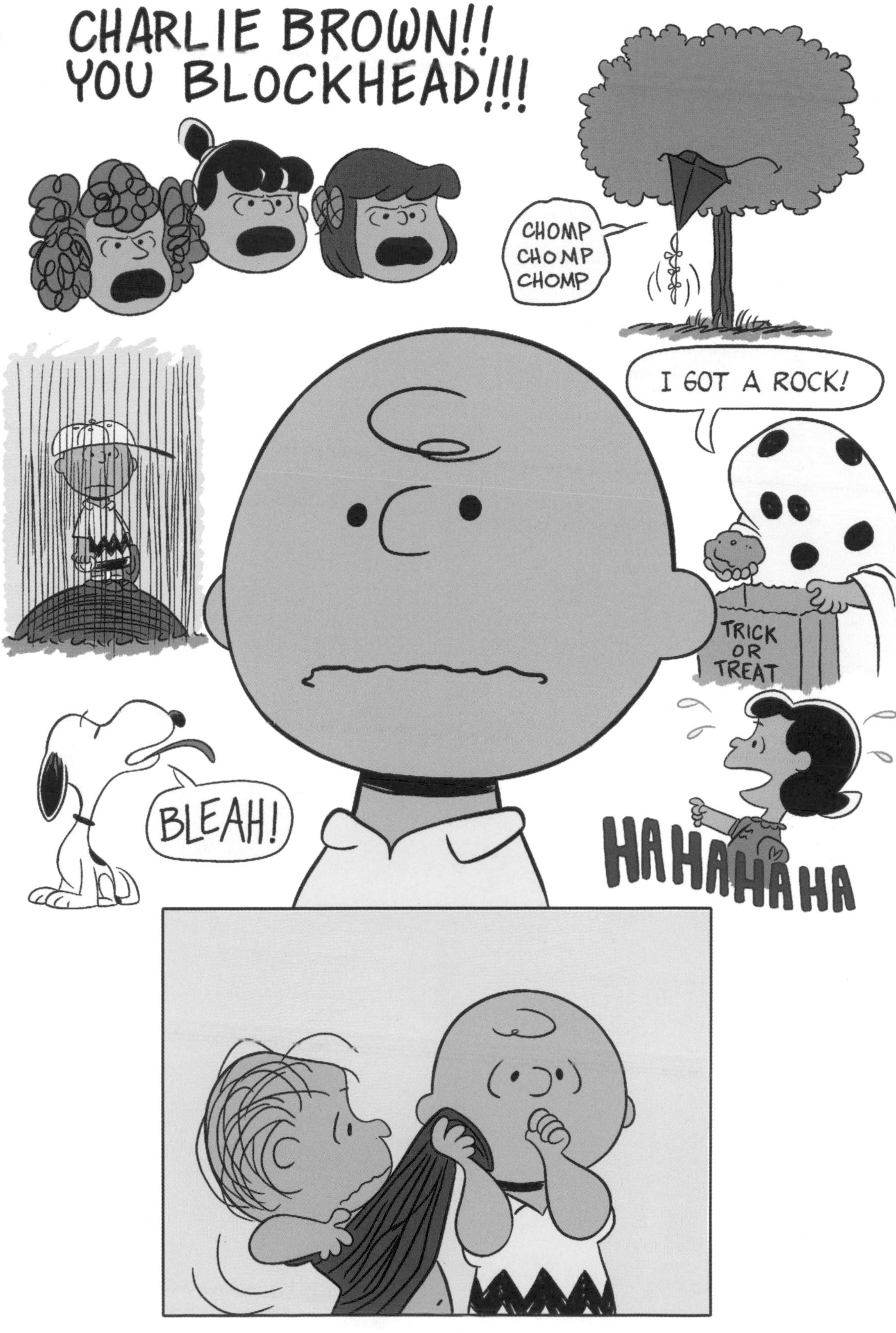
CHARLIE BROWN!!
YOU BLOCKHEAD!!!
CHOMP
CHOMP
CHOMP
I GOT A ROCK!
TRICK
OR
TREAT
BLEAH!
HAHAHAHA

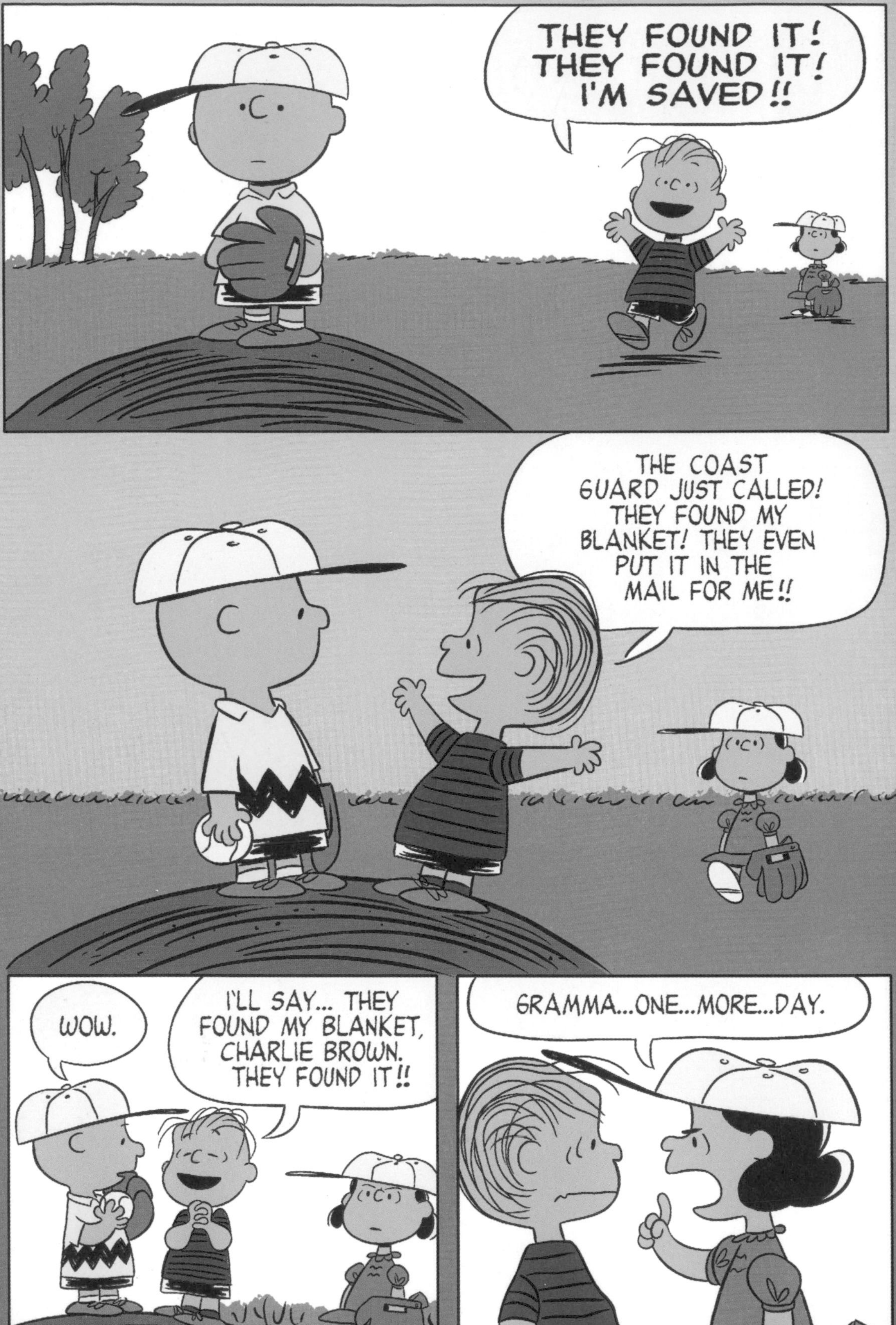
THEY FOUND IT! THEY FOUND IT! I'M SAVED!!
THE COAST GUARD JUST CALLED! THEY FOUND MY BLANKET! THEY EVEN PUT IT IN THE MAIL FOR ME!!
WOW.
I'LL SAY... THEY FOUND MY BLANKET, CHARLIE BROWN. THEY FOUND IT!!
GRAMMA...ONE...MORE...DAY.

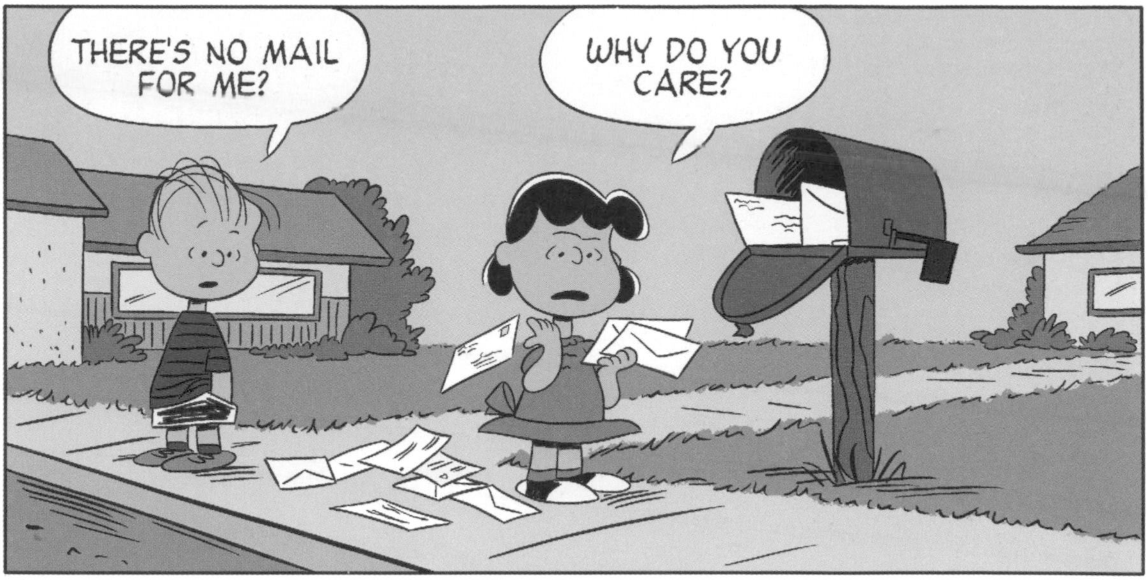
THERE'S NO MAIL FOR ME?
WHY DO YOU CARE?

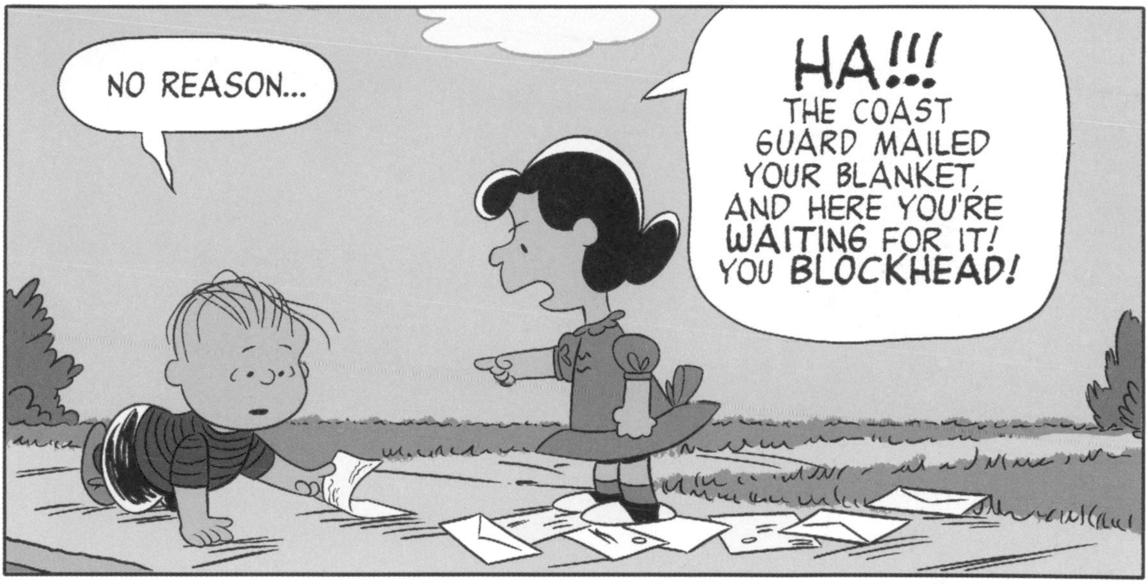
NO REASON...
HA!!! THE COAST GUARD MAILED YOUR BLANKET, AND HERE YOU'RE WAITING FOR IT! YOU BLOCKHEAD!

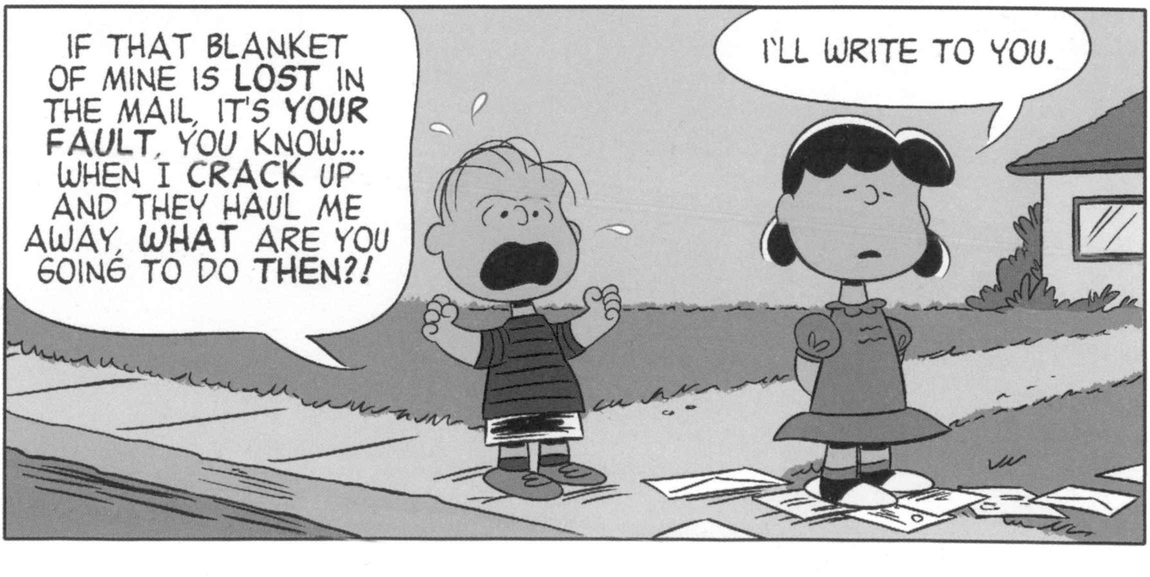
IF THAT BLANKET OF MINE IS LOST IN THE MAIL, IT'S YOUR FAULT, YOU KNOW... WHEN I CRACK UP AND THEY HAUL ME AWAY, WHAT ARE YOU GOING TO DO THEN?!
I'LL WRITE TO YOU.

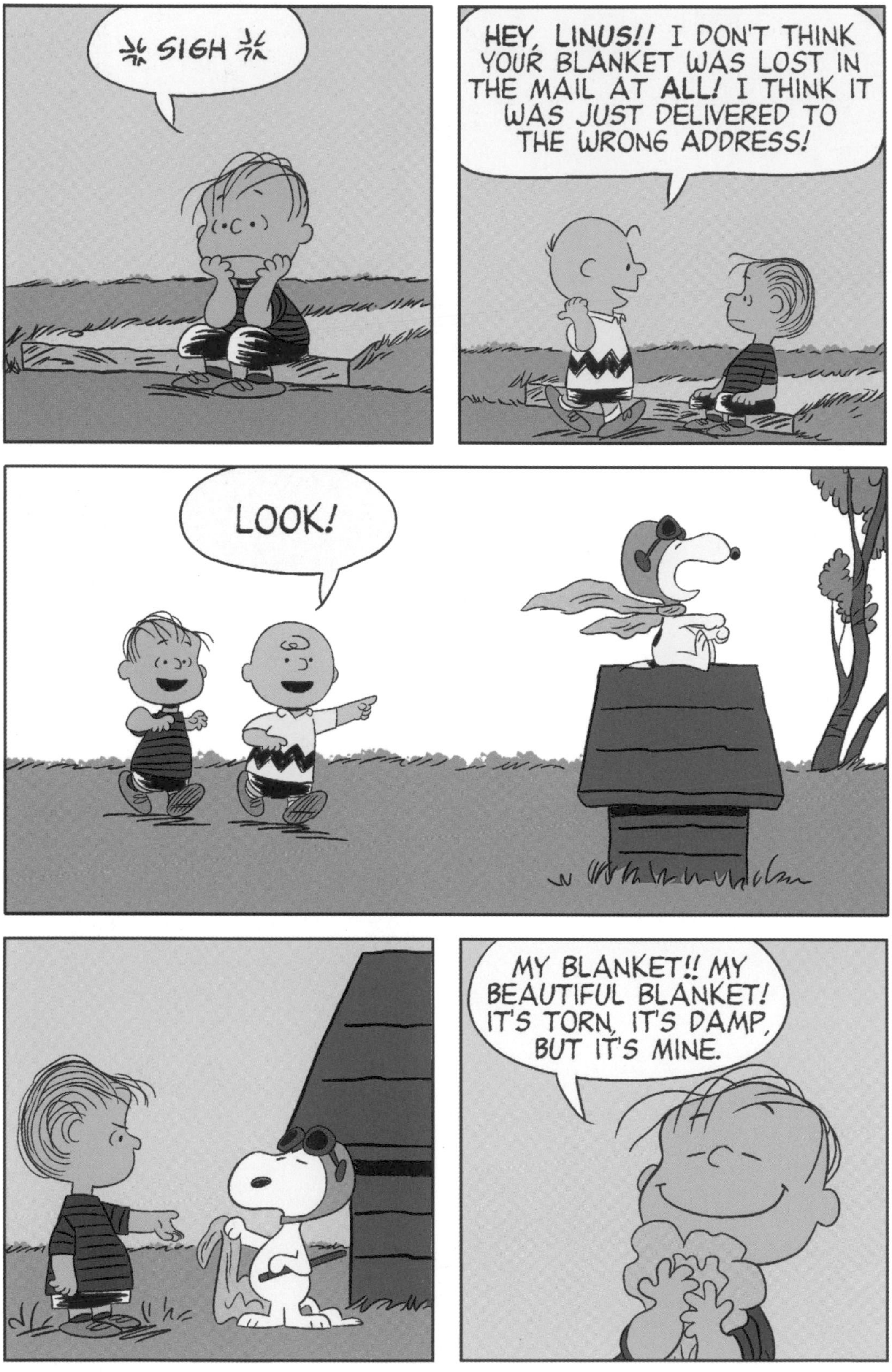
SIGH
HEY, LINUS!! I DON'T THINK YOUR BLANKET WAS LOST IN THE MAIL AT ALL! I THINK IT WAS JUST DELIVERED TO THE WRONG ADDRESS!
LOOK!
MY BLANKET!! MY BEAUTIFUL BLANKET! IT'S TORN, IT'S DAMP, BUT IT'S MINE.

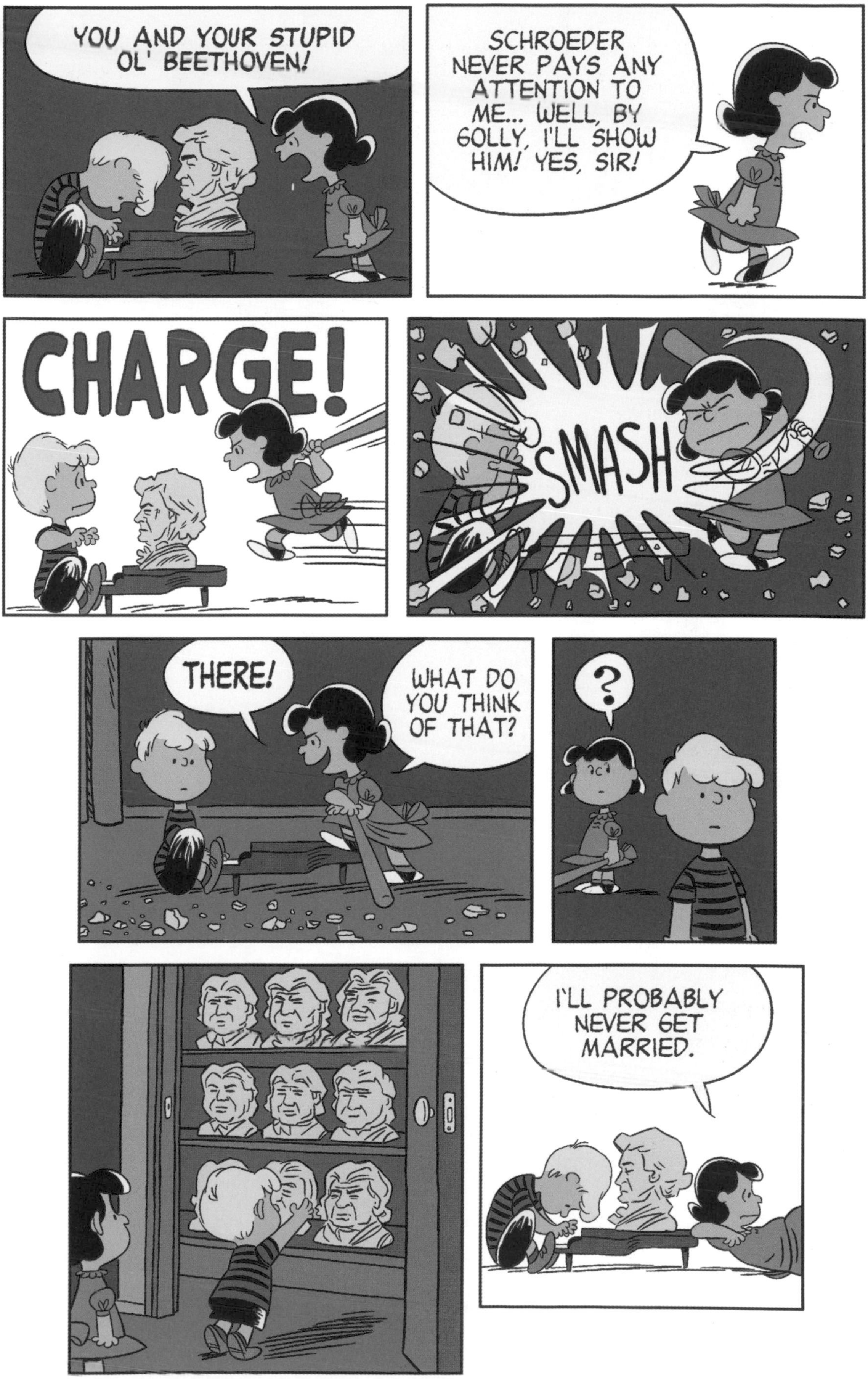
YOU AND YOUR STUPID OL' BEETHOVEN!
SCHROEDER NEVER PAYS ANY ATTENTION TO ME... WELL, BY GOLLY, I'LL SHOW HIM! YES, SIR!
CHARGE!
SMASH
THERE!
WHAT DO YOU THINK OF THAT?
?
I'LL PROBABLY NEVER GET MARRIED.

WELL, THAT'S THAT.

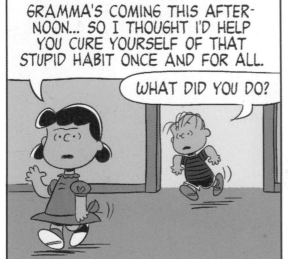

GRAMMA'S COMING THIS AFTERNOON... SO I THOUGHT I'D HELP YOU CURE YOURSELF OF THAT STUPID HABIT ONCE AND FOR ALL.

WHAT DID YOU DO?

I BURIED IT.

YOU CAN'T DO THAT! I JUST GOT IT BACK!

I HAD NO CHOICE. GRAMMA EXPECTS YOU TO BE DONE WITH THAT DUMB BLANKET BEFORE SHE GETS HERE.

TELL ME WHERE YOU BURIED IT! TELL ME TELL ME TELL ME TELL ME!! TELL ME ME TELL ME TELL

I'VE GOTTA FIND THAT BLANKET, CHARLIE BROWN!

LUCY WON'T TELL ME WHERE SHE BURIED IT SO I'VE GOTTA DIG 'TIL I FIND IT!

I'VE JUST GOTTA DIG AN' DIG AN' DIG UNTIL I FIND IT!

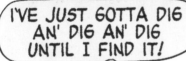

GOOD LUCK!

GOTTA FIND IT! GOTTA FIND IT!

?

GOTTA DIG EVERYWHERE UNTIL I FIND THAT BLANKET! GOTTA FIND IT! GOTTA FIND IT!

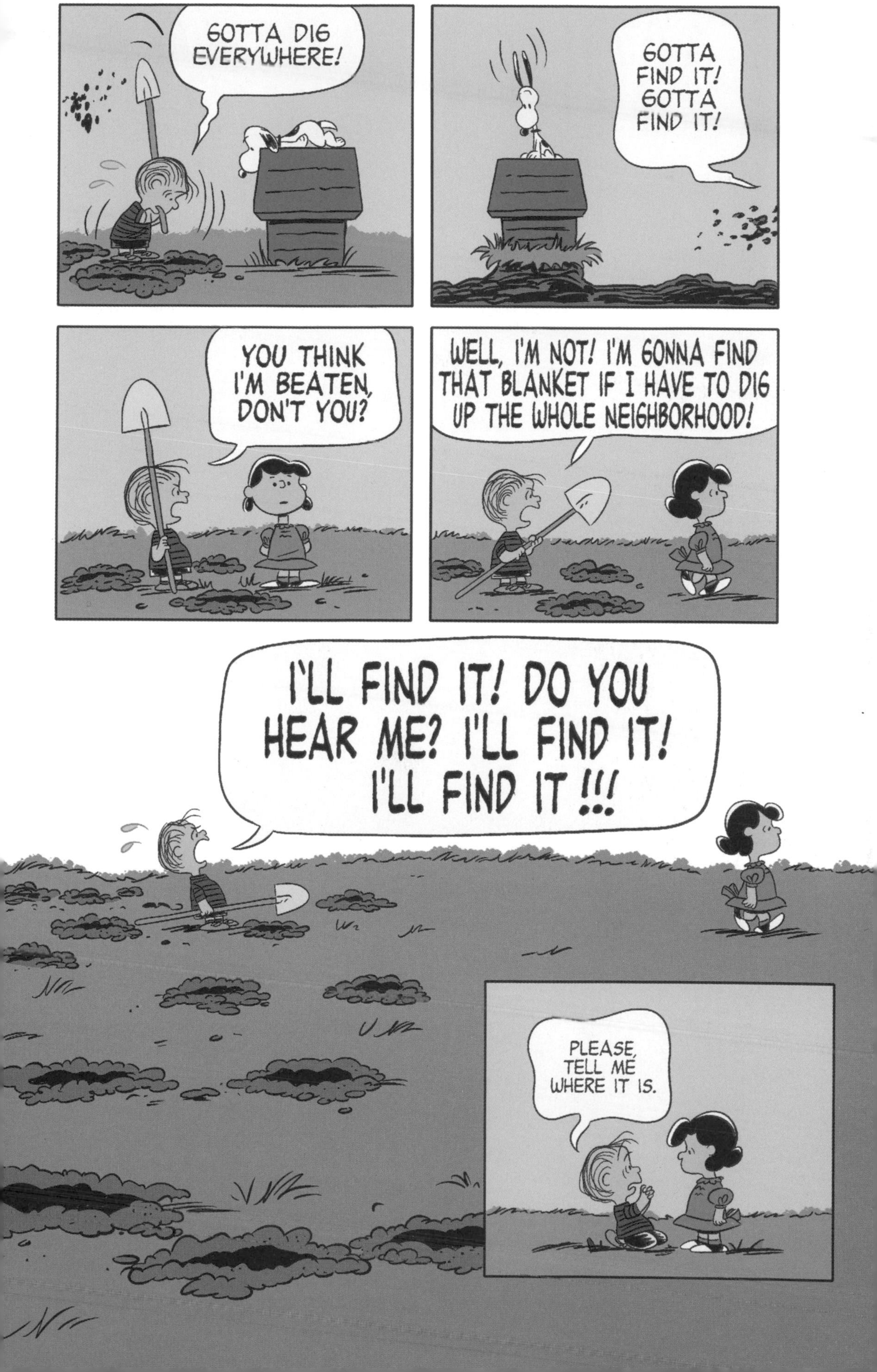
GOTTA DIG EVERYWHERE!
GOTTA FIND IT! GOTTA FIND IT!
YOU THINK I'M BEATEN, DON'T YOU?
WELL, I'M NOT! I'M GONNA FIND THAT BLANKET IF I HAVE TO DIG UP THE WHOLE NEIGHBORHOOD!
I'LL FIND IT! DO YOU HEAR ME? I'LL FIND IT! I'LL FIND IT !!!
PLEASE, TELL ME WHERE IT IS.

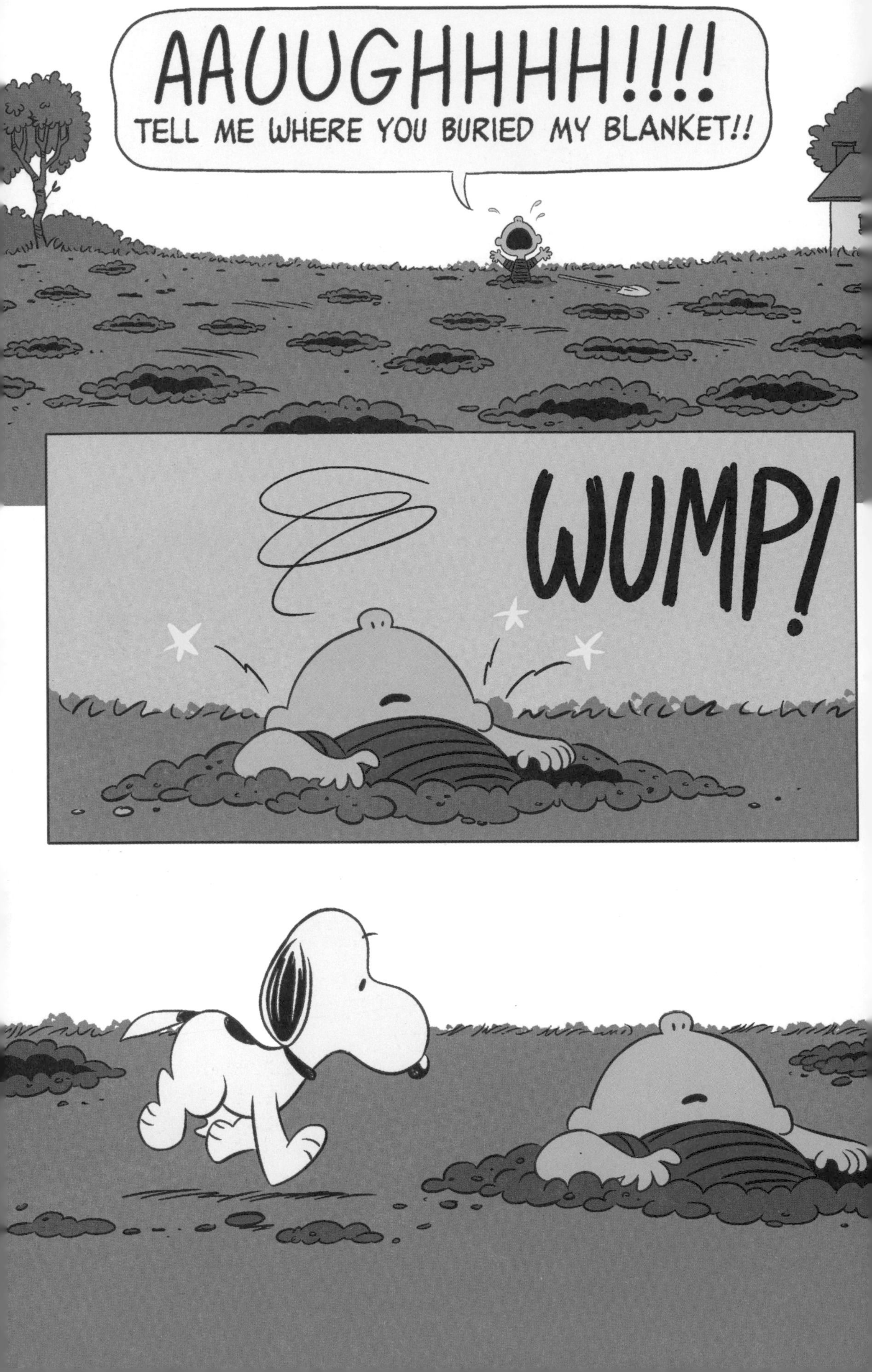
AAUUGHHHH!!!!
TELL ME WHERE YOU BURIED MY BLANKET!!
WUMP!

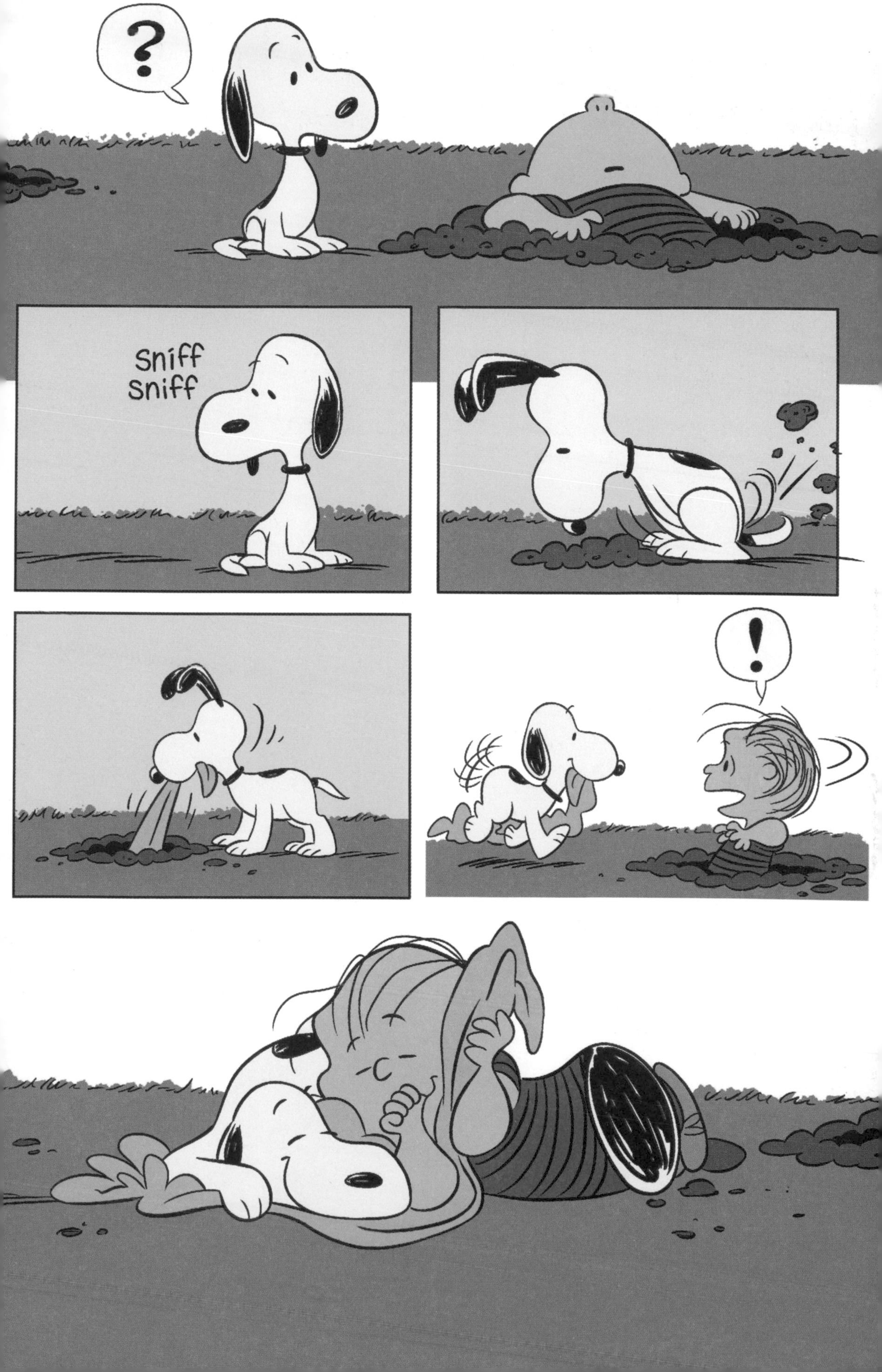
?
Sniff
sniff
!

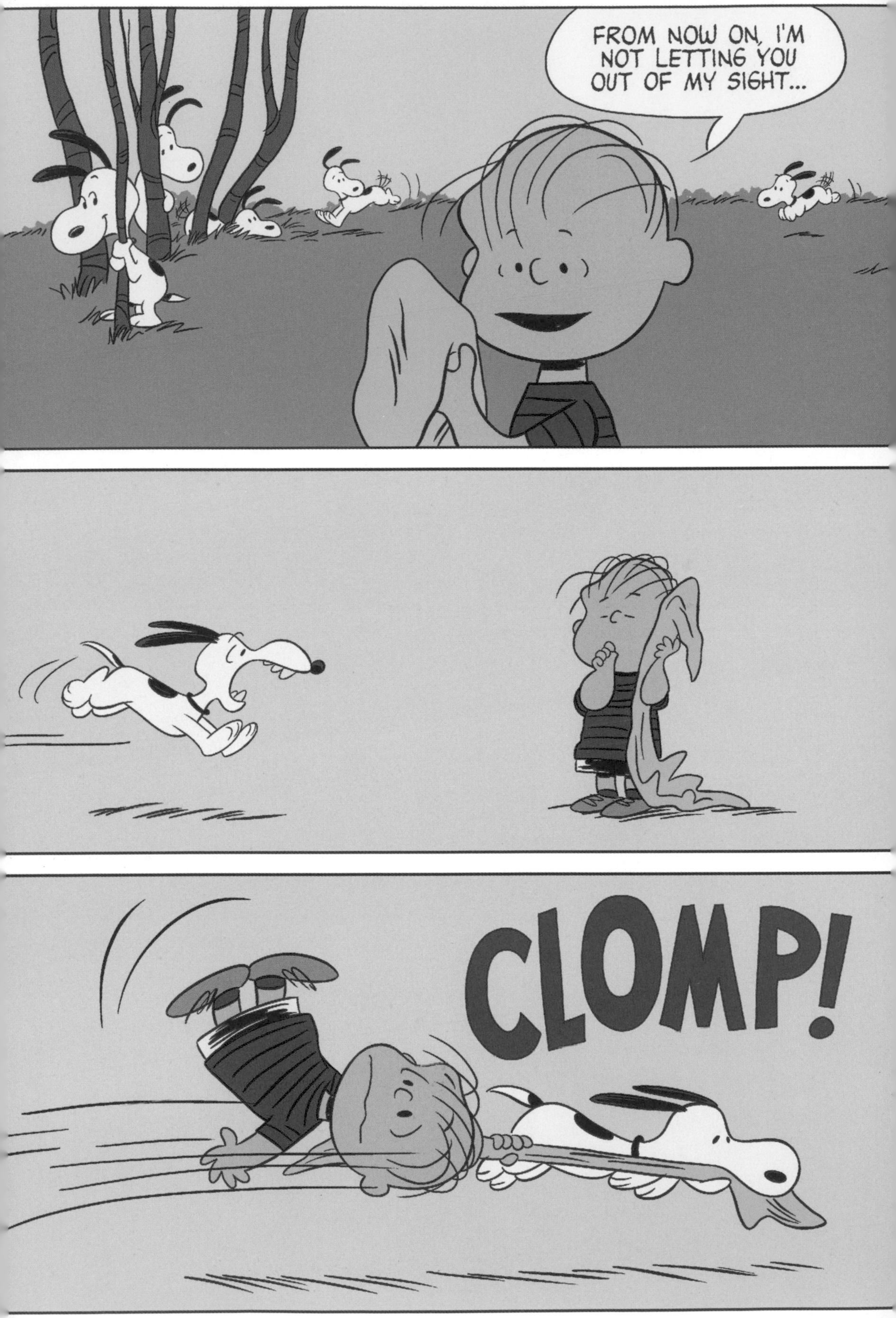
FROM NOW ON, I'M NOT LETTING YOU OUT OF MY SIGHT...
CLOMP!

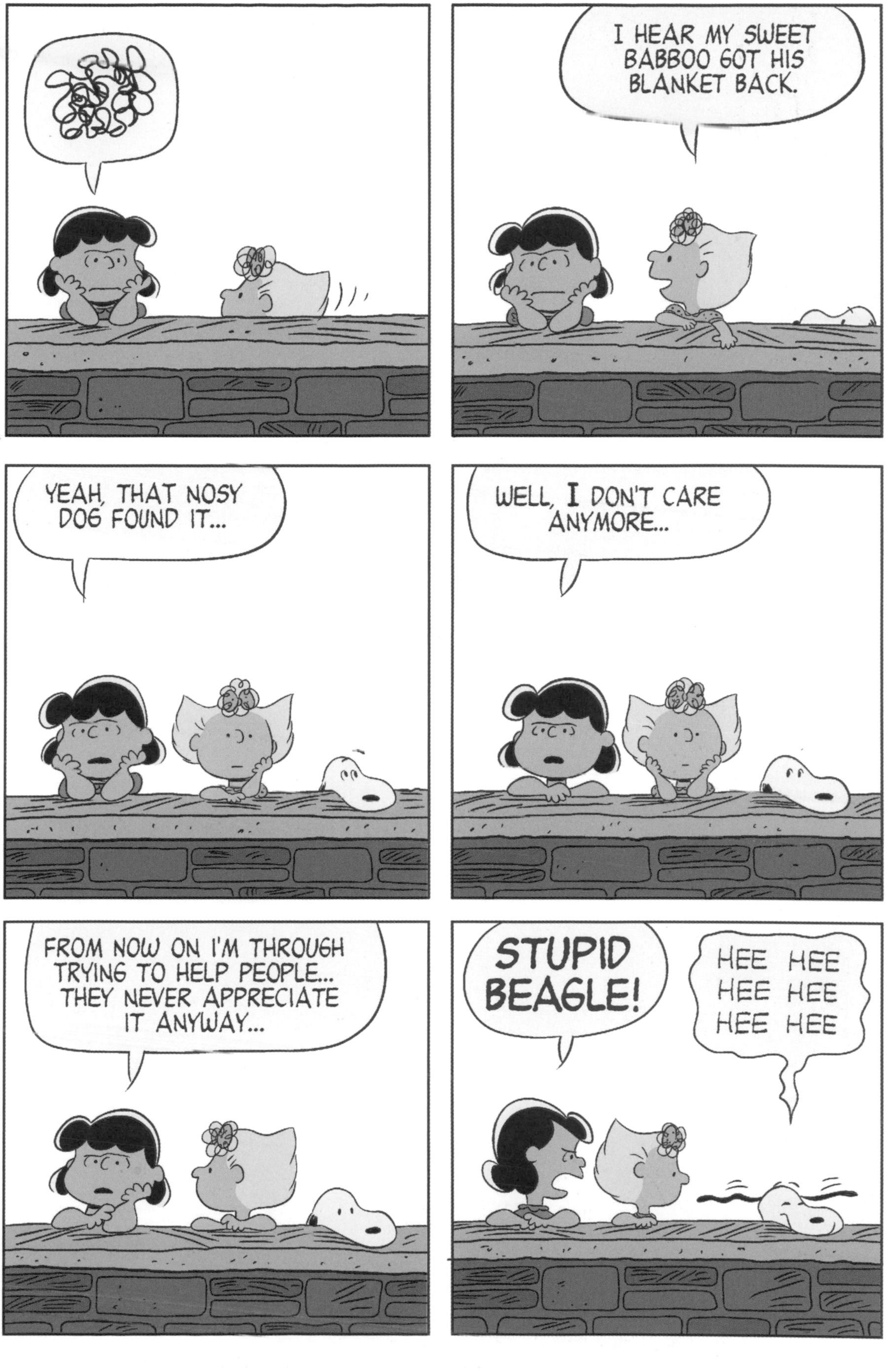
I HEAR MY SWEET BABBOO GOT HIS BLANKET BACK.
YEAH, THAT NOSY DOG FOUND IT...
WELL, I DON'T CARE ANYMORE...
FROM NOW ON I'M THROUGH TRYING TO HELP PEOPLE... THEY NEVER APPRECIATE IT ANYWAY...
STUPID BEAGLE!
HEE HEE HEE HEE HEE HEE

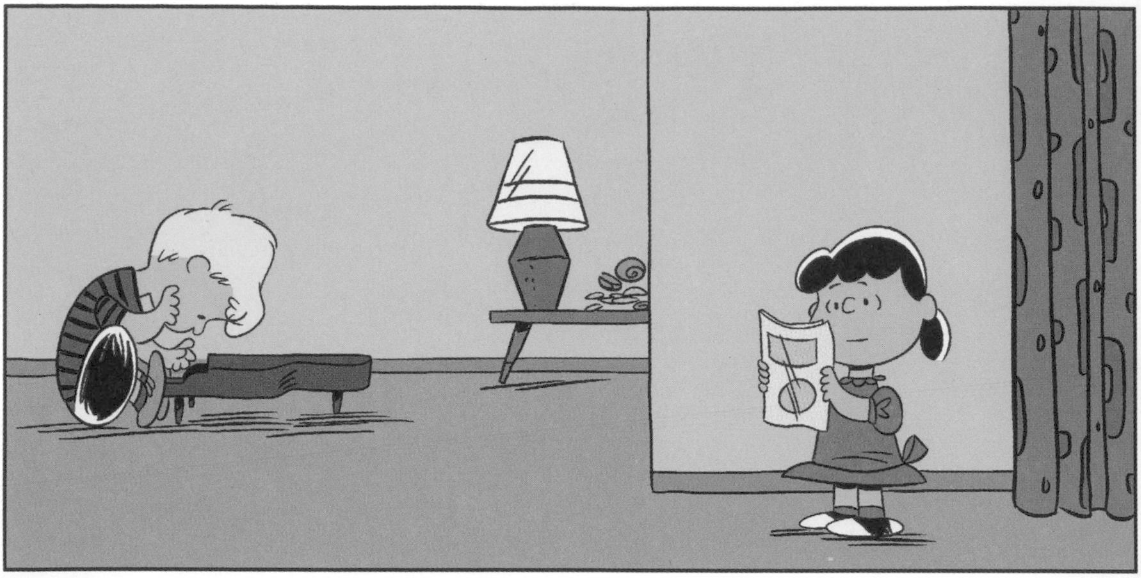

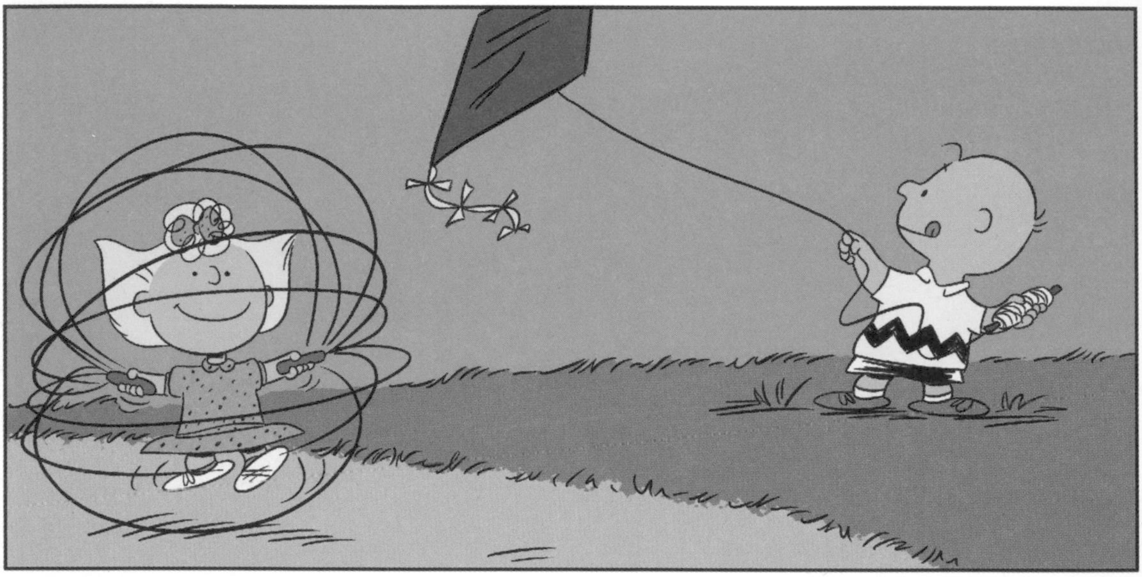

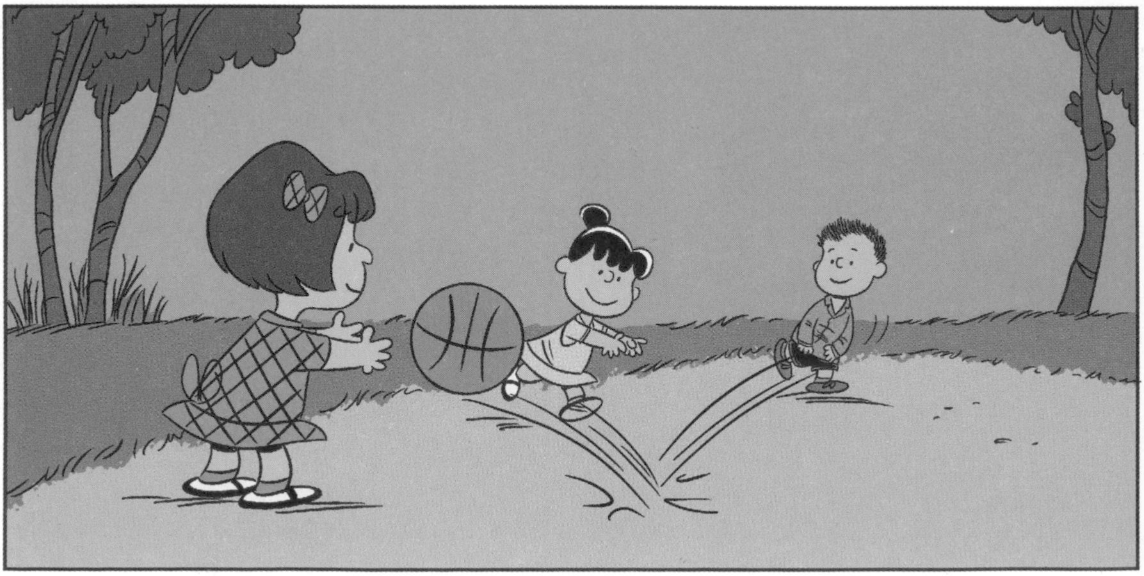

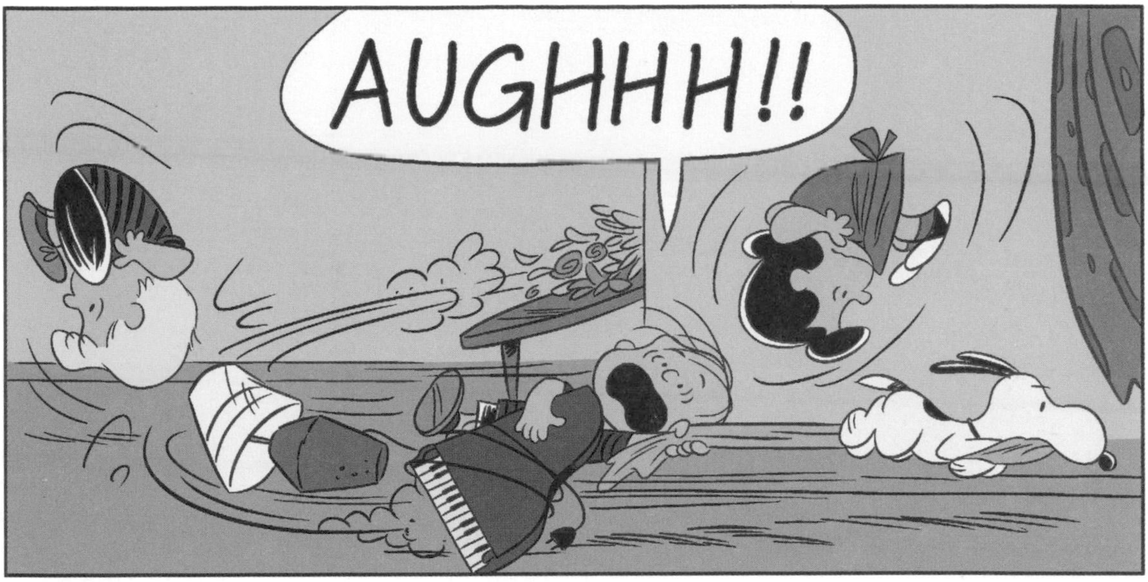
AUGHHH!!

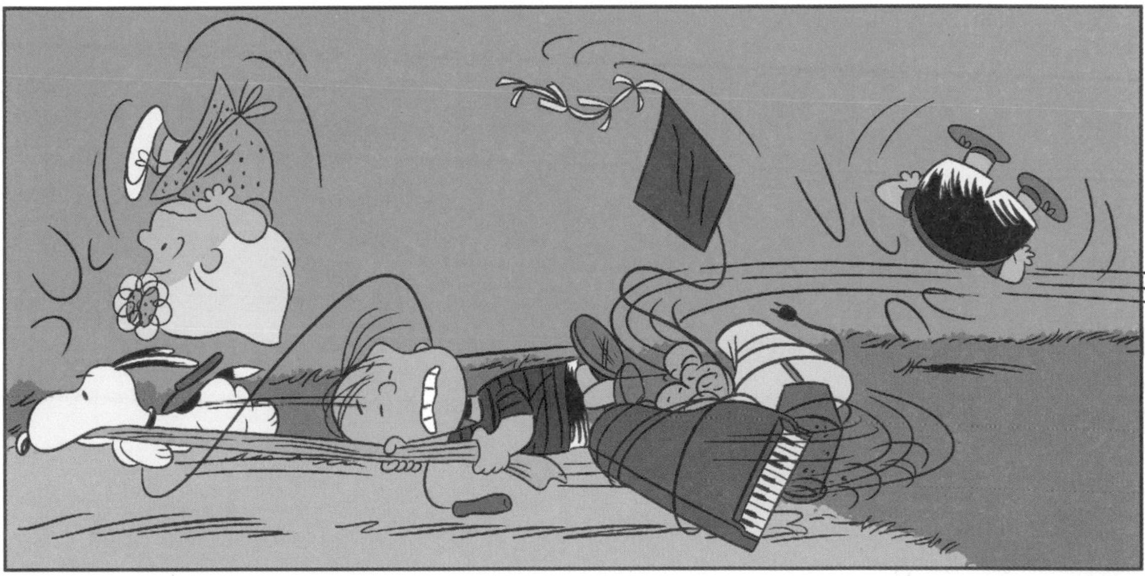

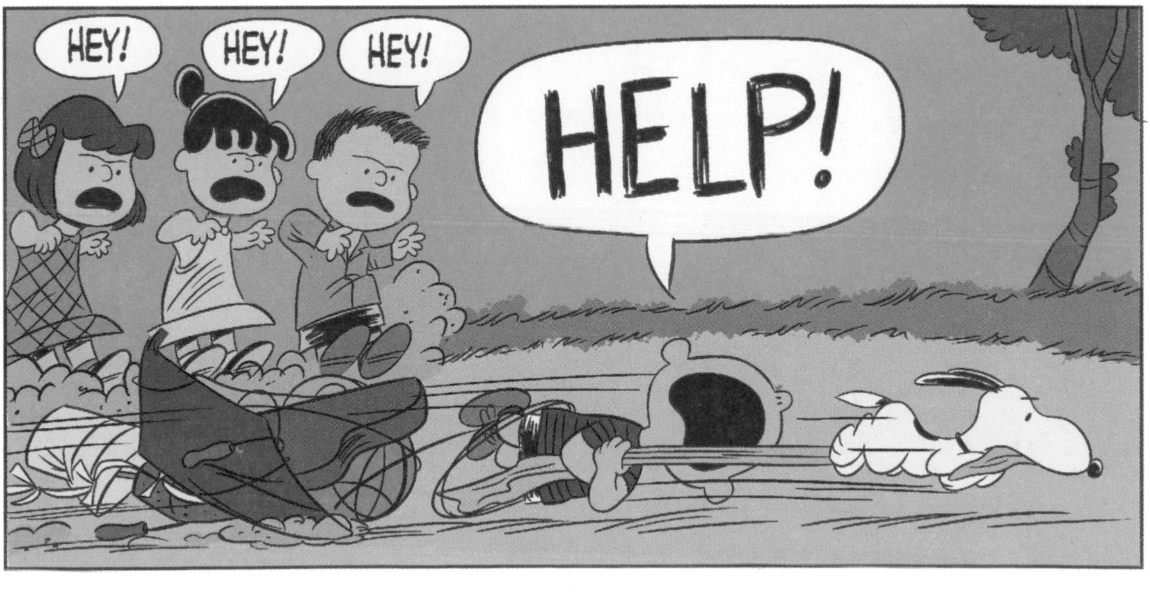
HEY!
HEY!
HEY!
HELP!

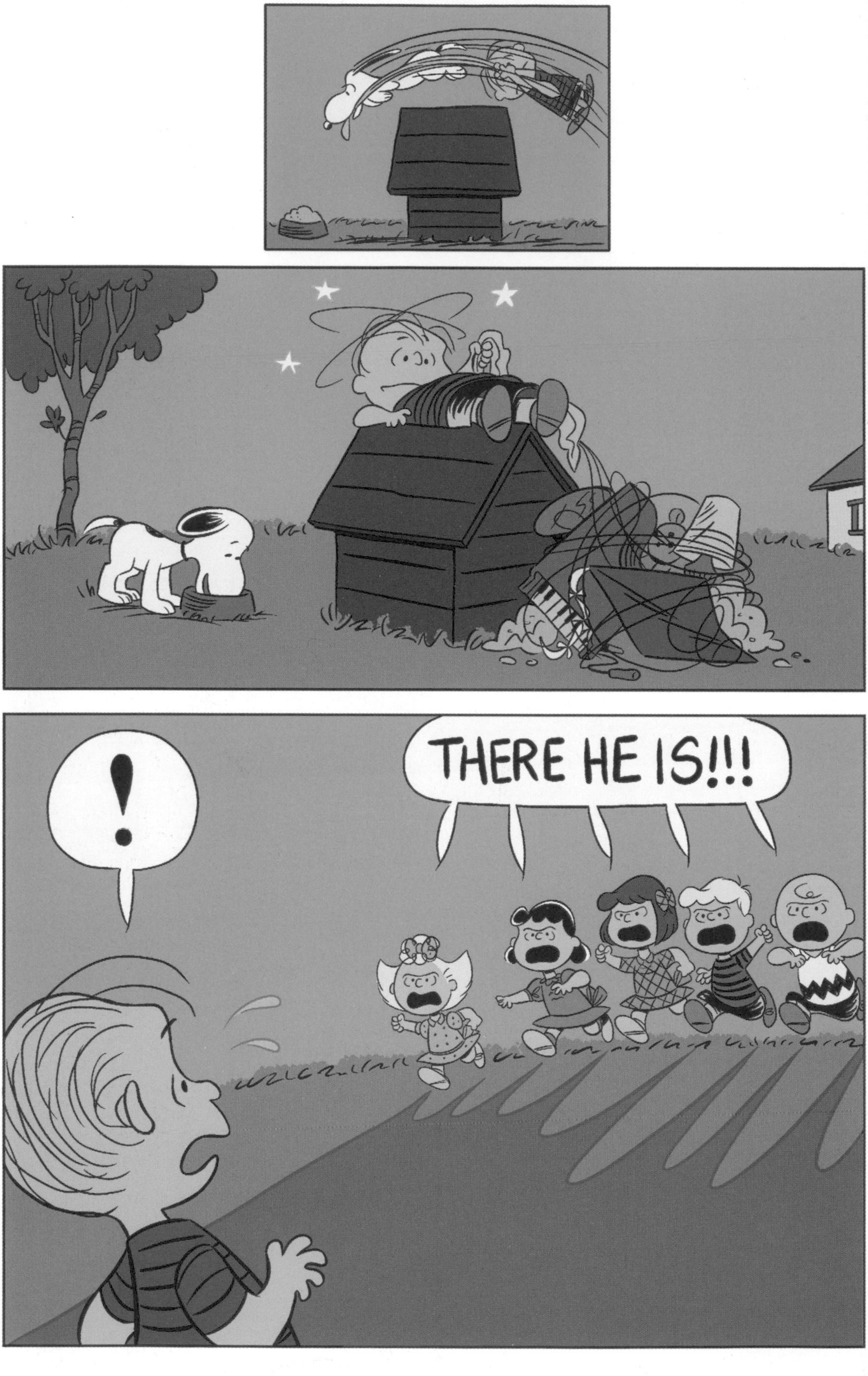
!
THERE HE IS!!!

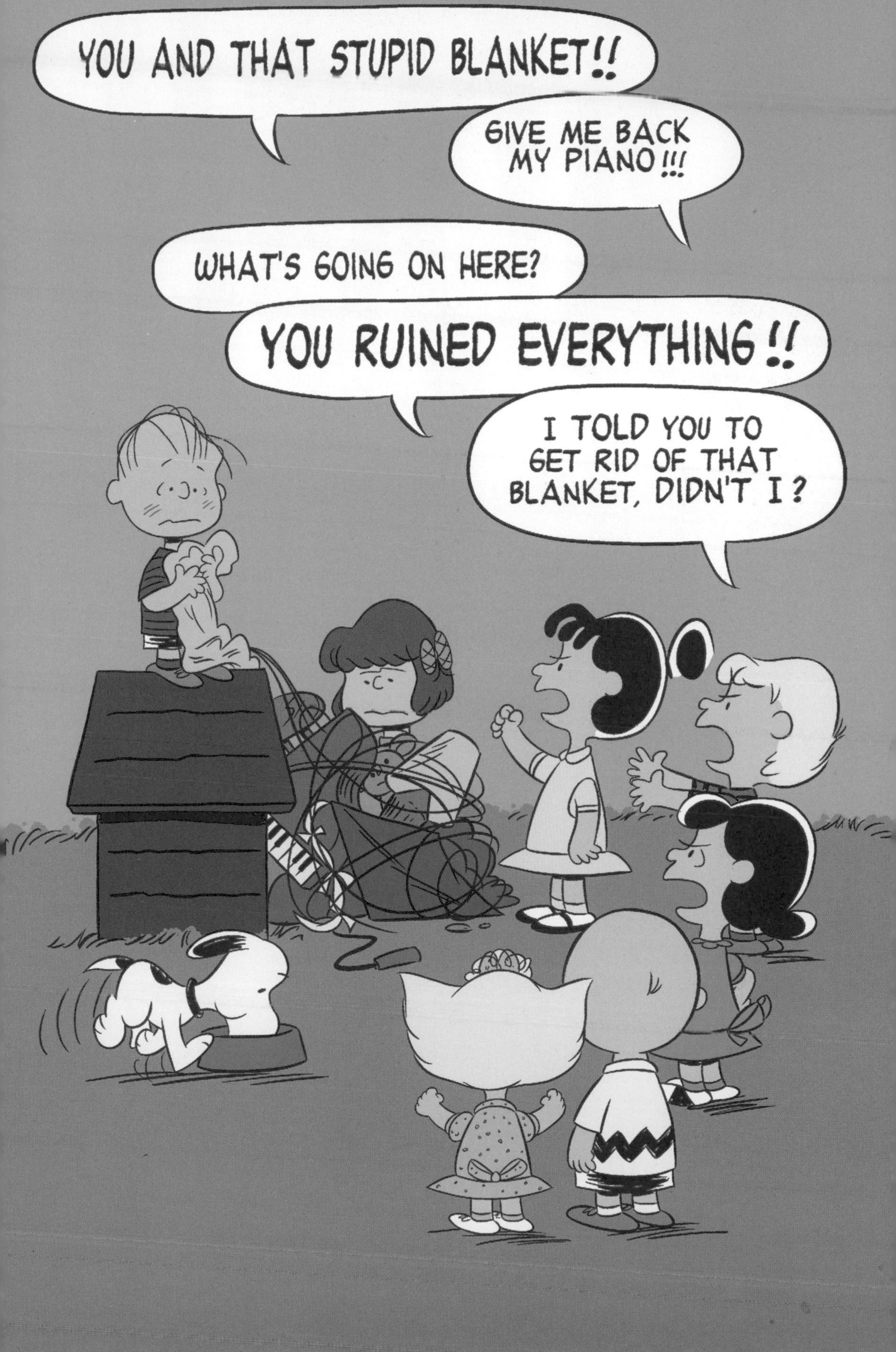
YOU AND THAT STUPID BLANKET!!
GIVE ME BACK MY PIANO!!!
WHAT'S GOING ON HERE?
YOU RUINED EVERYTHING!!
I TOLD YOU TO GET RID OF THAT BLANKET, DIDN'T I?

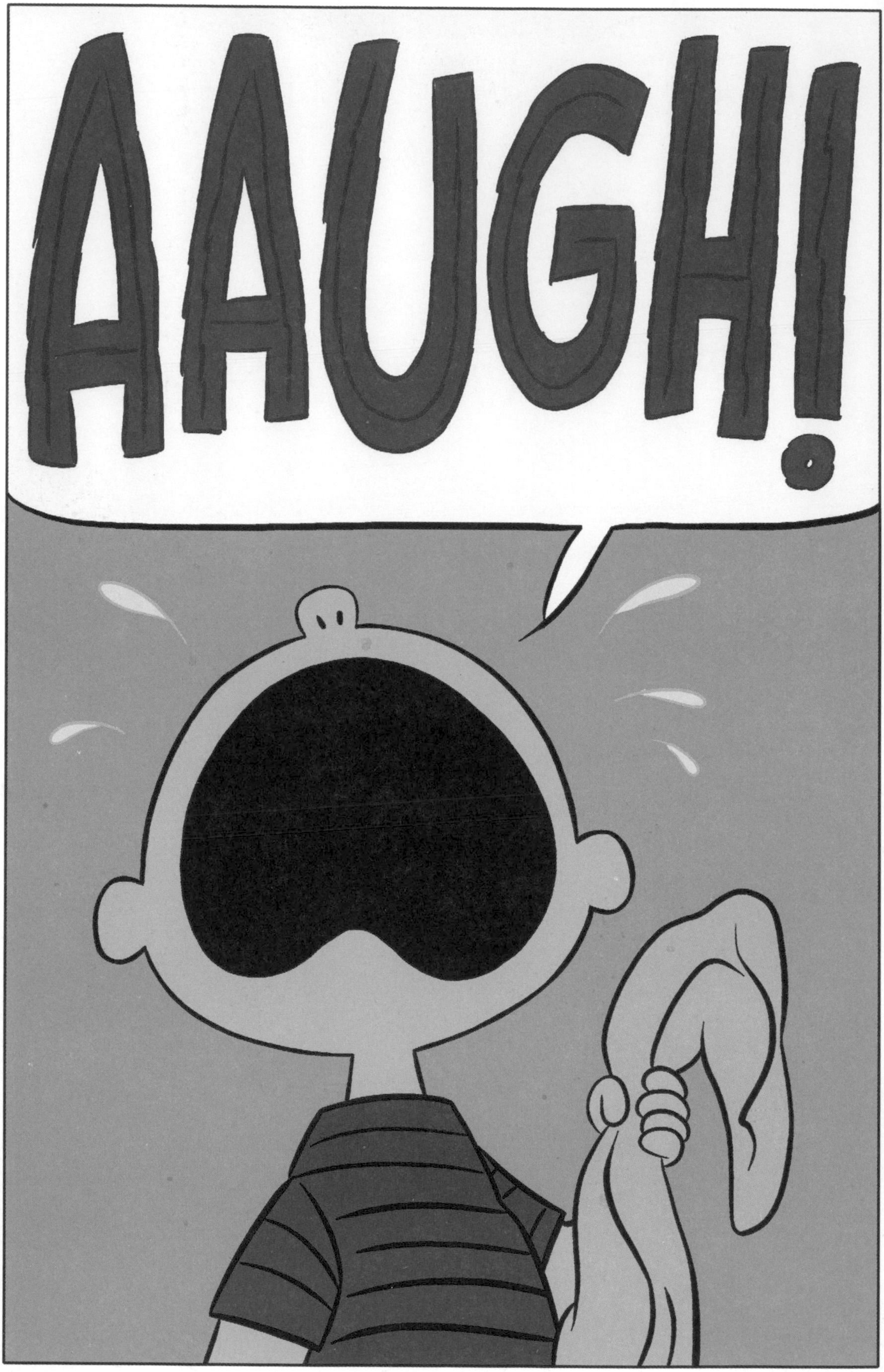
AAUGH!

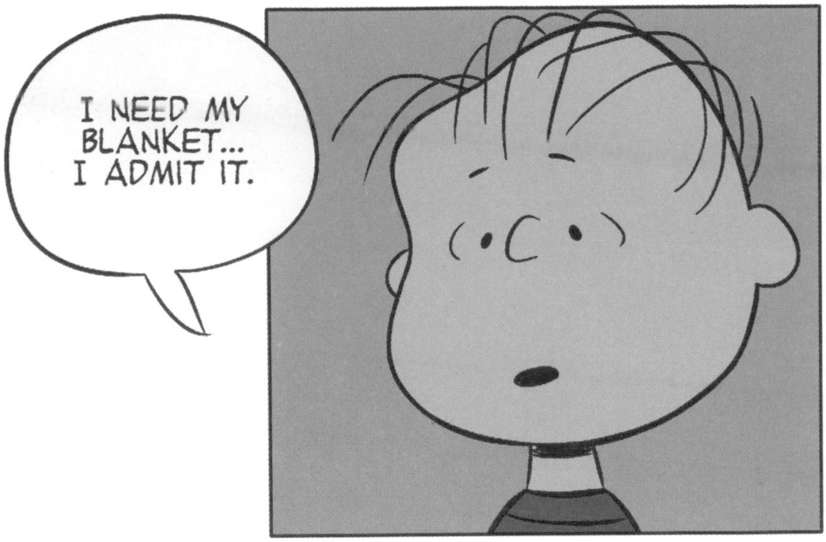
I NEED MY BLANKET... I ADMIT IT.

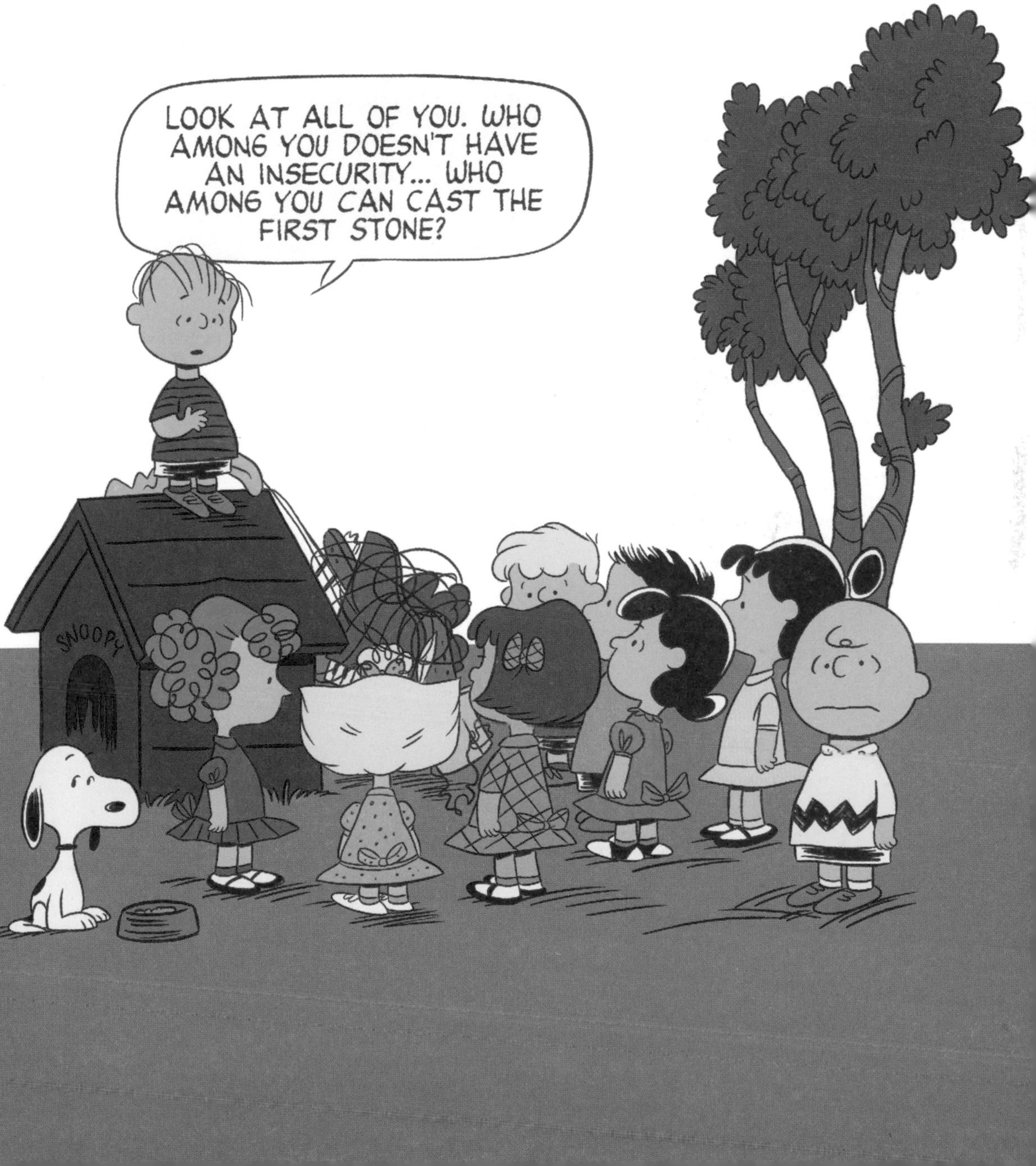
LOOK AT ALL OF YOU. WHO AMONG YOU DOESN'T HAVE AN INSECURITY... WHO AMONG YOU CAN CAST THE FIRST STONE?
SNOOPY

WHO AMONG YOU DOESN'T DEPEND ON SOMEONE OR SOMETHING TO HELP YOU GET THROUGH THE DAY?

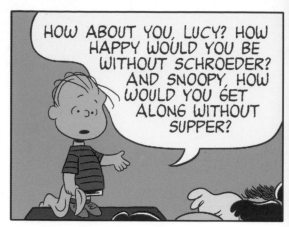

HOW ABOUT YOU, LUCY? HOW HAPPY WOULD YOU BE WITHOUT SCHROEDER? AND SNOOPY, HOW WOULD YOU GET ALONG WITHOUT SUPPER?

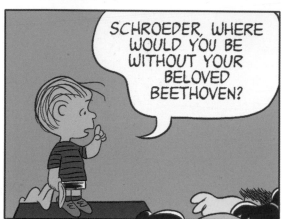

SCHROEDER, WHERE WOULD YOU BE WITHOUT YOUR BELOVED BEETHOVEN?

SALLY, DON'T YOU NEED YOUR SWEET BABBOO?

DON'T WE ALL NEED SOMETHING?... WHAT DO YOU WANT FROM ME? DO YOU **WANT** TO SEE ME UNHAPPY? DO YOU **WANT** TO SEE ME INSECURE? DO YOU **WANT** TO SEE ME END UP LIKE CHARLIE BROWN?

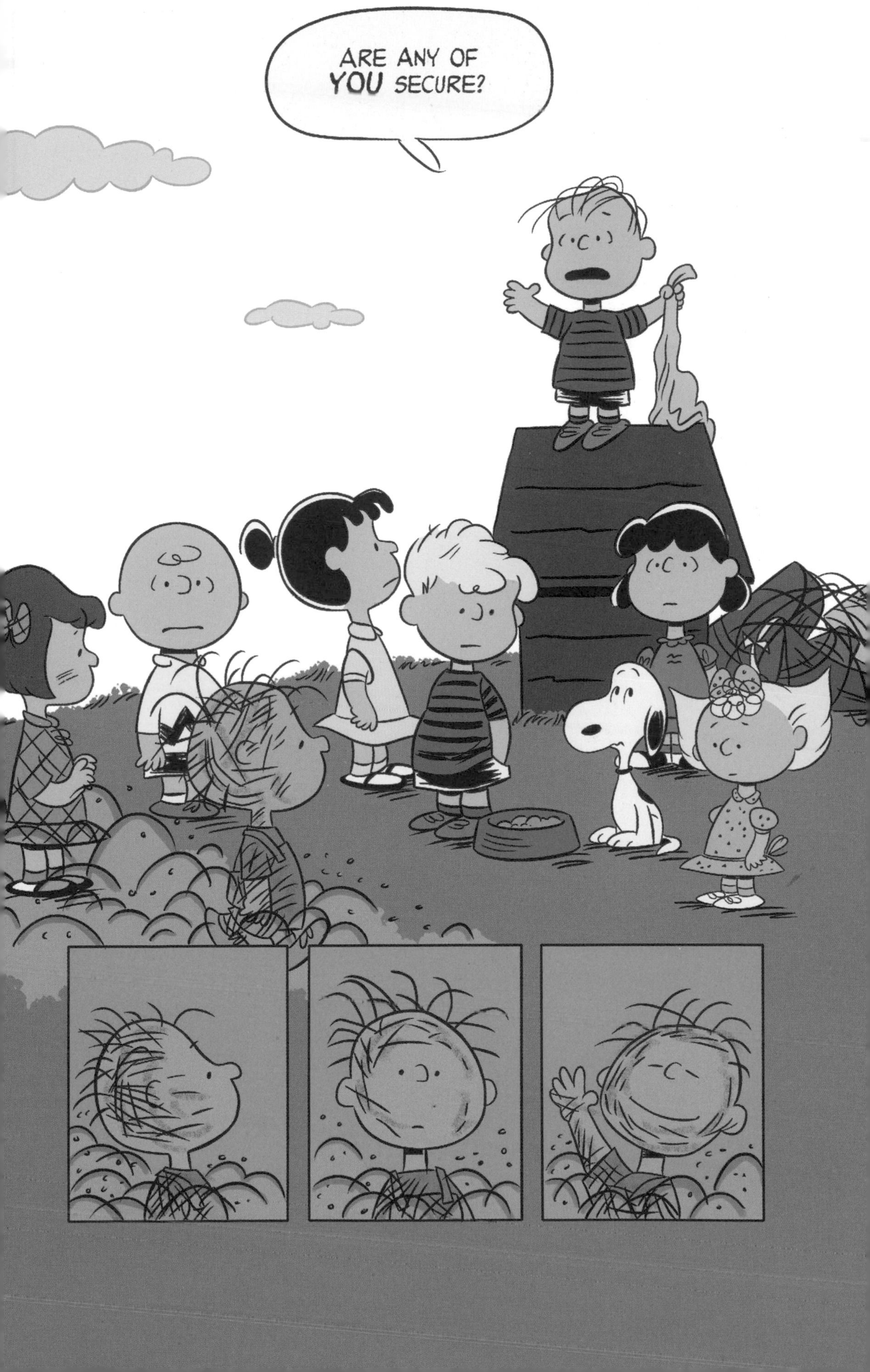
ARE ANY OF YOU SECURE?

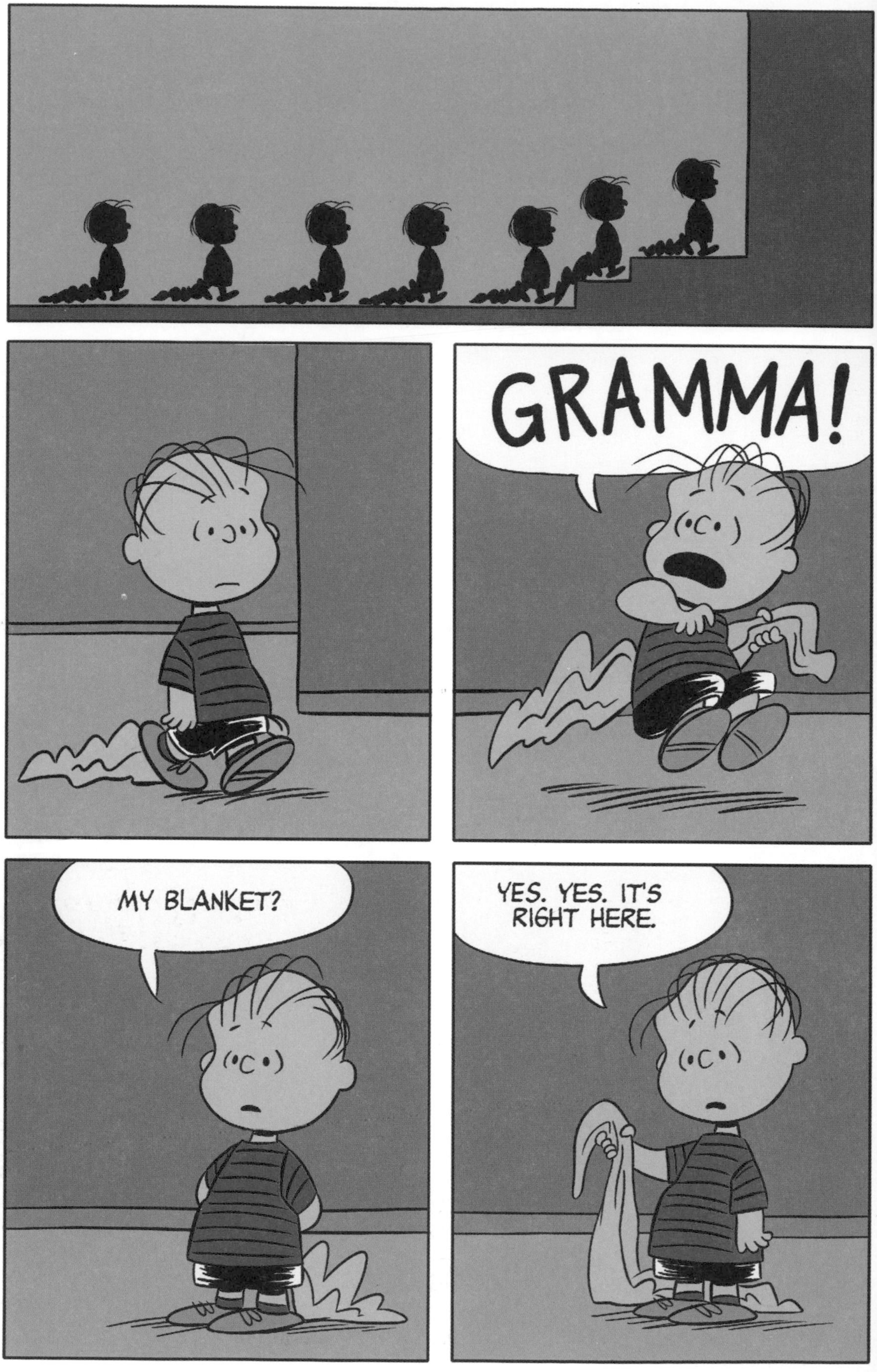
GRAMMA!
MY BLANKET?
YES. YES. IT'S RIGHT HERE.

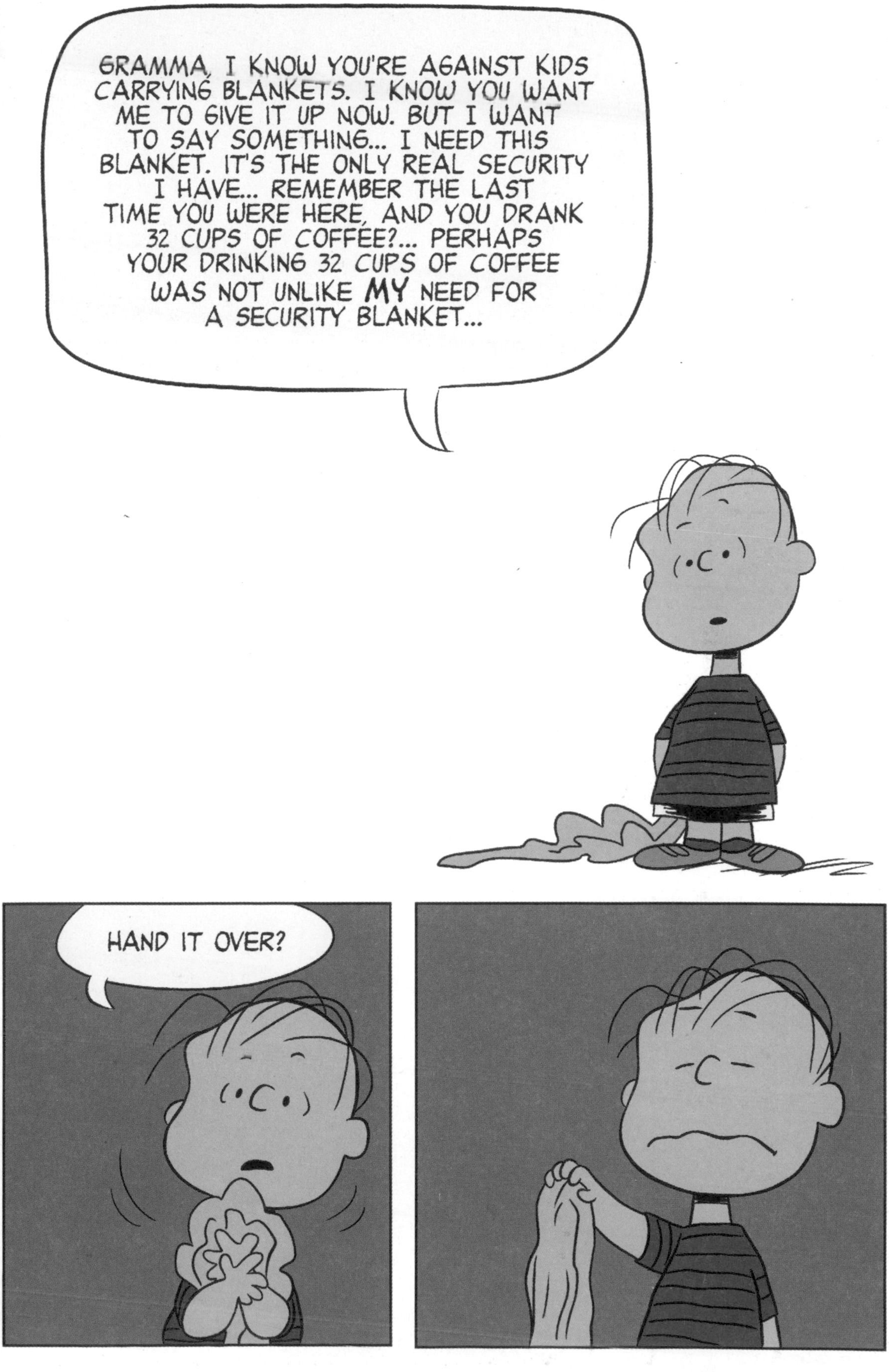
GRAMMA, I KNOW YOU'RE AGAINST KIDS CARRYING BLANKETS. I KNOW YOU WANT ME TO GIVE IT UP NOW. BUT I WANT TO SAY SOMETHING... I NEED THIS BLANKET. IT'S THE ONLY REAL SECURITY I HAVE... REMEMBER THE LAST TIME YOU WERE HERE, AND YOU DRANK 32 CUPS OF COFFEE?... PERHAPS YOUR DRINKING 32 CUPS OF COFFEE WAS NOT UNLIKE MY NEED FOR A SECURITY BLANKET...
HAND IT OVER?

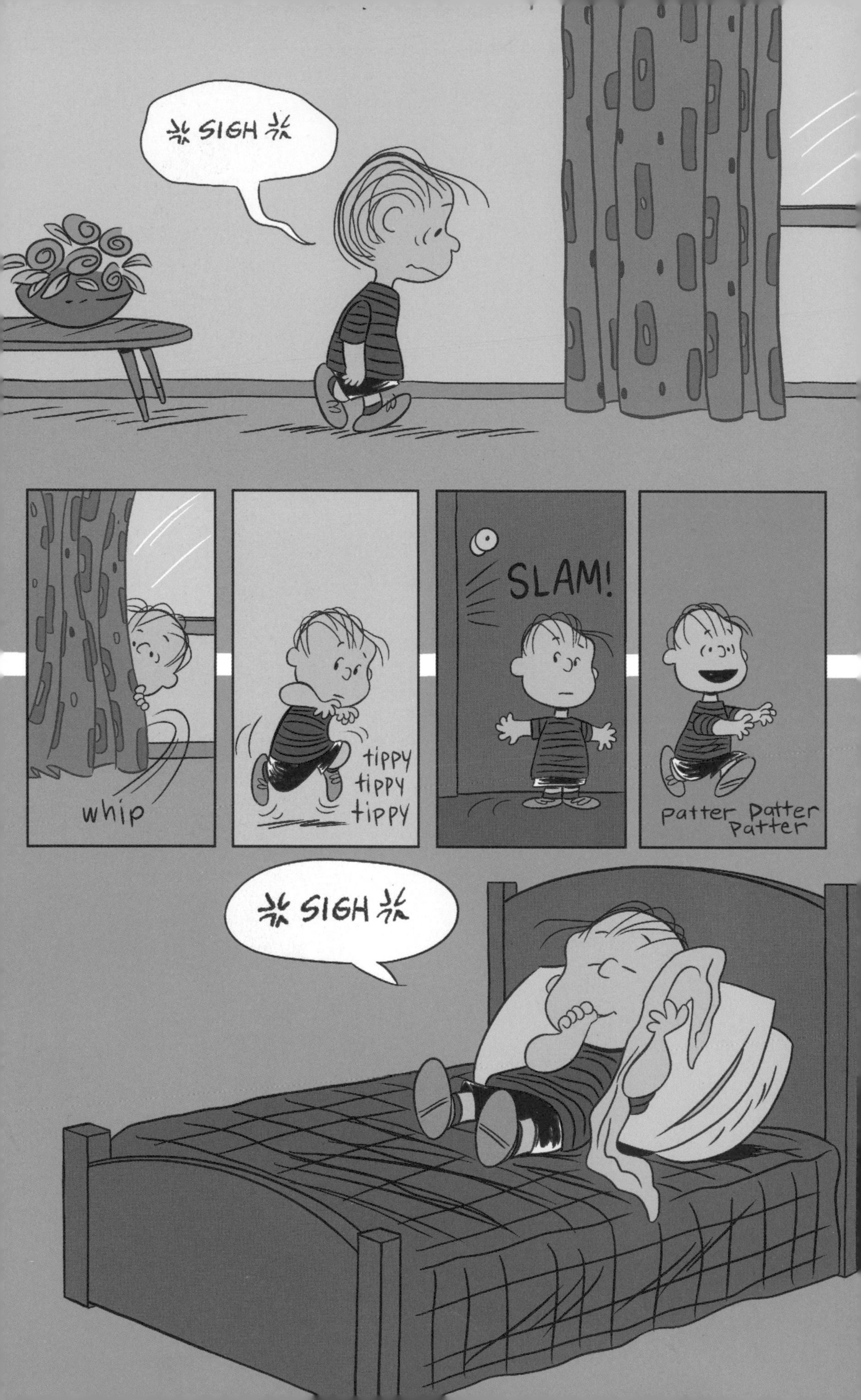
SIGH
whip
tippy
tippy
tippy
SLAM!
patter patter
patter
SIGH

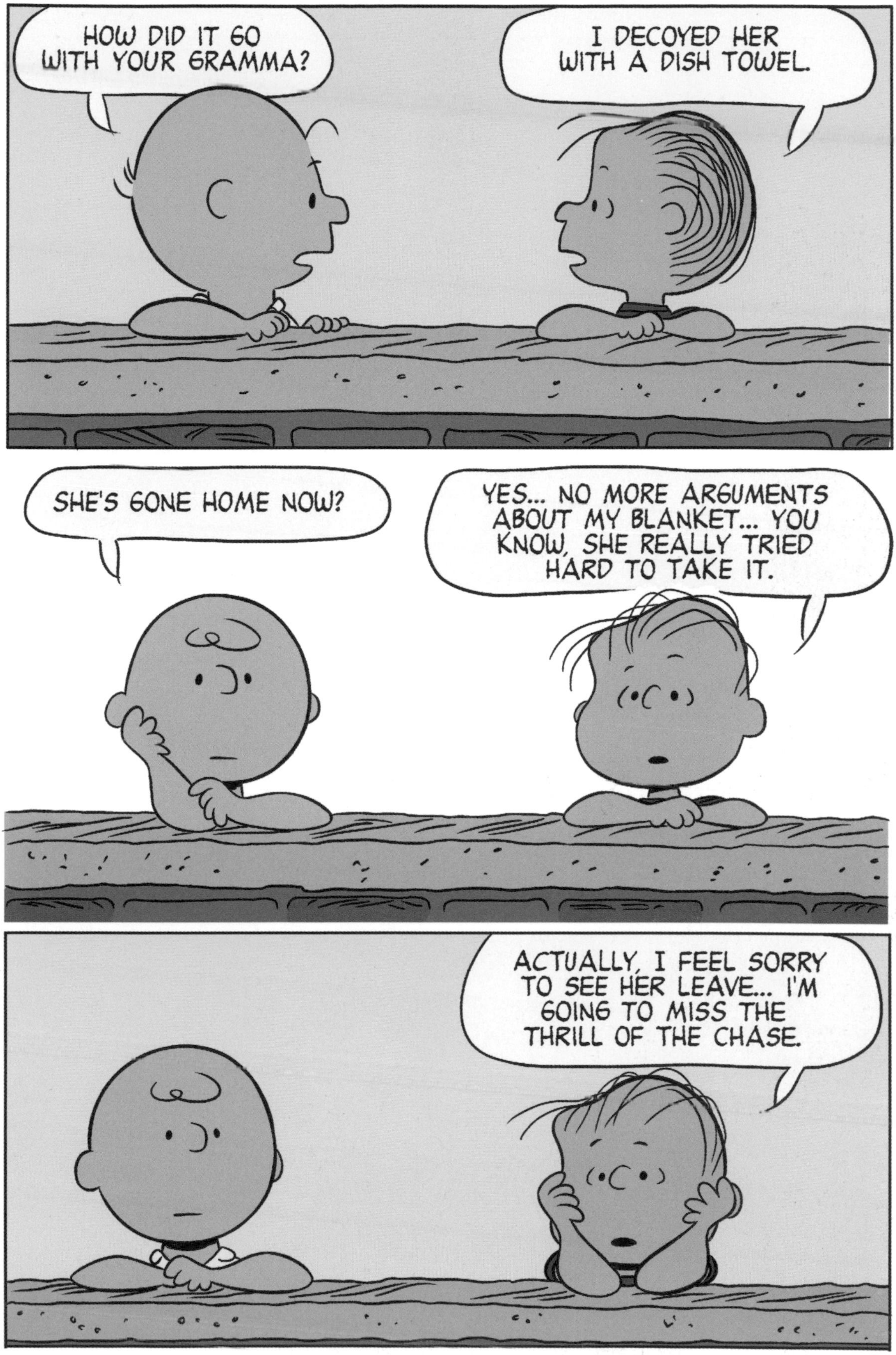
HOW DID IT GO WITH YOUR GRAMMA?
I DECOYED HER WITH A DISH TOWEL.
SHE'S GONE HOME NOW?
YES... NO MORE ARGUMENTS ABOUT MY BLANKET... YOU KNOW, SHE REALLY TRIED HARD TO TAKE IT.
ACTUALLY, I FEEL SORRY TO SEE HER LEAVE... I'M GOING TO MISS THE THRILL OF THE CHASE.

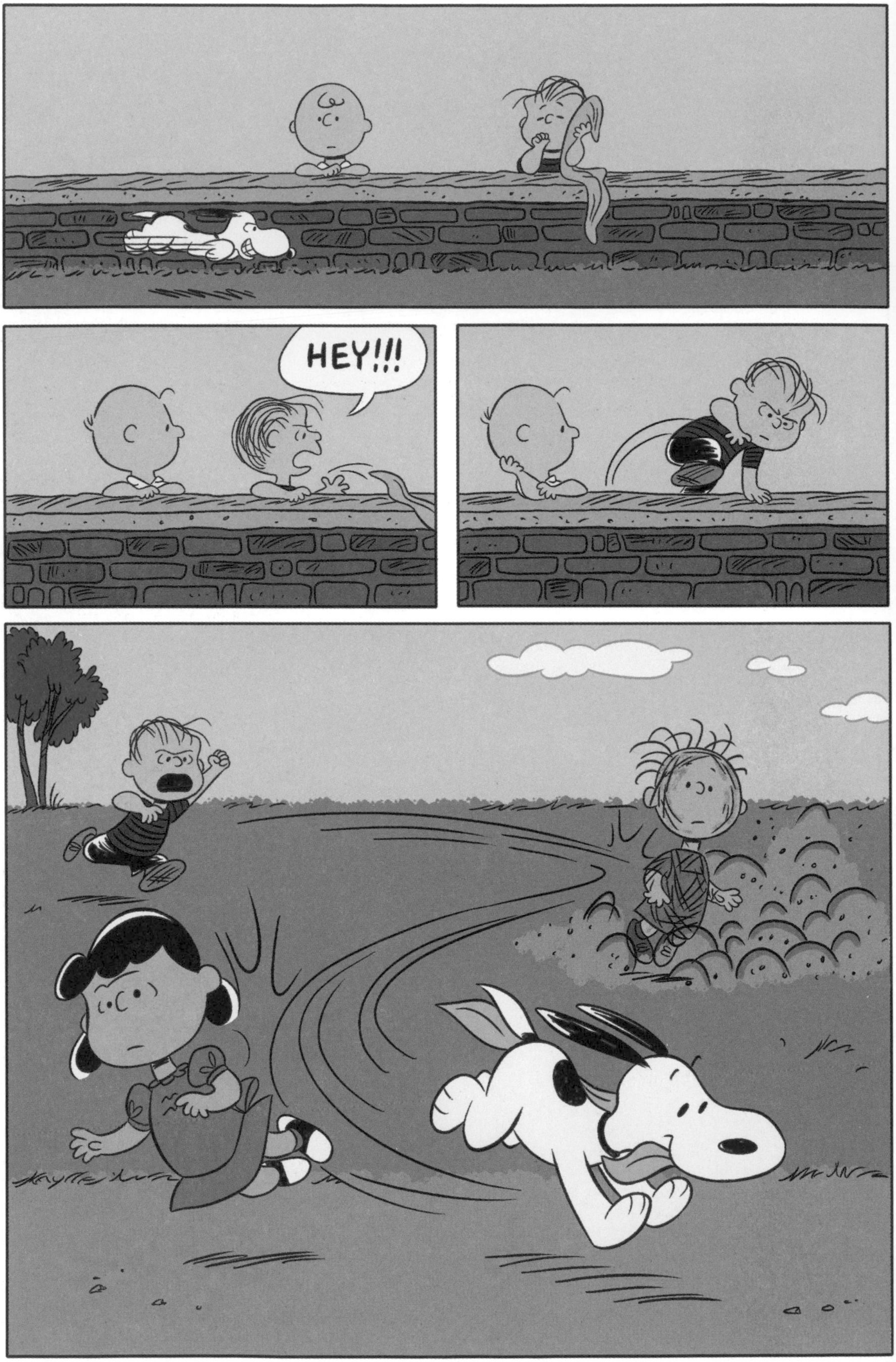
HEY!!!

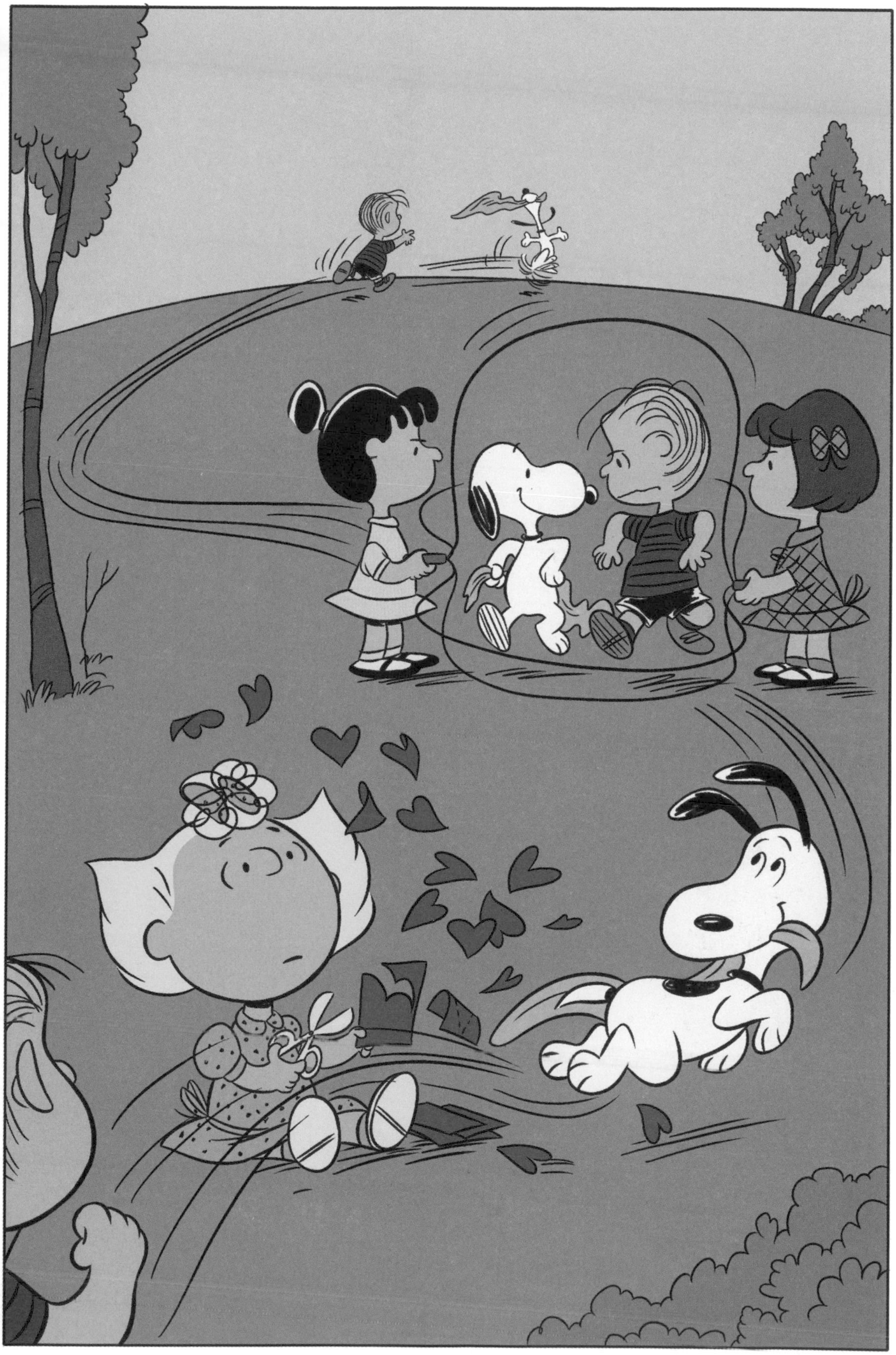

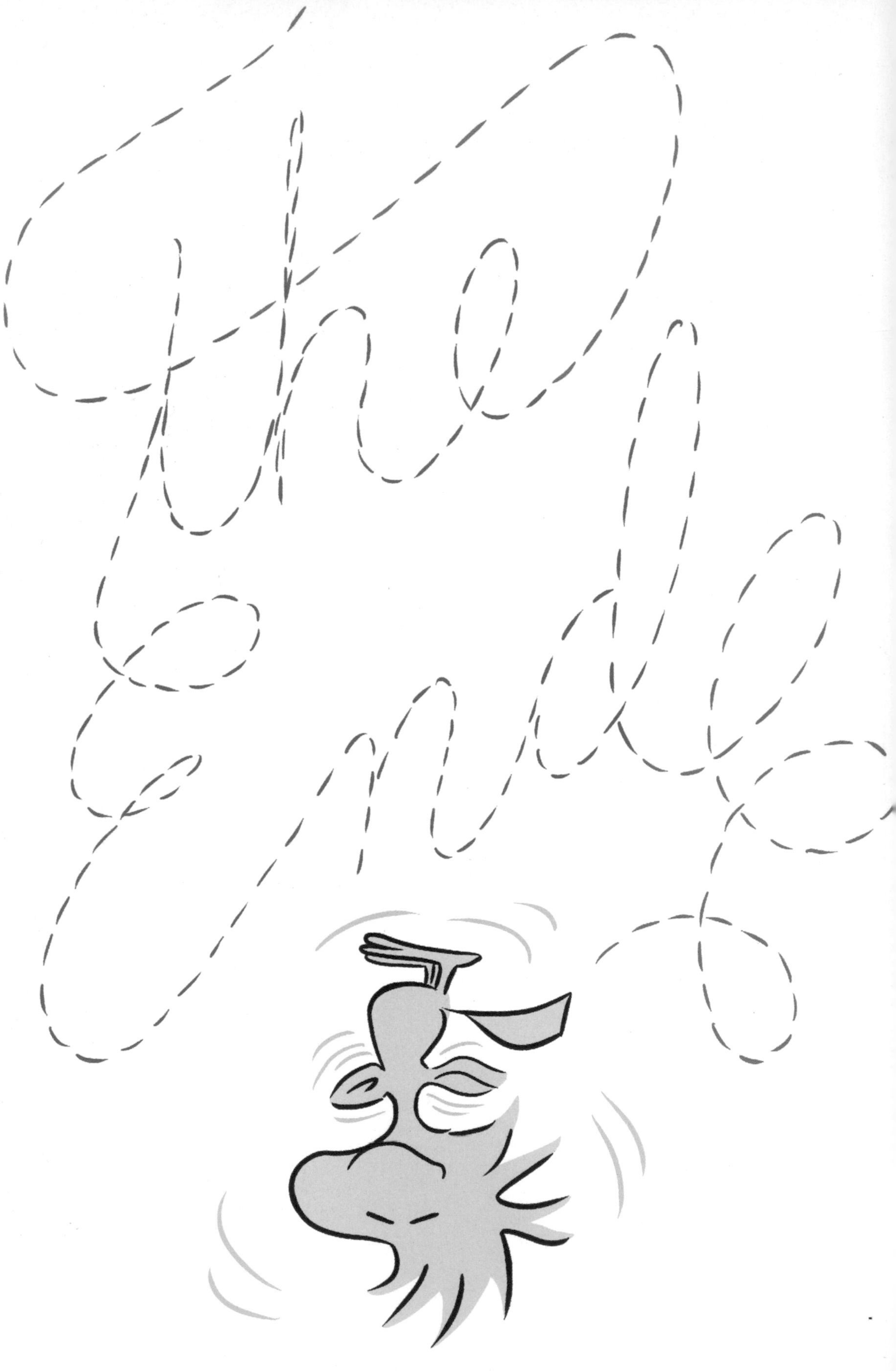
The End

BEHIND-THE-SCENES

Happiness
is a warm
Blanket
Charlie Brown™

ANIMATED SPECIAL

Happiness is a Warm Blanket, Charlie Brown is the first all-new animated special from *Peanuts* in over five years. Adapted from Charles M. Schulz's comic strip, the story is centered on Linus and his security blanket woes. Directed by Andy Beall and Frank Molieri, the special is a throwback to some of the best *Peanuts* animated specials: *A Charlie Brown Christmas, It's the Great Pumpkin, Charlie Brown*, and *Charlie Brown's All-Stars*.

The following model sheets, character poses and reference material was all part of the production on this newest *Peanuts* animated special.

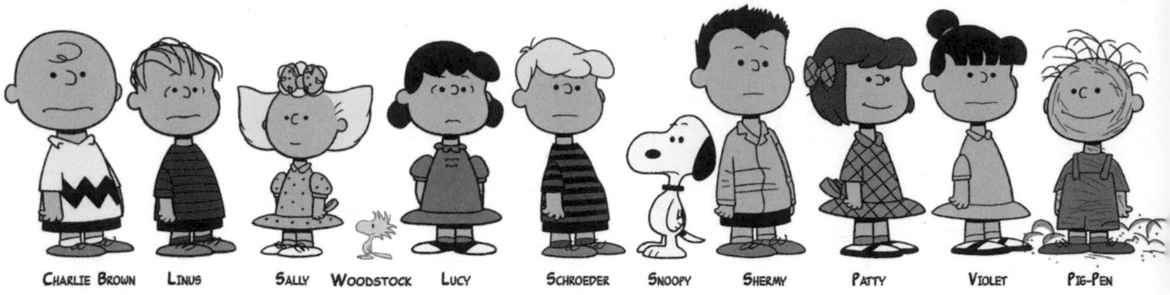
CHARLIE BROWN
LINUS
SALLY
WOODSTOCK
LUCY
SCHROEDER
SNOOPY
SHERMY
PATTY
VIOLET
PIG-PEN

Above The cast of characters for *Blanket*; the look is derived from *Peanuts* comic strips circa1963-64.

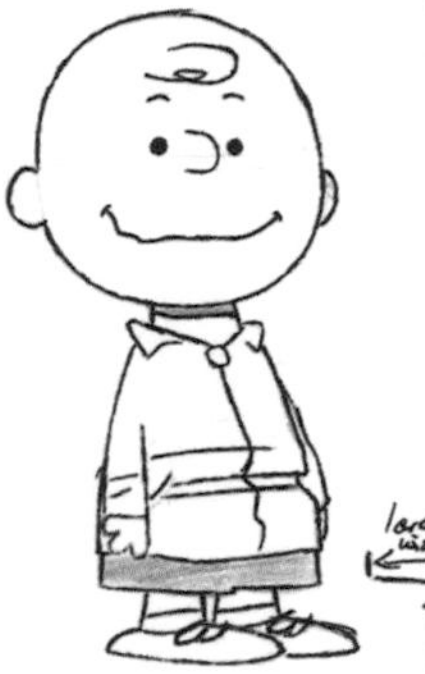

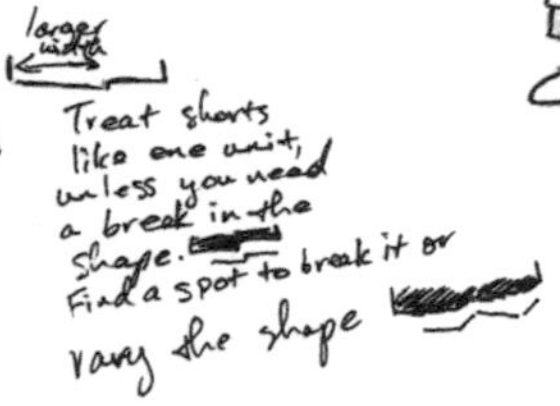
Treat shorts like one unit, unless you need a break in the shape.
Find a spot to break it or vary the shape

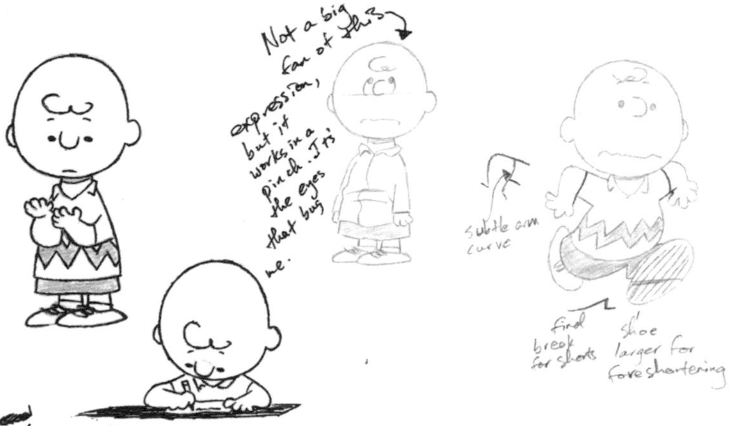
Not a big fan of this expression, but it works in a pinch. It's the eyes that bug me.
subtle arm curve
find break for shorts
shoe larger for foreshortening

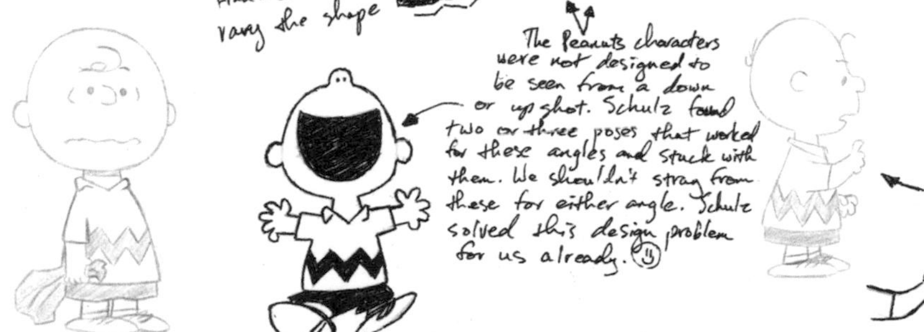
The Peanuts characters were not designed to be seen from a down or up shot. Schulz found two or three poses that worked for these angles and stuck with them. We shouldn't stray from these for either angle. Schulz solved this design problem for us already.

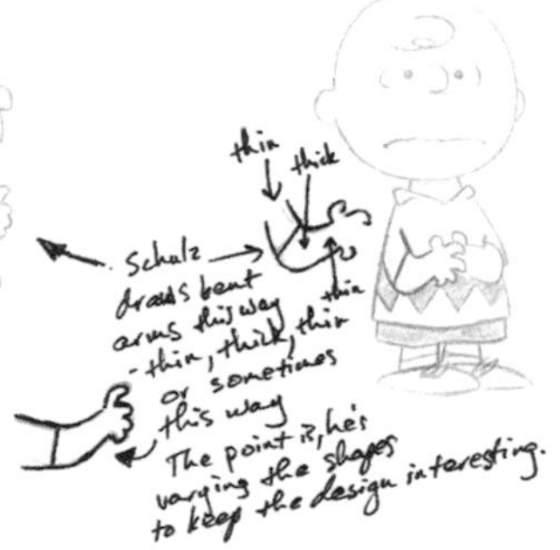
thin
thick
Schulz draws bent arms this way - thin, thick, thin or sometimes this way
The point is, he's varying the shapes to keep the design interesting.

Above & Below Development sketches of Charlie Brown and Snoopy, by Andy Beall.

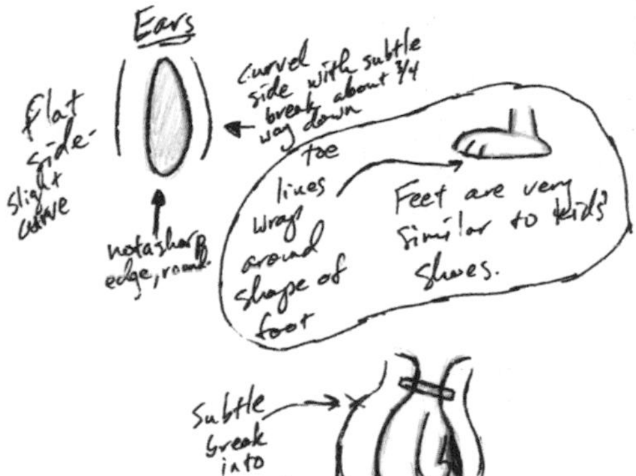
Ears
Flat side - slight curve
curved side with subtle break about 3/4 way down
not a sharp edge, round.
toe lines wrap around shape of foot
Feet are very similar to kids' shoes.
Subtle break into curve

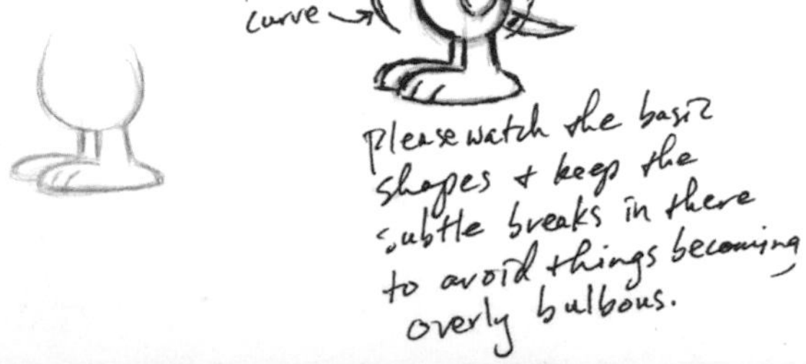
Please watch the basic shapes & keep the subtle breaks in there to avoid things becoming overly bulbous.

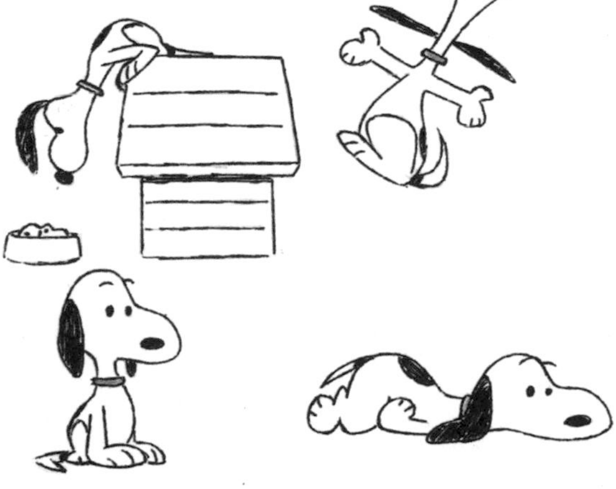

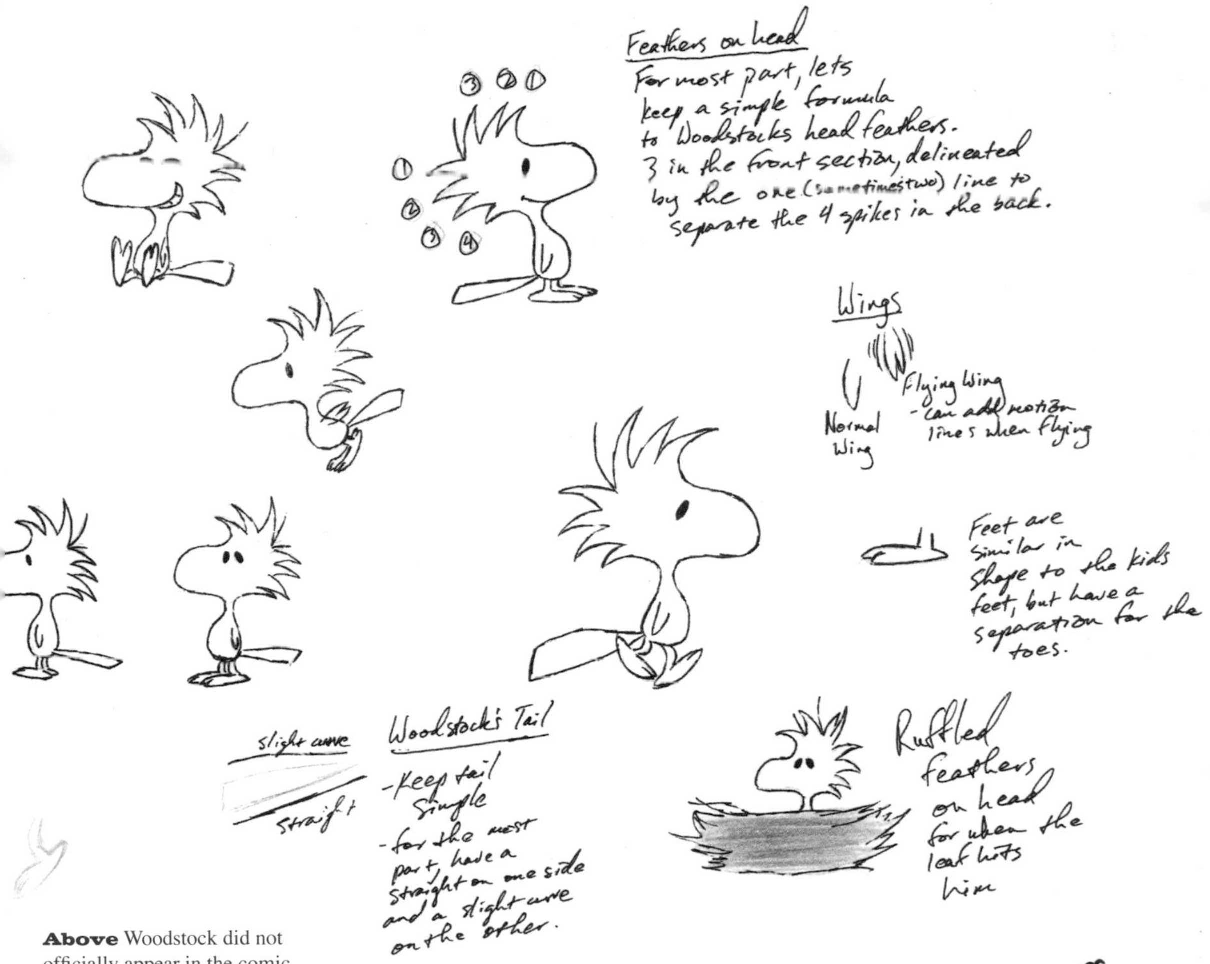
Feathers on head
For most part, lets keep a simple formula to Woodstocks head feathers. 3 in the front section, delineated by the one (sometimestwo) line to separate the 4 spikes in the back.
Wings
Normal Wing
Flying Wing - can add motion lines when flying
Feet are similar in shape to the kids feet, but have a separation for the toes.
slight curve
straight
Woodstock's Tail
- Keep tail simple
- for the most part, have a straight on one side and a slight curve on the other.
Ruffled feathers on head for when the leaf hits him

Above Woodstock did not officially appear in the comic strip until 1967 but has a cameo in this new animated special. Development sketches by Andy Beall.

Below A turnaround of Patty by Andy Beall.

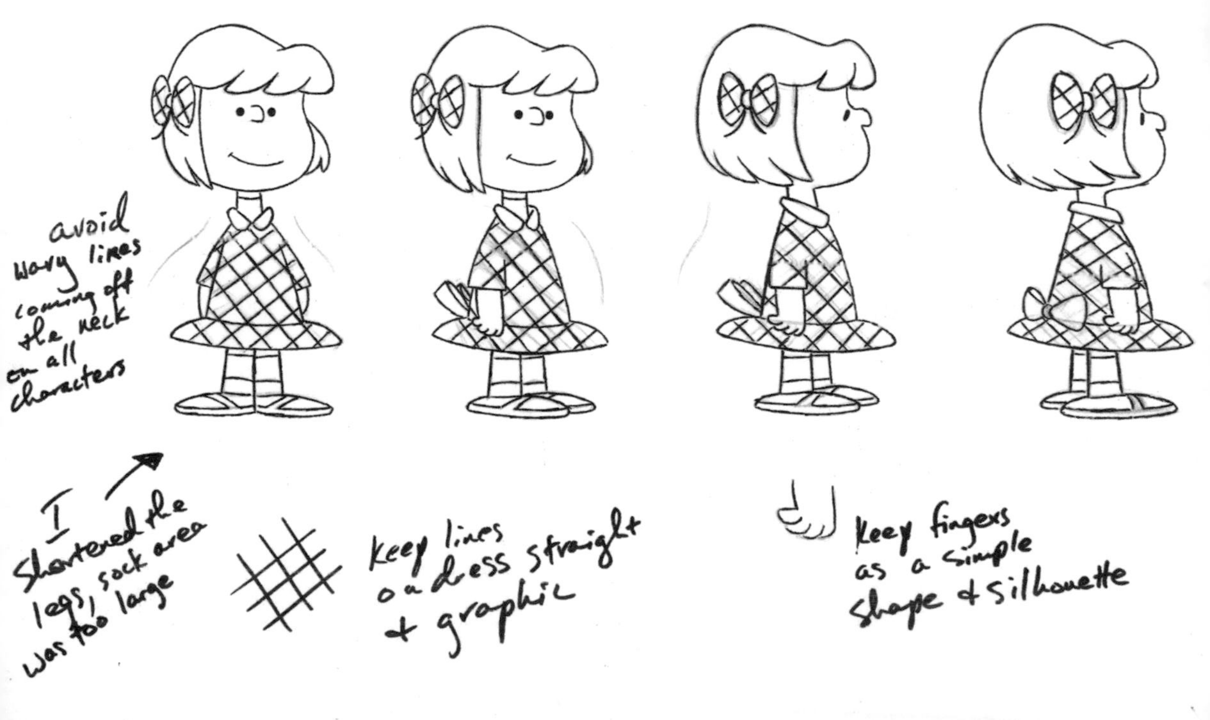
Don't make hair tufts too round, think straights against curves.
avoid wavy lines coming off the neck on all characters
I shortened the legs, sock area was too large
keep lines on dress straight + graphic
keep fingers as a simple shape & silhouette

LINUS' HEAD CONSTRUCTION

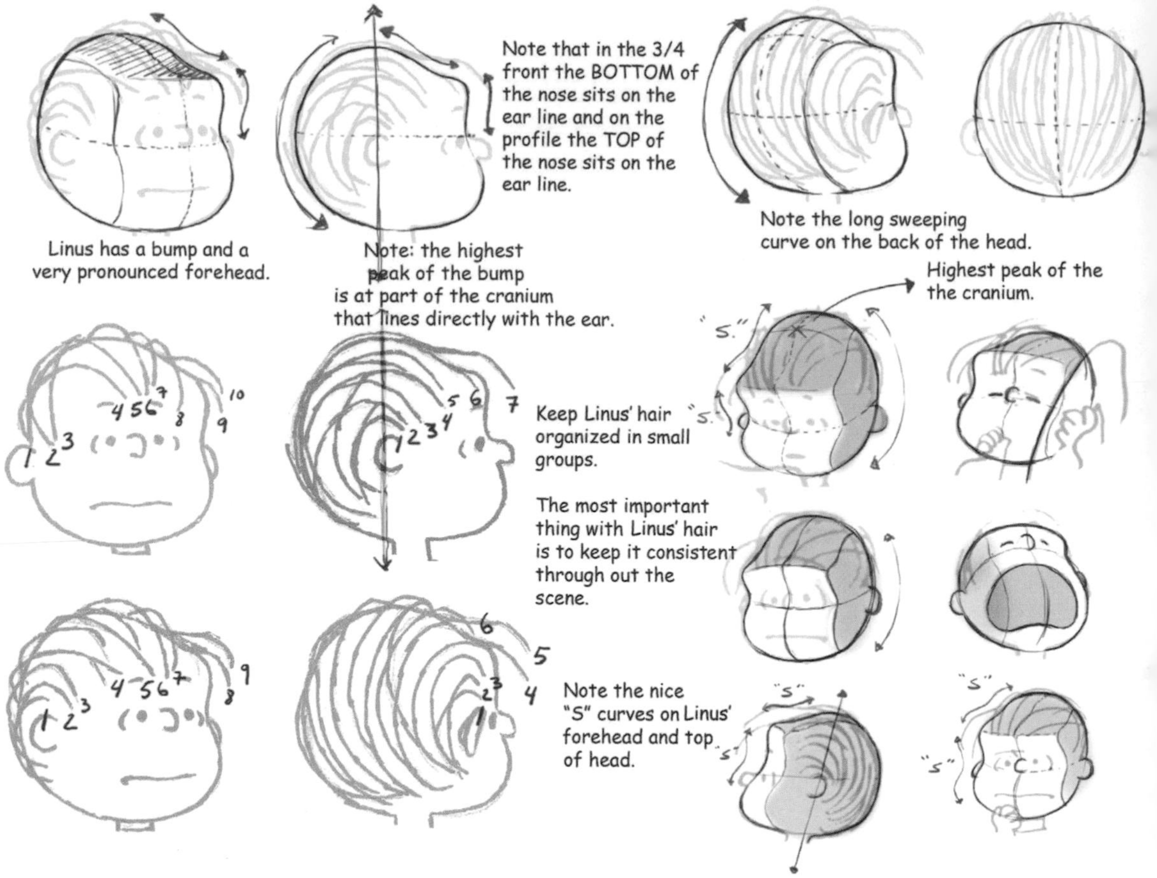
Note that in the 3/4 front the BOTTOM of the nose sits on the ear line and on the profile the TOP of the nose sits on the ear line.
Linus has a bump and a very pronounced forehead.
Note: the highest peak of the bump is at part of the cranium that lines directly with the ear.
Note the long sweeping curve on the back of the head.
Highest peak of the the cranium.
"S."
Keep Linus' hair organized in small groups.
The most important thing with Linus' hair is to keep it consistent through out the scene.
Note the nice "S" curves on Linus' forehead and top of head.
"S"

SHOES

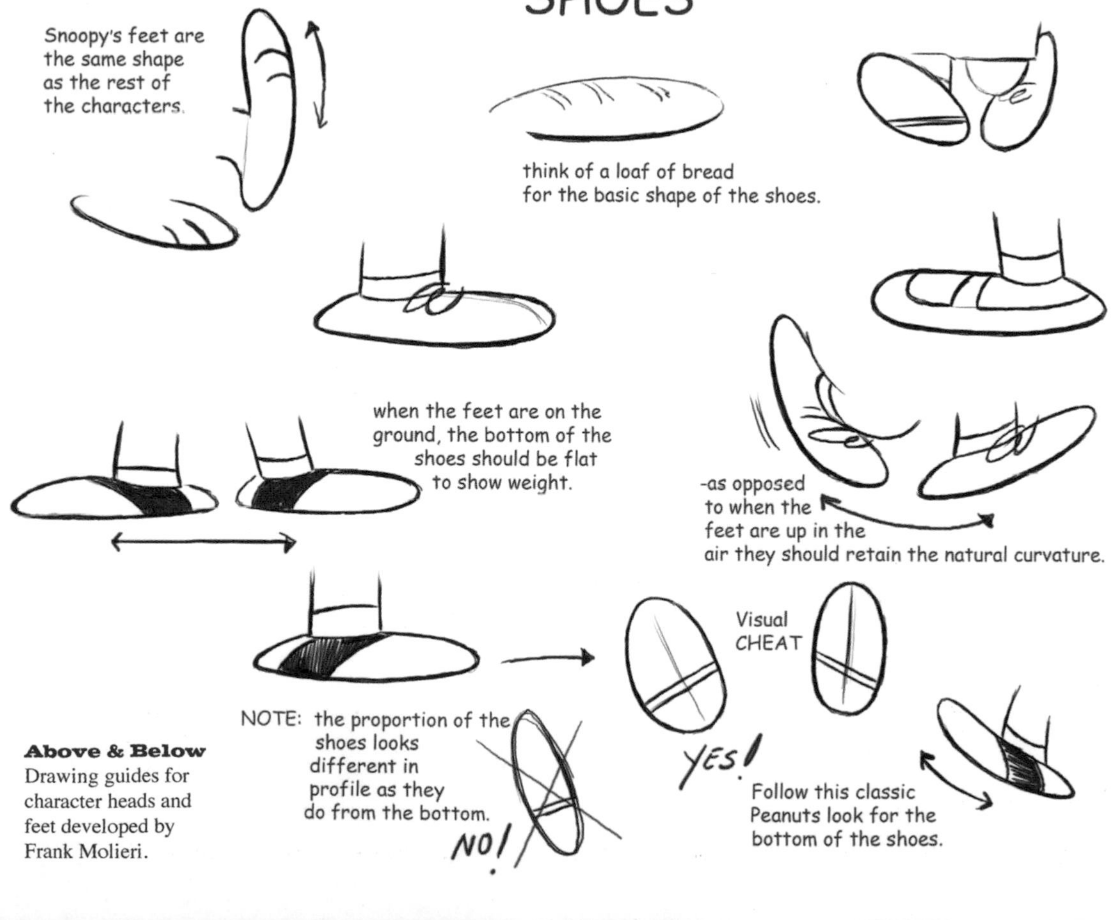
Snoopy's feet are the same shape as the rest of the characters.
think of a loaf of bread for the basic shape of the shoes.
when the feet are on the ground, the bottom of the shoes should be flat to show weight.
-as opposed to when the feet are up in the air they should retain the natural curvature.
Visual CHEAT
NOTE: the proportion of the shoes looks different in profile as they do from the bottom.
YES!
NO!
Follow this classic Peanuts look for the bottom of the shoes.

Above & Below
Drawing guides for character heads and feet developed by Frank Molieri.

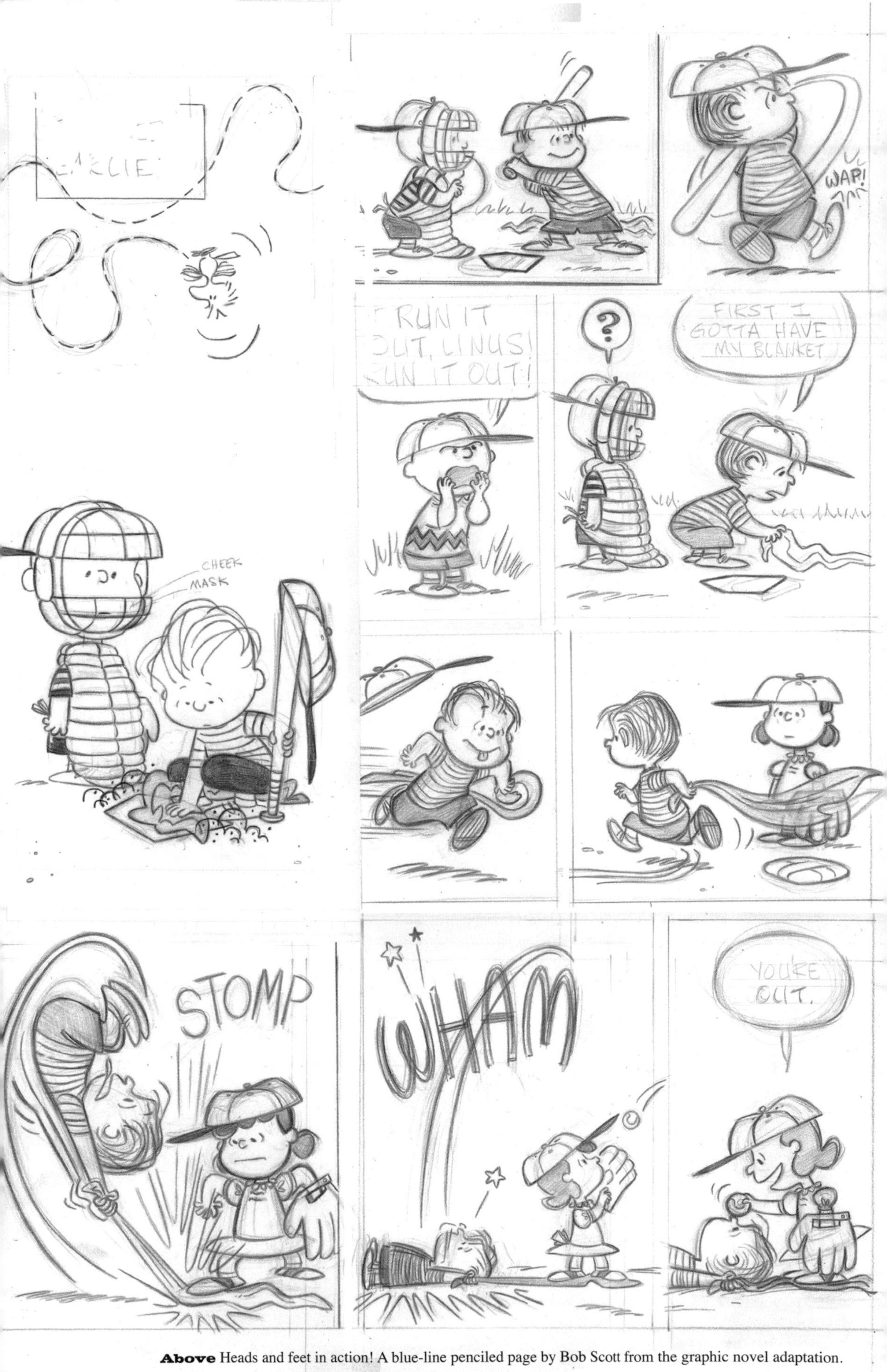
WAP!
RUN IT OUT, LINUS! RUN IT OUT!
?
FIRST I GOTTA HAVE MY BLANKET
CHEEK
MASK
STOMP
WHAM
YOU'RE OUT.

Above Heads and feet in action! A blue-line penciled page by Bob Scott from the graphic novel adaptation.

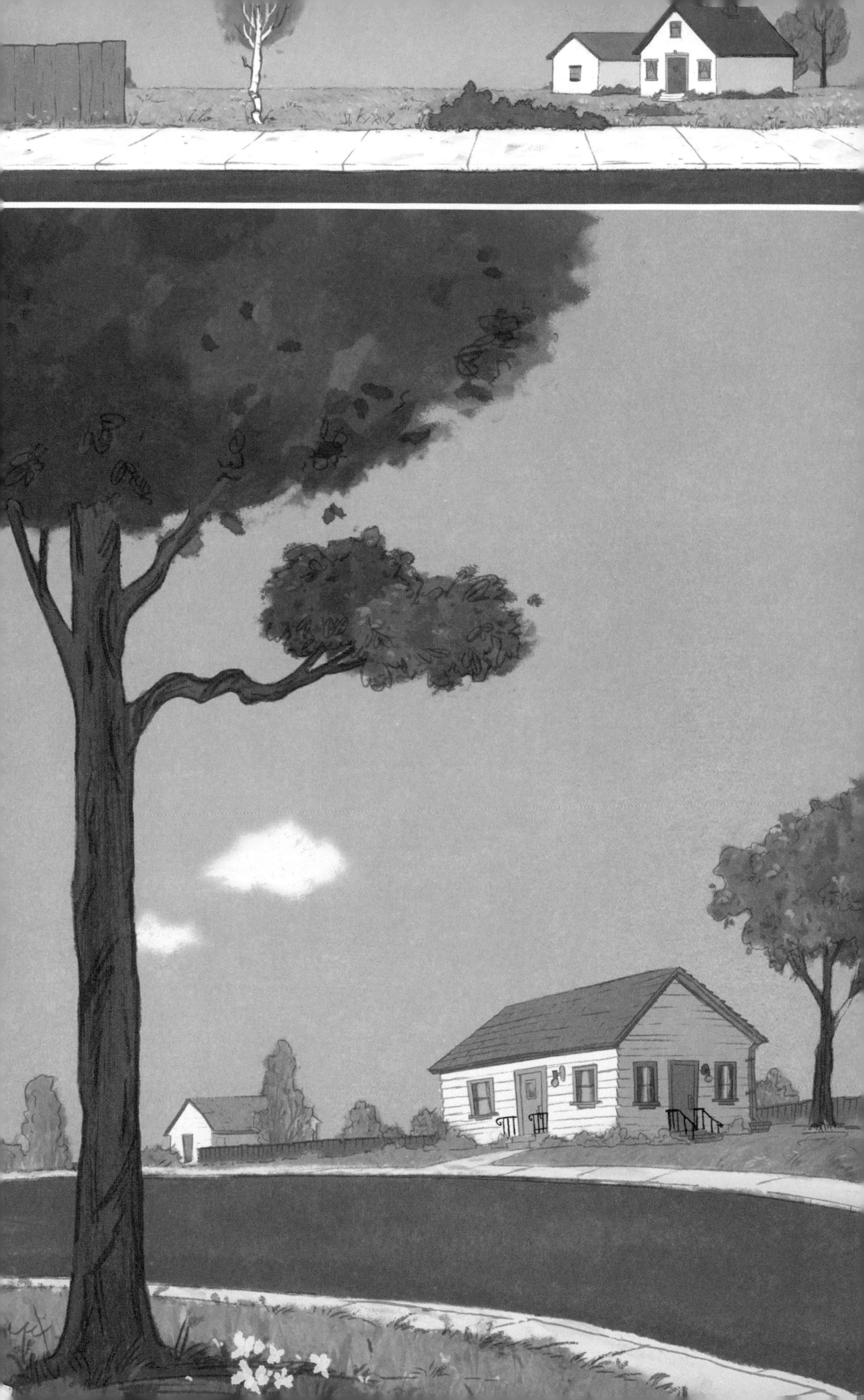

Opposite The *Peanuts* neighborhood: designed by layout artist Edgar Carlos and painted by Rozalina Tchouchev.

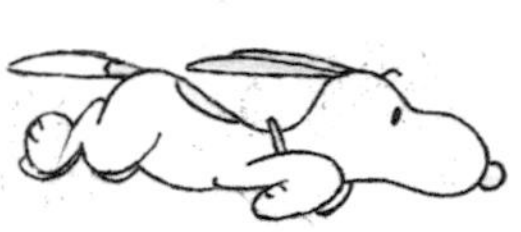

Above Snoopy, by Andy Beall.

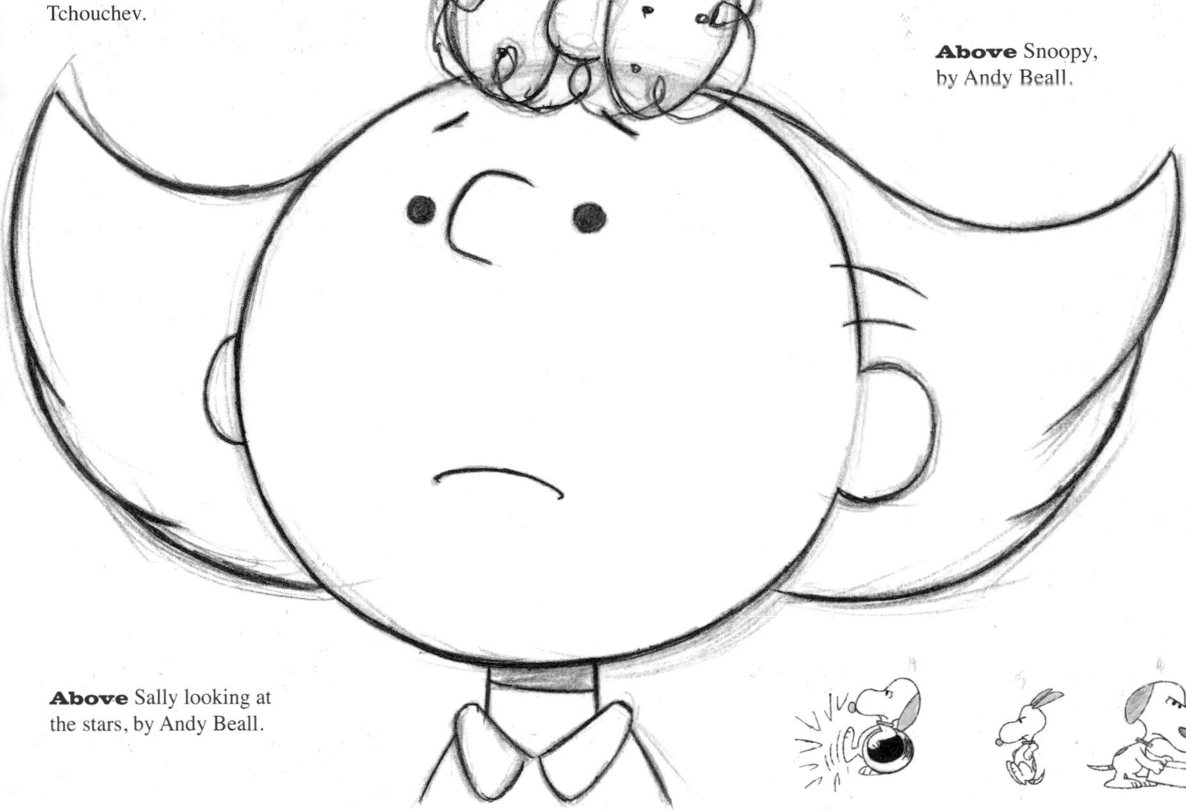

Above Sally looking at the stars, by Andy Beall.

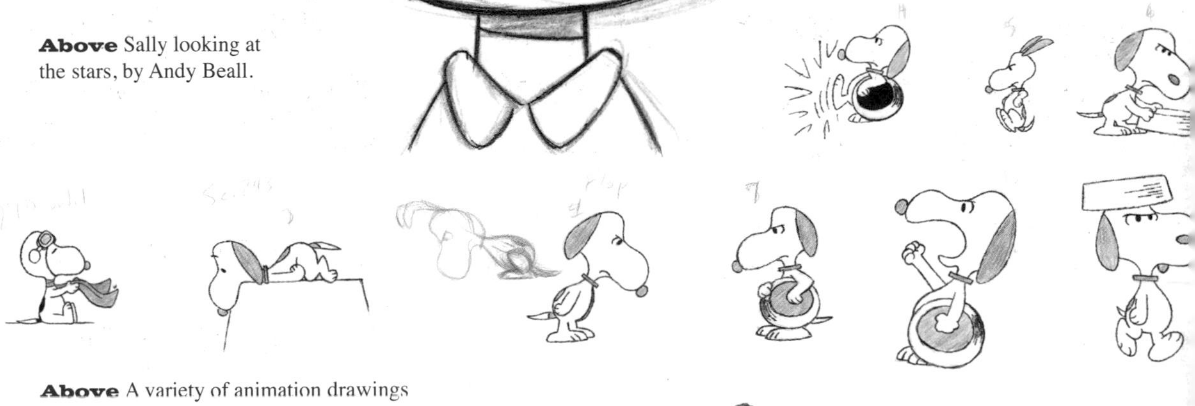

Above A variety of animation drawings of Snoopy, by Andy Beall.

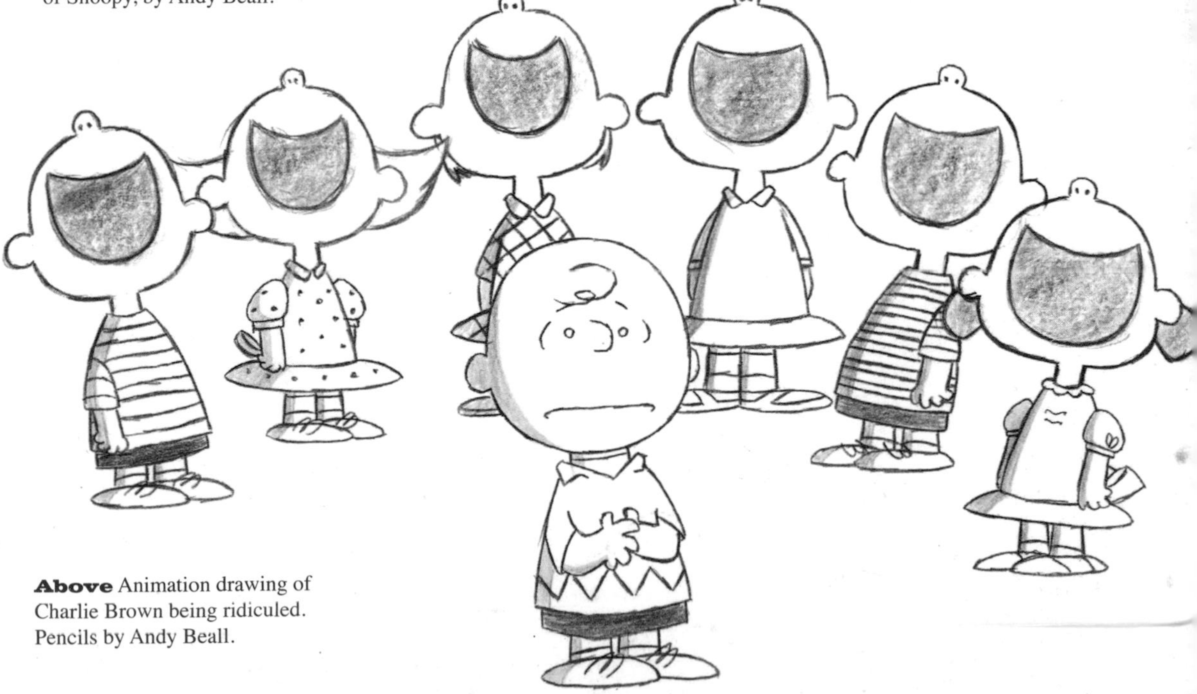

Above Animation drawing of Charlie Brown being ridiculed. Pencils by Andy Beall.

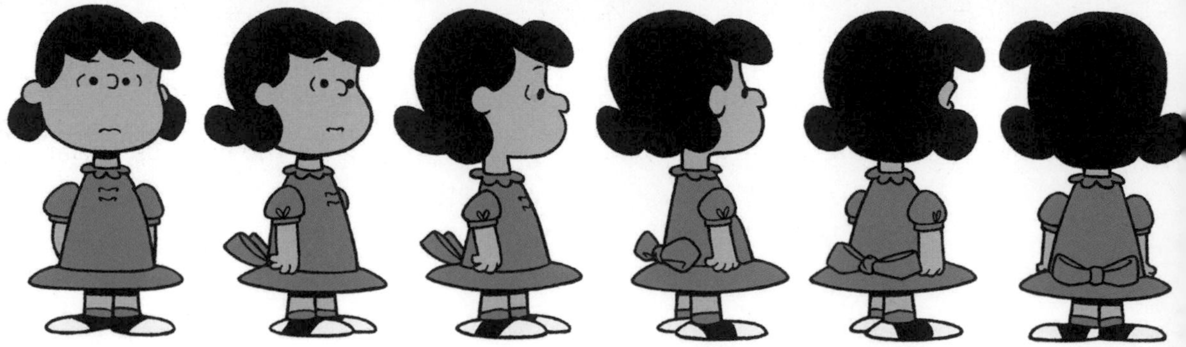

Above & Below Turnarounds of Lucy Van Pelt and Charlie Brown, by Andy Beall.

Opposite The *Peanuts* neighborhood: *(top)* layout by Edgar Carlos painted b Rozlina Tchouchev. *(below)* layouts by Edgar Carlos, painted by Seonna Hong.

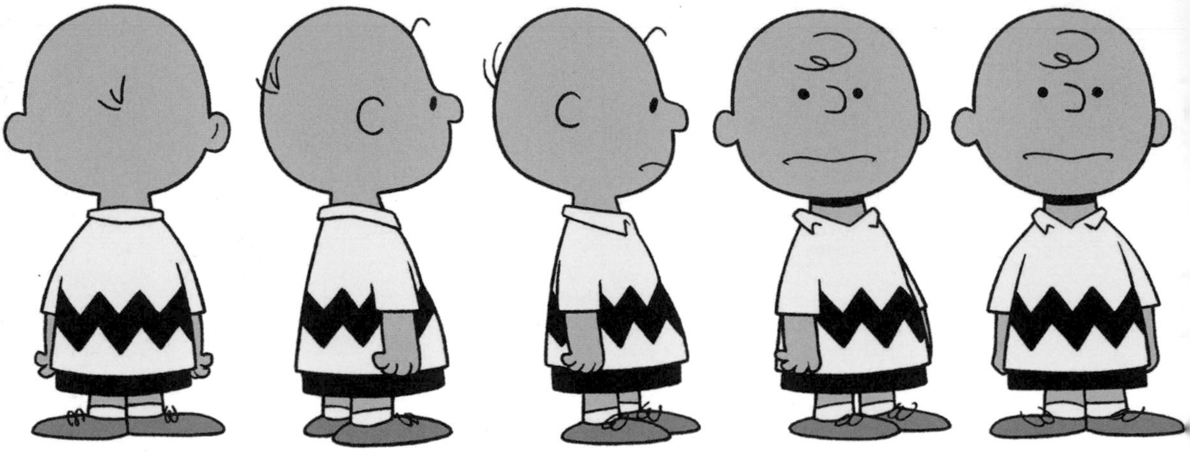

Below Drawing guide by Frank Molieri.

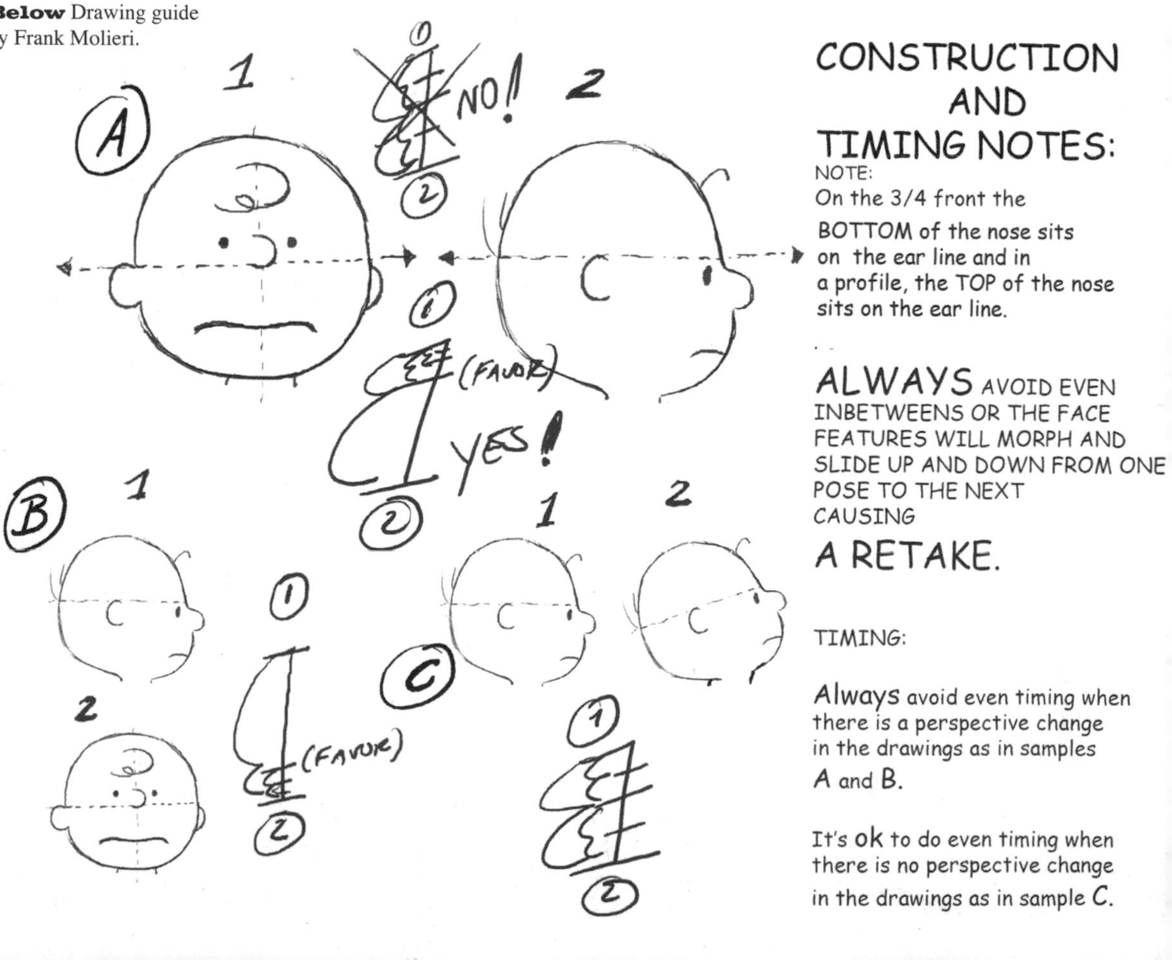

A
1
NO!
2
(FAVOR)
YES!
B
1
2
(FAVOR)
C
1
2
CONSTRUCTION AND TIMING NOTES:
NOTE:
On the 3/4 front the BOTTOM of the nose sits on the ear line and in a profile, the TOP of the nose sits on the ear line.
ALWAYS AVOID EVEN INBETWEENS OR THE FACE FEATURES WILL MORPH AND SLIDE UP AND DOWN FROM ONE POSE TO THE NEXT CAUSING
A RETAKE.
TIMING:
Always avoid even timing when there is a perspective change in the drawings as in samples A and B.
It's ok to do even timing when there is no perspective change in the drawings as in sample C.

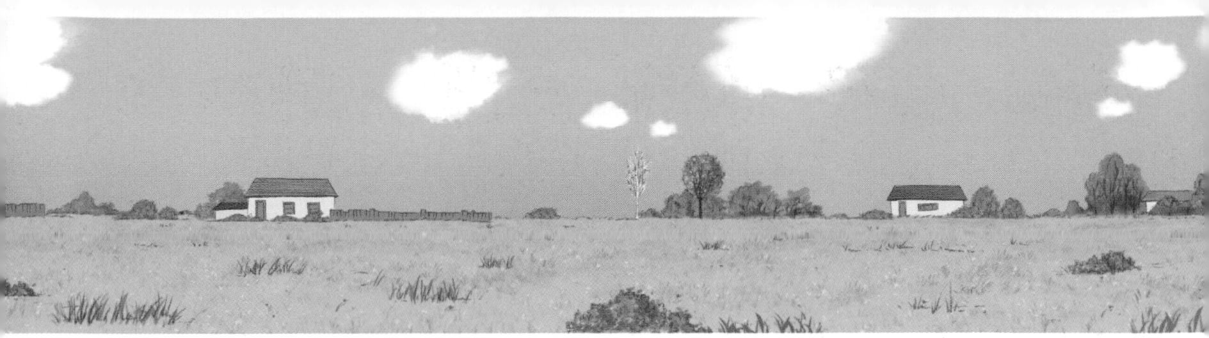

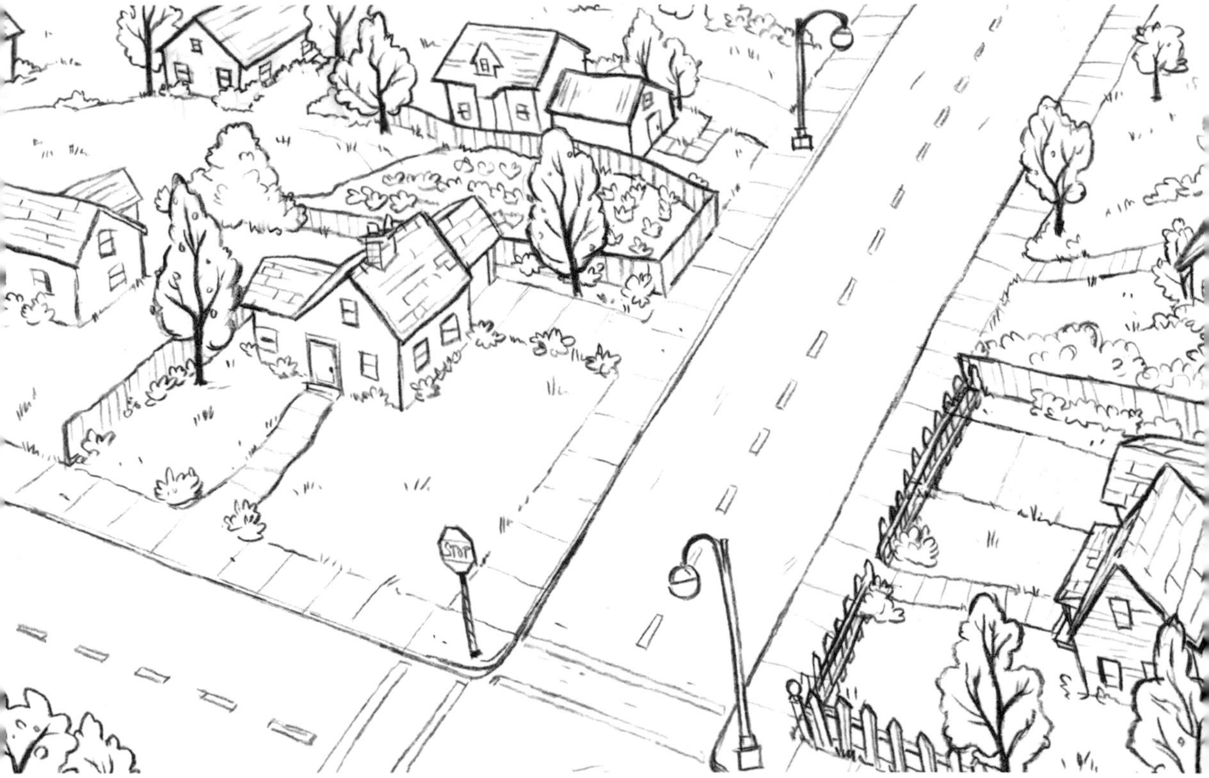
STOP

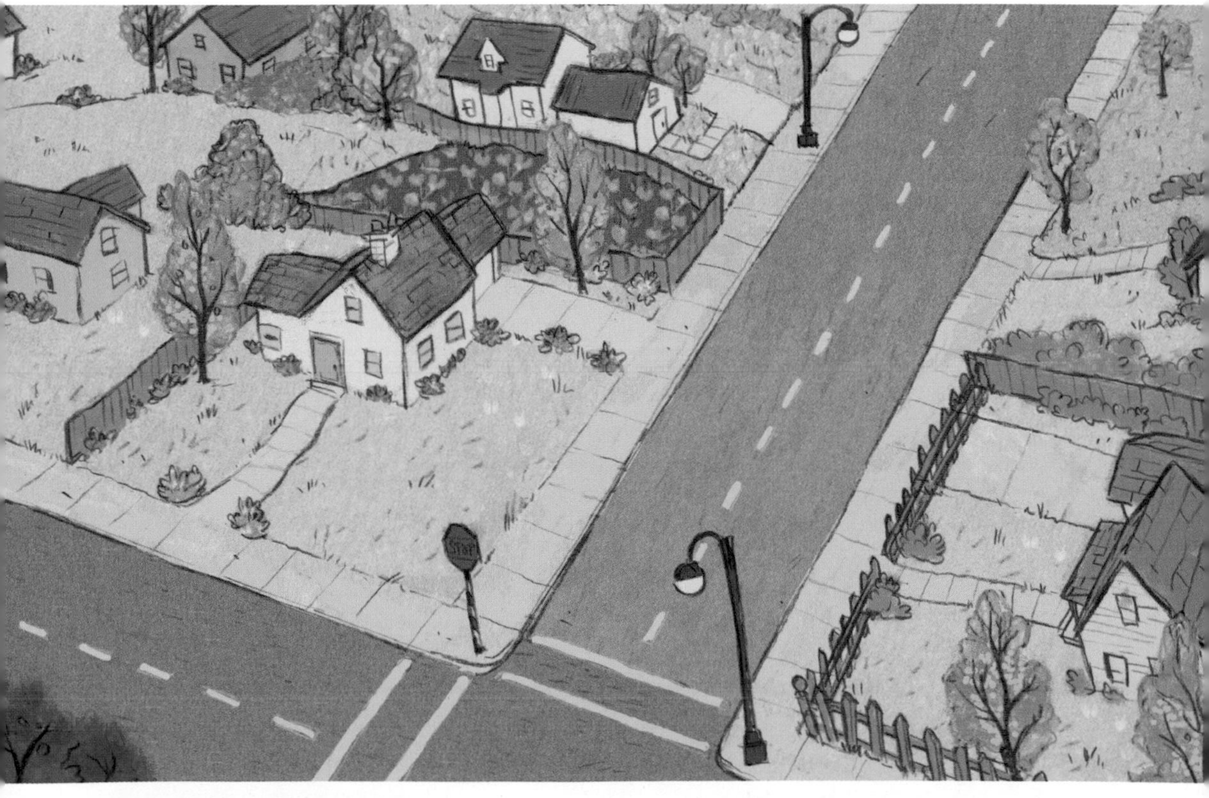
STOP

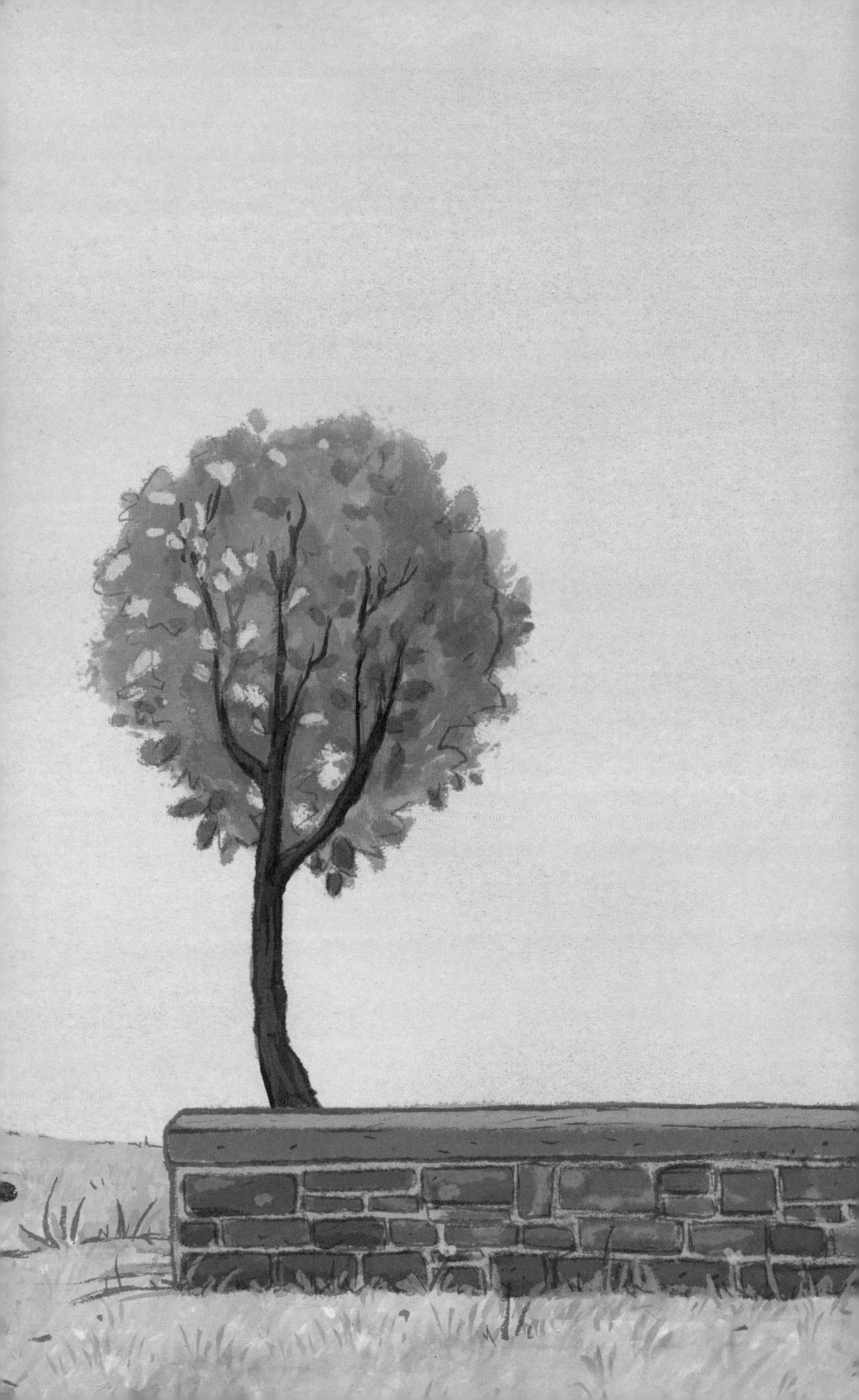

Charles M. Schulz once described himself as "born to draw comic strips." Born in Minneapolis, at just two days old, an uncle nicknamed him "Sparky" after the horse Spark Plug from the Barney Google comic strip, and throughout his youth, he and his father shared a Sunday morning ritual reading the funnies. After serving in the Army during World War II, Schulz's first big break came in 1947 when he sold a cartoon feature called "Li'l Folks" to the *St. Paul Pioneer Press*. In 1950, Schulz met with United Feature Syndicate, and on October 2 of that year, PEANUTS, named by the syndicate, debuted in seven newspapers. Charles Schulz died in Santa Rosa, California, in February 2000—just hours before his last original strip was to appear in Sunday papers.